Research Methods for Social Justice and Equity in Education

BLOOMSBURY RESEARCH METHODS FOR EDUCATION SERIES

Edited by Melanie Nind, University of Southampton, UK

The *Bloomsbury Research Methods for Education* series provides overviews of the range of sometimes interconnected and diverse methodological possibilities for researching aspects of education such as education contexts, sectors, problems or phenomena. Each volume discusses prevailing, less obvious and more innovative methods and approaches for the particular area of educational research.

More targeted than general methods textbooks, these authoritative yet accessible books are invaluable resources for students and researchers planning their research design and wanting to explore methodological possibilities to make well-informed decisions regarding their choice of methods.

Also available in the series

Research Methods for Pedagogy, Melanie Nind, Alicia Curtin and Kathy Hall

Place-Based Methods for Researching Schools, Pat Thomson and Christine Hall

Research Methods for Education in the Digital Age, Maggi Savin-Baden and Gemma Tombs

Research Methods for Understanding Professional Learning, Elaine Hall and Kate Wall

Forthcoming

Research Methods for Classroom Discourse, Jenni Ingram and Victoria Elliott

Research Methods for Early Childhood Education, Rosie Flewitt and Lynn Ang

Research Methods for Educational Dialogue, Ruth Kershner, Rupert Wegerif, Ayesha Ahmed and Sara Hennessy

BLOOMSBURY RESEARCH METHODS FOR EDUCATION

Research Methods for Social Justice and Equity in Education

LIZ ATKINS AND VICKY DUCKWORTH

BLOOMSBURY ACADEMIC
LONDON · NEW YORK · OXFORD · NEW DELHI · SYDNEY

BLOOMSBURY ACADEMIC
Bloomsbury Publishing Plc
50 Bedford Square, London, WC1B 3DP, UK
1385 Broadway, New York, NY 10018, USA

BLOOMSBURY, BLOOMSBURY ACADEMIC and the Diana logo are trademarks
of Bloomsbury Publishing Plc

First published in Great Britain 2019
Reprinted 2019, 2020 (twice)

Series design by Clare Turner

A catalogue record for this book is available from the British Library.

A catalog record for this book is available from the Library of Congress.

ISBN: HB: 978-1-3500-1545-6
PB: 978-1-3500-1546-3
ePDF: 978-1-3500-1548-7
eBook: 978-1-3500-1547-0

Series: Bloomsbury Research Methods for Education

Typeset by Newgen KnowledgeWorks Pvt. Ltd., Chennai, India
Printed and bound in Great Britain

To find out more about our authors and books visit www.bloomsbury.com
and sign up for our newsletters.

Dedicated to the joys of Grace and James Hailey and Elkana Duckworth and with love to Craig, Anna and Niamh Ludlow

Vicky Duckworth

For Ray and for Charlotte with love

Liz Atkins

CONTENTS

ACKNOWLEDGEMENTS

We would like to express our thanks to our families for their personal support during the writing of this book and the always helpful team at Bloomsbury, especially Maria Giovanna Brauzzi. We would also like to thank Professor Melanie Nind, series editor, for her encouragement.

In particular we would like to thank the participants whose voices are heard in this text, as well as all those colleagues who have shared discussions about their own perspectives on research for and about social justice and who have contributed to the writing of the book. They are:

Bally Kaur, Birmingham City University

Chelsea Swift, University of York

Clare Woolhouse, Edge Hill University

Curtis Chin, Hollywood and New York University

Fergal Finnegan, Maynooth University, Southern Ireland

Fiona Hallett, Edge Hill University

Francesca Bernardi, Edge Hill University

Francis Farrell, Edge Hill University

Garth Stahl, University of South Australia

Janet Lord, Manchester Metropolitan University

Joanne Clifford-Swan, Northumbria University

Julie Sealy, latterly Fielding Graduate University and now Edge Hill University

Katerina Matziari, Manchester Metropolitan University

Kay Heslop, Northumbria University

Laura Louise Nicklin, University of York

Mark Vicars, Victoria University, Australia

Mary McAteer, Edge Hill University

Rob Smith, Birmingham City University

Tony Capstick, Reading University

Vini Lander, Roehampton University

Virginie Thériault, University of Strathclyde, Glasgow

Our grateful thanks to you all.

ABBREVIATIONS

AR	Action Research
BERA	British Education Research Association
BME	British, Black and Minority Ethnic
CMC	Computer-Mediated Communication
CRT	Critical Race Theory
DBIS	Department for Business Innovation and Skills
DfE	Department for Education
DfEE	Department for Education and Employment
DfES	Department for Education and Skills
ECU	Equality Challenge Unit
EEA	European Economic Area
ESRC	Economic and Social Research Council
FE	Further Education
GCSE	General Certificate of Secondary Education
HE	Higher Education
IMF	International Monetary Fund
ITE	Initial Teacher Education
MTeach	Master of Teaching
NEET	Not in Employment, Education or Training
NGO	Non-government Organizations
OECD	Organisation for Economic Cooperation and Development
OfSTED	Office for Standards in Education, Children's Services and Skills
PAR	Participatory Action Research
PDI	Parent Development Interview
PGCE	Postgraduate Certificate in Education
PIAAC	Programme for the International Assessment of Adult Competencies
PICCOLO	Parenting Interactions with Children: Checklist of Observations Linked to Outcomes

PR	Practitioner Research
RE	Religious Education
RISE	Research in Special Education
SEN	Special Educational Needs
SEN/D	Special Educational Needs and/or Disabilities
SHSAT	Specialized High School Admissions Test
SID	Small Island State
SMSC	Spiritual, Moral, Social and Cultural
STEMM	Science, Technology, Engineering, Mathematics and Medicine
UCU	University College Union
UN	United Nations
UNCRC	United Nations Convention on the Rights of the Child
UNCRPD	United Nations Convention on the Rights of Persons with Disabilities
UNESCO	United Nations Educational, Scientific and Cultural Organization
UNICEF	United Nations Children's Fund
WEA	Workers Education Association

SERIES FOREWORD

The idea of the *Bloomsbury Research Methods for Education* series is to provide books that are useful to researchers wanting to think about research methods in the context of their research area, research problem or research aims. While researchers may use any methods textbook for ideas and inspiration, the onus falls on them to apply something from social science research methods to education in particular, or from education to a particular dimension of education (pedagogy, schools, the digital dimension, practitioner learning, to name some examples). This application of ideas is not beyond us and has led to some great research and also to methodological development. In this series though, the books are more targeted, making them a good place to start for the student, researcher or person wanting to craft a research proposal. Each book brings together in one place the range of sometimes interconnected and often diverse methodological possibilities for researching one aspect or sector of education, one research problem or phenomenon. Thus, readers will quickly find a discussion of the methods they associate with that bit of education research they are interested in, but in addition they will find less obvious and more innovative methods and approaches. A quick look at the opening glossary will give you an idea of the methods you will find included within each book. You can expect a discussion of those methods that is critical, authoritative *and* situated. In each text the authors use powerful examples of the methods in use in the arena with which you are concerned.

There are other features that make this series distinctive. In each of the books the authors draw on their own research and on the research of others making alternative methodological choices. In this way they address the affordances of the methods in terms of real studies; they illustrate the potential with real data. The authors also discuss the rationale behind the choice of methods and behind how researchers put them together in research designs. As readers you will get behind the scenes of published research and into the kind of methodological decision-making that you are grappling with. In each of the books you will find yourself moving between methods, theory and data; you will find theoretical concepts to think with and with which you might be able to enhance your methods. You will find that the authors develop arguments about methods rather than just describing them.

Readers drawn to this title will appreciate the impossibility of studying social justice in education without reflecting on how the research design and methods support, undermine or otherwise interact with the social justice agenda. In *Research Methods for Social Justice and Equity in Education*, Liz Atkins and Vicky Duckworth explore how researchers have understood social justice and equity in education and translated their interest and passion for pursuing this into fitting research methods. Readers will find in this book examples from a range of educational phases, settings, cultures, contexts and collaborators, each of which illustrates how marginalized communities of learners and educationalists can be treated respectfully by researchers. With a chapter dedicated to global perspectives this book will appeal to people researching in different geopolitical environments. The question of reflexive, ethical implementation of social research methods is considered throughout, and Liz and Vicky repeatedly demonstrate their ethical stance in narratives about their own work. In common with other books in the series these authors also point to creative and innovative adaptations of established methods and to additional reading to enable methods of interest to be followed up with ease.

This book will not be the only book you need to read to formulate, justify and implement your research methods. Other books will cover alternative methods or provide different kinds of detail. The aim for this series, though, is to provide books that take you to the heart of the methods thinking you will want and need to do. They are books by authors who are equally passionate about research methods as they are about their substantive topic and they are books that will be invaluable for inspiring deep and informed methods thinking.

Melanie Nind
Series Editor

Introduction

This book is concerned with research that is undertaken from a perspective which aims to address issues of social justice and (lack of) equity. The notion of social justice and the ideologies that underpin it are highly contested, and our first challenge in the writing of this book has been to explore some of the debates and contradictions associated with it. Our second challenge was to establish what 'counts' as socially just research. Is it research which aims to inform policy and practice? Is it research which is participative and where the researched have equal control over the research process? Is it only research with marginalized communities? As these questions imply, the writing of this book was never going to be a linear exploration. Therefore, in this introduction, we have positioned the book in relation to some of the key questions posed throughout the text. In addition to exploring understandings of social justice and equity, this includes addressing questions about their implications for undertaking educational research that is both moral and ethical, the contribution that research for equity and social justice can make to new and emerging methods and methodologies, and the ways in which researchers can implement socially just research methods from what is often a position of power and privilege. We firmly believe that it is important to bring debates about the issues associated with research for social justice and equity into the public domain. There are two primary reasons for this. First, the opportunity it presents through our case examples to highlight the many issues which engender and reify in/equalities in different education contexts. Secondly, the opportunity it offers to illustrate not only how different researchers are addressing the personal and theoretical challenges that undertaking socially just research presents but how many are also working with new and emerging methodologies as they seek to make and influence emancipatory change and challenge hegemony. In doing this, we draw on case examples contributed by a wide range of colleagues in the field, to exemplify some of those challenges, and the methods and methodological approaches different researchers choose to address them.

Theoretically, key issues which arise in research concerned with social justice and equity are often those associated with ethics, power relations, reflexivity and positionality. In this book we are concerned with foregrounding moral and ethical research as being fundamental to socially just approaches. We argue that positionality, power relations and reflexivity are all central to conceptions of ethics and ethical research. Therefore, in response to our own arguments, we begin this text by outlining our own positionality in relation to the book.

Personal positionality, shared values

This book arose from our shared commitment to socially just research and our recognition that, as education professionals, we are in a unique position in terms of being able to address some of the inequalities influencing our students. Our commitment to social justice arose from parallel personal historical experiences. We both had difficult early education experiences, Liz due to the physical and social impacts of stigmatized disability, Vicky due to the limited educational opportunities and expectations for working-class girls (and boys). We both wanted to train as nurses and overcame our individual personal barriers and the wider structural inequalities that had shaped our individual trajectories to do so. Liz trained as a psychiatric nurse and Vicky as a registered nurse and a midwife, both roles that expose the professional to every form of human inequality and its consequences. For different reasons, we both eventually moved to work in Further Education (FE). FE has traditionally been based in colleges but now extends to a wide range of private training providers. It is idiosyncratic to the UK, although a similar system exists in Australia. It caters for anyone aged 14+ and, in England alone, in 2017/18 educated 2.2 million people (AoC, 2017). It is also a sector which is heavily classed and gendered (Colley, 2006) and historically known as the sector of the 'second chance' (see Atkins, 2010b) in recognition of the way in which it can transform lives (e.g. see Duckworth, 2013; Duckworth and Smith, 2018a, b, c) for those students who have not flourished and have often been failed by the compulsory system. We would position it as often being the only chance for many marginalized communities to offer resistance to structural inequalities such as class, gender and ethnicity, which constrain their personal agency. It can also offer opportunities for educators and students to participate in a larger, problem-solving, dialogic community discourse (Duckworth and Maxwell, 2015).

However, FE is paradoxical in that while it has a transformative effect on many who engage with it, the fact that it offers vocational education and training, which may be viewed as being held in lower esteem in comparison to traditional 'academic' programmes, and provides fewer opportunities than academic education means that for many students the sector is complicit in processes of class and labour reproduction.

It is not possible to work in this sector, as we did, without recognizing the lack of equity in how education is structured and enacted and wanting to address that. We both sought to do this through our teaching and research (and Vicky with her activism). As FE students, having been labelled as non-achievers at school, we both thrived, felt valued and developed a sense of belonging. Later, as FE teachers our personal histories motivated us: Vicky's 'Insiderness' was a key motivation to becoming a adult literacy teacher and undertaking research with marginalized communities, while Liz's personal experience of being labelled as a 'failure' at school inspired her interest in, and commitment to, level 1 learners – those with the lowest educational positioning in the mainstream sector post-16.

Working in FE demanded of us that we became more critical, questioning a society in which so many were much less equal than others. Ultimately, our journeys led to us both registering for doctoral study in which we used different perspectives to understand and address a number of the issues facing some of the most marginalized students. Undertaking that research was, in itself, transformational for both of us, offering us a deepened insight and perspective on education locally, nationally and globally. Unknown to us at that time, our perspectives on social justice located us within a small group of scholars who were beginning to explore the possibilities of using theoretically sound research to work on issues of social justice and inform policy with 'the purpose of redressing a variety of historically reified oppressions in modern life' (Denzin and Lincoln, 2013: 580). Such oppressions included not only issues around class, gender and racism but also more subtle forms of discrimination which impact on education and its outcomes including, for example, economic injustices, homelessness or the impact of low attainment in a highly credentialized society. Early work in this field included that by Morwenna Griffiths (1998), who influenced both our thinking in this area. Today, many scholars working within a range of paradigms seek to uncover and address issues of inequality and 'exposing how historic social structures reify and re-invent discriminatory practices, and proposing new forms of social structures that are less oppressive. The turn toward social justice, of course, is directly linked with the turn toward more critical stances in interpretation and representation' (Denzin and Lincoln, 2013: 580).

Our commitment to social justice has been driven by moral and ethical beliefs, and that is reflected in this book. We are both committed to research which informs the development of more equitable education systems as a means of developing a more equitable society. We see research which uncovers and addresses oppression as being fundamental to that. Working in education, we believe that all educators and researchers have a moral imperative to act in ways that promote equity and social justice. For this reason, we place an emphasis on socially just research as an ethical and moral undertaking throughout this book. We also acknowledge that the nature of research and, more specifically, qualitative approaches position the researcher as the data collection instrument. In this context, the researcher cannot be separated from the research as their positionality, in terms of characteristics such as beliefs, assumptions, political ideologies, gender, ethnicity, class, socioeconomic status, educational background and so on, is an important variable that may impact on the research process in different ways. Indeed, as our participants' experiences are embedded in sociocultural contexts, so too are our own as researchers. This highlights the importance of reflecting on, and making explicit, our own positionality. For example, are we insiders or outsiders (see Chapter 4)? How does our positioning influence the methodological approach we adopt? Clifford (1986) has argued that we are never truly outsiders, yet never wholly insiders either; however, we are always partial in examining our research results (ibid.: 7). While the 'partiality' that Clifford alludes to is influenced by positionality, Wilkinson (2016) highlights the importance of 'personality' in shaping the research process and argues that 'a lack of focus on the researcher's personality is an egregious oversight, as personality is capable of shaping both the research process and the final outcome' (116). In her research on a CASE studentship concerned with young people and community radio, she states that she believes that her 'social and emotional qualities enabled a close relationship to be developed between myself and the young participants' (Wilkinson, 2016: 116). In terms of our own positionality, we believe that we are, as Clifford argues, a fundamental part of our research. This, together with our commitment to social justice, which we explore throughout this text, inclines us towards a wide range of qualitative and ethnographic methods, such as those illustrated in this book. We believe that qualitative methods, particularly when implemented in the context of research which involves some degree of participation and/or collaboration (thus implying researching *with* the participants), are more easily applied in ways which are consistent with social justice than some large-scale quantitative methods (such as, e.g. surveys) which present greater difficulty in implementing in ways consistent with social justice (e.g. they assume a certain level of literacy) and thus imply researching *on* the participants. Of course, this may not always be the case, but our experience suggests that smaller scale research which utilizes a range of qualitative methods more readily highlights and addresses some of the challenges facing marginalized learners and their communities. Our privileged positioning as researchers in relation to those communities demands that we reflect on our positionality in relation to our overall methodological approach and the individual methods we adopt. It is essential to remember that both who we are and the way in which we interact with the world shape our lens since 'greater reflection on the part of the researcher might produce more inclusive, more flexible, yet philosophically informed methodologies sensitive to the power relations inherent in fieldwork' (England, 2008: 251).

Positioning the book

Social justice and equity are slippery concepts, something we discuss at length in Chapter 1. This makes it important that we introduce this book by establishing our position in terms of what social justice and equity mean in relation to research. In the book we variously use the terms 'equity', 'socially just research' and 'research for social justice'. Equity is a concept which is inseparable from social justice. The concept of equity is generally considered to be associated with justice and fairness, thus moving it beyond notions of equality and 'sameness'. Ideas of fairness emphasize the individual and individual needs and abilities. The notion of fairness has also been conflated with, or used to define, notions of justice throughout history (see Chapter 1). An equitable world would be a socially just world, and an equitable education system would promote this. However, most education systems globally fail in this respect, either because they reproduce and reify the historical oppressions inherent in them (such as the English system, which has always differentiated educational opportunity by social class) or, as in some Asian and African contexts, because they enforce cultural or societal norms (such as denying girls an (equal) education) which are contrary to social justice. Therefore, where in this book we discuss the inequalities uncovered and addressed in educational research, we see a state of equity as being the opposite of this and social justice as the means to achieve that equity. This is driven by a moral sense of what is right (equity) and what is wrong (oppression and inequality), thus emphasizing the moral and ethical underpinnings of research which claims social justice as part of its process or purpose. This places a particular responsibility on the researcher in terms not only of undertaking work which is rigorous, credible and theoretically sound but also of considering the moral and ethical implications for the research throughout and beyond the research process. That means undertaking a critical and reflexive approach which involves, continually posing questions to oneself about the rightness of the research and the way in which it is contributing to equity and social justice. This moral responsibility has significant implications for the way in which research is conceived, planned, conducted, analysed, written and disseminated, and throughout the book, we draw on case examples offered by colleagues from diverse contexts and cultures in order to illuminate this.

We use the term 'socially just research' in relation to research that claims social justice in the way in which it is conducted as well as its aims. Many examples of this are participative and/or collaborative studies which involve and seek to empower all participants at all stages of the research process, often on a co-researcher basis, something which can have the added advantage of providing new and different insights into the process and the data. In contrast, the term 'research for social justice' might be used to apply to a wide range of studies which, while not involving other participants as co-researchers, has aims and questions that seek to uncover or illuminate issues of concern in relation to social justice. This would include critical studies from a wide range of theoretical perspectives which address issues of in/equality and oppression and, crucially, inform pedagogy and/or policy in terms of developing a more socially just education system. We emphasize the broad range of perspectives, which each offer different opportunities to illuminate different issues in different ways, and we do not assume that any particular perspective, including those we work with, is in any way especially 'good' or better at illuminating a situation or phenomenon. We accept Denzin and Lincoln's (2013: 189) argument that paradigms are human constructions and, as such, no single perspective can be established in terms of its 'ultimate truthfulness'. This is critically important in terms of research which claims social justice as part of its aim or purpose, because valorizing one perspective over another has consequences in terms of the power that bestows not upon the researchers but upon the discourses surrounding a particular perspective. As Patai (1994: 63) has argued, claims of 'rightness' in terms of methodological perspective 'carry troubling implications [that this type of claim] presumes the utter rightness of its own beliefs and its ability to legitimately valorize one discourse over another', something we would argue is contrary to conceptions of social justice.

In terms of method, some would argue that research methods are methods and thus there cannot be socially just methods. We would accept this argument up to a point. We believe that no method, in and of itself, can be described as socially just, since social justice refers more broadly to the philosophical underpinnings of the research. Therefore, it is, we believe, the application of particular methods which determines the extent to which they are, or are not, socially just. In this context, we believe that the use of qualitative and ethnographic methods can more easily be utilized in a socially just manner. For example, we have suggested that surveys and many questionnaires might be less accessible to individuals with limited levels of literacy and thus in contexts involving marginalized groups – who form the focus of much research for social justice – could not be described as socially just methods. However, methods such as interview or photo-elicitation might more easily be implemented in ways that could be consistent with social justice. In contrast, 'quicker' methods such as undertaking surveys might be more appropriate (so long as they can answer the research questions) with some time-poor professional groups, such as in research around medical education, which would normally involve only highly qualified (and literate) participants. Therefore, the researcher who is concerned with social justice needs to give consideration to methods' 'fitness for purpose' (see Wellington, 2015) not only in terms of generating data which will answer the research questions but also to the extent to which the chosen methods are (or are not) socially just in the context of the research and all its potential participants. For example, are the methods accessible? What assumptions and values are inherent in their design? Do they patronize? Are they respectful? Are they cognizant of issues around intersectionality? Are they consistent with 'doing'[1] social justice?

These questions, which should be considered reflexively in the context of your own research, illustrate the fact that while all methods, potentially, are value laden (Kemmis and McTaggart, 2005), they can be utilized in ways which are socially just, a point which is explored in Chapter 1. The social justice perspectives we take in our own research direct our methods and our philosophy, as well as the *process* of the research. In relation to process, Lyons et al. (2013) suggest that:

> researchers that aspire to be equitable might reflect on the research process (e.g. are certain research tasks valued above others? If utilizing a research team, can team members take on tasks that capitalize on their strengths?), the content and focus of the research (e.g. choosing to study traditional healing practices for people of the African diaspora, gender inequalities in executive pay), or on research outcomes (e.g., Do the findings accurately represent the experiences of the community members? How can the findings be disseminated to the necessary stakeholders?).

---

[1] See Chapter 1 for further elaboration on social justice as a verb.

Adopting the type of approach advocated by Lyons et al. will certainly involve addressing methods, as well as all other aspects of the research, from a critically reflexive perspective which considers the impact of both the researcher and the method on the researched, particularly when they are members of marginalized groups. Using methods in a socially just way will also involve engaging in dialogical processes with researched communities which re-conceptualize notions of 'expert' and question dominant discourses in research, thus disrupting embedded power relationships in which the power is located with the researcher. In the context of dominant discourses of research some people (e.g. children and parents) become objects of study. Other parties to the research include teachers and other education professionals who are supposed to be 'informed' by the research and the researchers who produce the knowledge (Gitlin and Russell, 1994: 184), a significant divide which continues to exist in Higher Education departments across the UK – a generation after the publication of Gitlin and Russell's book. The persistence of this divide emphasizes the need for the participative, dialogical and socially just approaches to method and methodology advocated in this book, in order to facilitate research which avoids the risk of method becoming power (Patai, 1994).

Ultimately, it is the responsibility of the researcher, in dialogue with the other participants, to question the methods used and the extent to which they can be described as socially just. At a practical level, are they accessible to the other participants or do they assume levels of education and/or literacy among the participant group? To what extent are they culturally acceptable and/or appropriate and who is making that judgement? It is worth noting here that we use culture in its broadest sense to recognize subtle differences, often arising from social class or education, between individuals or sub-groups who are often seen as homogenous. From a more moral and theoretical perspective, however, a whole different set of questions arises. What is my positionality in relation to this study? How has that informed/influenced the development of the methods? How can I be certain my study is both ethical and moral? Who has ultimate control over the choice, development and use of the methods? What implications does this have for power relations? To what extent was the development of the methods a dialogic and participatory process? However, we should also take note of Patai's

(1994: 70) warning that 'we do not escape from the consequences of our positions by talking about them endlessly'.

Patai's concerns relate to the very significant issues of power inherent in any form of research, also alluded to by Gitlin and Russell (as discussed above). Power relations are inextricably intertwined with research that is concerned with social justice: issues of equity and in/equality are by definition associated with issues of where power is located in societies and their education systems. Yet, if we accept the arguments proposed by Patai, and by Gitlin and Russell, we see that undertaking research – albeit with the best of intentions – often reifies those power differentials because of the already privileged positioning of the researcher. This raises questions about the extent to which any research can be truly equitable but paradoxically also demands, in the name of social justice, that we continue working to develop new, creative – and possibly transgressive – approaches to method and methodology as a means of addressing issues of power. We address these issues throughout the book, giving extensive consideration to debates on power relations, proposing some of the ways in which unequal power relations can be ameliorated while acknowledging that issues of power continue to present challenges to researchers concerned with social justice and equity.

Structure of the book

We begin the book with a chapter which explores the often confused and confusing nature of the terms 'social justice' and 'equity'. Chapter 1 provides the theoretical underpinning to these terms and outlines the ways in which educational research might be framed within a socially just context. It gives consideration to the fact that conceptions of social justice and equity are not fixed or static but 'slippery' terms which are adopted and utilized by different groups and individuals at different times and for whom they can have very different meanings. Thus we explore questions such as whether social justice is a reciprocal concept or not and how it relates to individual positioning and power in terms of gender, race, notions of ability and so on. We move from this to more philosophical questions, such as where does social justice reside? Is it an ontological or philosophical position? Does it sit in the research questions and/or in the use we put our data to? In the absence of clear definitions that facilitate a single coherent theory, this chapter considers these issues in the context of the historical, philosophical and political meanings attributed to the terms 'equity' and 'social justice'. In particular, it explores the ancient concept of justice from which they are derived and considers them in the light of education, and more particularly educational research. We build on this discussion in Chapter 2 with an exploration of some of the issues in society and education which compel us to undertake our research in the context of a socially just paradigm.

We begin by examining various equity and social justice issues and analysing strategies for bringing about positive social change. In doing so we consider methodological concepts such as those of Power and of Voice and explore the implications of utilizing socially just research methods to theorize and shed light on these. We recognize that within all contemporary societies there are groups that struggle to gain equality of opportunity and social justice in their local and in front of national educational systems and consider this in the context of power relations and the implications of these relationships for socially just research methods and methodology. We position socially just educational research as a key driver for developing a more equitable, critical and democratic education system. We argue that this is one of the ways in which teachers and researchers can contribute to the collective responsibility of a free and just society, to ensure that civil and human rights are preserved and protected for each individual regardless of notions of difference. In this context, we demonstrate ways of exploring individuals, families, communities and regions using socially just research methods. We also explore how engaging with socially just research methods can support people's agency to change their social and economic circumstances where this is constrained by various forms of structural inequality.

Research for social justice is usually concerned with forms of oppression and marginalization which have an impact on educational access, experience and/or outcomes. However, such research also includes, for example, work on in/equalities which explores and seeks to understand advantage, as this is also a necessary prerequisite to the development of more equitable education systems, or pedagogic research which seeks to improve outcomes for all children and young people. Thus, socially just research is not necessarily about the study of marginalized communities. However, it all forms part of an ethical endeavour to improve educational access, experience and/or outcomes. Thus, what all educational research for equity and social justice has in common is a strong moral foundation, and this is explored in depth in Chapter 3.

Chapter 3 addresses issues of ethics and morality, which we argue are fundamental to social justice and equity. We explore in depth notions of reflexivity arguing that using socially just methods from a perspective of commitment to equity provides an opportunity to participate in an ethical and reflexive process which questions traditional understandings and scrutinizes existing educational values, processes, practices and ideological frameworks. Reflexive processes, however, give rise to the 'double-edged sword' of using socially just methods to give (mediated) Voice to marginalized groups: it is important to address these issues from a perspective of social justice, and so we discuss the ethical implications of this. We also engage with the issue of philosophical/sociological and economic drivers of research in education and discuss the tensions and parallels between the various value positions leading to and informing educational research. For example, to what extent is research socially just where it is funded by an organization with an ideological agenda (which may or may not be contrary to the researcher's notions of social justice)? These are significant issues which require careful consideration. We also discuss differing conceptions of ethics: while we emphasize the importance of moving beyond instrumental institutional ethics processes which emphasize the procedural at the expense of the moral, we acknowledge the problematic issues that this raises and explore them in this chapter. These three chapters provide the theoretical underpinning to the book: subsequent chapters explore the methodological and ethical implications of utilizing particular methodological approaches in research for social justice and equity.

Chapter 4 explores Insider Research. Much educational research – in particular that conducted by postgraduate students – is conducted as an 'insider researcher'. This chapter addresses some of the issues associated with undertaking research from an insider perspective and the complexities and tensions that might be addressed when doing so from a perspective of social justice which may bring the researcher into conflict with other actors in the institution. While this is a moral and ethical issue, we also discuss more broadly the politics of doing the research in relation to where and how the researcher is located. We then move on to discuss the notion of the insider/outsider and whether this is a false dichotomy or over-simplification given our multiple indices of difference in terms of our personal positioning in relation to research we may undertake. In this chapter we also examine the role of the researcher practitioner and the impact of this in developing as a critical educator who can contribute to the development of a more socially just and equitable education system. We discuss how this is located not only in the research questions but also in the methods and methodology and the way the research is carried out and how it is written. We position research as a political activity in terms of both its process and how it is written and disseminated. For example, accountability is central to this process, and we address the issue of to whom the researcher is accountable. We move from this chapter to one which explores some of the challenges of conducting socially just research with marginalized young people.

Chapter 5 draws on Liz's research to explore how marginalized and hard-to-reach young people can become valuable collaborators in the research process through developing a dynamic of respect and value for the individual. It considers some of the challenges in articulating the voice of marginalized populations and discusses this in the context of performing ethical and reflexive research which acknowledges the particular challenges of power relations. The chapter draws on individual narratives of young participants in order to illustrate some of the points made. It also discusses some of the methods used to develop data-generating instruments with the participants and the strategies used which facilitated them to contribute to data analysis while not requiring advanced levels of literacy.

Chapter 6 draws on Vicky's work with Adult Literacy. The chapter explores her concerns with fairness and equitability in relation to students and their families and communities. It also discusses empowerment and the ways in which socially just literacy research practice can often reach and change social conditions for different individuals and communities involved in research projects. The chapter goes on to discuss how participants' perceptions about their role in determining the course of their lives changed as a result of their research participation, illustrating how participation in research can support agentic action among disempowered individuals, their families and communities. This change is illustrated with individual stories and narratives which also reflect the economic, political, social and cultural impact of the study, emphasizing community building and empowerment. Chapter 6 concludes with proposals for ways in which communities can engage with participatory methods and methodology to promote and sustain the building of equitable networks, partnerships and collaborations. Both Chapters 5 and 6 emphasize the local. We move on to discuss how research concerned with social justice and equity is developing on a global scale. Chapter 7 draws on a number of international exemplars. These are drawn from contributors located in Western and developing nations and encompass educational contexts from early years, special and inclusive education, to adult education. We utilise them to illustrate how educational researchers from different contexts and working with diverse and marginalized populations understand and apply concepts of equity and social justice through their methods and methodologies. We also draw on these narratives to demonstrate some of the contrasting and creative ways in which researchers can reflect on and integrate principles of social justice in their methods and in their methodological decision making, with different global communities.

In Chapter 8 we explore recent moves to redress past mistakes through the development of more democratic and inclusive research methods to influence educational practice. New forms of research developed in a postmodern idiom recognize that researchers should understand that their actions have multiple meanings. The participatory paradigm fits quite naturally with a model of research in which equality is sought not solely in the distribution of this or that predetermined good but through the status and voice of the participants. In this chapter we explore research investigation that is critical of, and concerned with, deconstructing authoritative voices, those who speak for and on behalf of others. This includes the researchers deconstructing their own voices to critique their personal perceptions and explanations of what counts as inclusive practice. We illustrate this with examples of methods and approaches which new researchers can utilize in their own work, in particular drawing on Kay Heslop's innovative and inclusive approach to her doctoral research.

In Chapter 9 we move from participative to ethnographic approaches. It is, however, important to note that the two are not mutually exclusive. Here we explore the ways in which ethnographic methods can provide a vehicle for the enactment of socially just research practice when researchers are conscious and deliberate about their intentions. We provide examples of how ethnographic approaches can be designed and applied in an equitable and socially just manner. We offer practical examples from the literature and practice intended to demonstrate the socially just use of ethnographic methods with the understanding that the suggested practices may not be exclusively relevant to qualitative methodologies. We also discuss design, selecting research members, participant recruitment, data collection, gatekeepers, participation, data analysis, participant voice and dissemination together with ethical issues such as power and voice.

In recent years, many ethnographic approaches which were once marginalized and criticized (such as the use of some visual methodologies) have become more accepted as mainstream. In our quest for a more socially just and equitable education system, we suggest that it is important to continue developing creative and transgressive methodological approaches which are often better suited to engaging with researched communities, which demonstrate respect, for example, or have capacity for equitable participation, or are able to tell a story to a much wider audience. To this end, our final chapter explores methodological creativity for social justice.

In this chapter, we present a range of creative approaches to research design. This includes, for example, the use of approaches such as images and diaries, as well as other methods which are appropriate to the needs and wishes of other participants in the research process. We also consider strategies which are able to reach much wider audiences, drawing on the narrative provided by our colleague Curtis Chin, whose research is represented as documentary films. We emphasize the importance of 'fit for purpose' ideas for collaboration with researched communities and discuss ways in which researchers and participants can work together to develop methods which fit into a socially just paradigm. Finally, we include a discussion about the processes involved in the collection, collation, analysis and writing up of data with participants. The conclusion of the book draws together these themes and considers the ideas put forward in the book. Drawing on this, we propose a range of methods and methodologies that researchers could use to challenge inequality and work towards social justice and equity.

To start using the book, we recommend reading Chapters 1 to 3, which provide theoretical underpinning in relation to debates around social justice, equity and ethics. From the early, theoretical chapters, we recommend that you move on to read those which are most closely related to your own area of interest. In conclusion we need to comment about the limitations of a book of this nature. The debates around research concerned with social justice are wide-ranging. Thus, limited by the scope of a complex and multilayered subject which is of significant importance, we have attempted to capture the *essence* of key contemporary debates around research for social justice and equity as methodological approaches underpinned by this philosophy continue to emerge and develop. We have illustrated how these are enacted by drawing on vignettes or case studies generously provided by colleagues working in this field. We hope that our readers find this approach helpful and engaging in informing their own socially just research practice.

PART ONE

Theorizing social justice and equity in educational research

CHAPTER ONE

Theoretical conceptions of social justice and equity

This chapter will explore the theoretical conceptions of social justice and equity and their relationship with research methodology. A pertinent place to start is with the conception of philosophy; all philosophical positions and their associated methodologies, whether implicit or indeed explicit, offer a lens to notions of 'reality' which then determines what can be regarded as legitimate knowledge. A question we may ask is, whose interest does the 'legitimate knowledge' serve, and why? hooks (2009) argues that when the tenets of knowledge which include notions of authority and progress are embraced and implemented in specific ways that support only the interests of the dominant group, they lead to either social inertia or regression. So, what does that mean for us as socially just researchers? Importantly, we need to address the framing and posing of our questions. This is essential in ensuring that we are listening to perspectives from hidden, marginalized and silenced voices that enable new and different critiques of the educational settings and other institutions that support and perpetuate the interests of the dominant group(s). With this in mind, a central role and methodological driver of socially just research is how research questions are posed and to whom. For example, when researching educational inequalities there needs to be an awareness through the questions posed – that education systems are punctuated with social inequalities and the questions we ask, the context and the participant group cannot be positioned in isolation from this. Critical questions may explore aspects of how and why the educational system is unjust, and to what extent does an unjust society influence and perpetuate this. Philosophical positioning will shape the generation of the questions and methodology. In the absence of clear understandings of these issues that facilitate a single coherent theory, this chapter considers these issues in the context of the historical, philosophical and political meanings attributed to the terms equity and social justice. In particular, it explores the ancient concept of justice from which they are derived and considers them in the light of education, and more particularly educational research.

The history and philosophy of social justice

The debated notion of Justice is evident from the earliest times and draws heavily on the works of the ancient Greek philosophers and, later, Judaeo-Christian traditions and scholarship. Plato's *Republic* (1955) is, essentially, an extended work which debates the nature of justice. However, in exploring the work of the early Greek philosophers, it is worth noting that the word 'justice' has a different – and wider – range of meanings and subtleties than its English translation. In Greek, it implies, among other things, morality and 'right conduct' (Lee in Plato, 1955). In addition to these constructs, Plato also debates whether Justice is a virtue or knowledge, and whether the act of being Just would make a man happy or unhappy. Similarly, Aristotle in his treatise *Nicomachean Ethics* begins by defining Justice as 'a moral state' (1998: 76) but develops this argument in the context of his debate around the notion of reciprocity, noting that the Pythagoreans defined *Just* as simply 'that which reciprocates with another' but arguing that this is not consistent with conceptions of 'Distributive or Corrective Just[ice]' (84). He comes to the conclusion that:

> Justice is the moral state in virtue of which the just man is said to have the aptitude for practicing the Just in the way of moral choice, and for making division between himself and another, or between two other men, not so as to give himself the greater and to his

neighbour the less share of what is choice-worthy, and contrary-wise of what is hurtful, but what is proportionably equal, and in like manner when adjudging the rights of two other men. (86/87)

Aristotle also differentiates between conceptions of Justice as an abstract and the 'Social Just', which is concerned with social relations, arguing that 'by proportionate reciprocity of action the social community is held together' (84).

Similar philosophies underpin teachings from all the Abrahamic religions: for example, Social Justice is central to Judaism, where the Torah commands both charitable giving and advocacy on the part of the poor (e.g. Proverbs, 31:9, 'speak up, judge righteously, champion the poor and needy'). Similarly, in Islam the tenets of social justice are set down in the Quran, and then in Hadith and Sunna (sayings and behaviour of the Prophet Mohammed), with later interpretations by Islamic scholars. The Quran includes specific exhortations in relation to social justice. For example, 'so as for the orphan, do not oppress him, and as for the petitioner, do not repel him' (Quran.com/93), while the Prophet said, 'he is not a Muslim who sleeps with his stomach full while his neighbour stays hungry' (Sunan al-Kubra 19049). In a Christian context, the works of Aristotle informed those of St Augustine of Hippo, which are considered fundamental to modern understandings of social justice.

Augustine (354–430) was the bishop of Hippo Regius in modern-day Annaba, Algeria. His concerns were broad, including addressing the needs of the poorest and most marginalized members of his community. Augustine remains one of the most prolific writers in history, and many of his works are still extant. Similarly to the ancient Greeks, whom he referenced in his work (e.g. *City of God*, 2:14) he understood justice as meaning not only right relationships but also a fairer distribution of goods, a concept which is given prominence in much contemporary Catholic teaching (e.g. see John Paul II's Catechism of the Catholic Church undated: 421) and which might also be understood to relate to concepts of equity. Augustine regarded a just person as one who sought to use things only for the end for which God appointed them, arguing that 'when the miser prefers his gold to justice, it is through no fault of the gold, but of the man; and so with every created thing' (*City of God* 15.22). Augustine's notion of justice is, in a sense, reciprocal, in terms of his emphasis on fairer distribution of goods (*Letters*,

CCXI, AD 423). However, his emphasis on responsibility for others, particularly where they are less advantaged, also has resonance with broader contemporary understandings of social justice, both within and beyond the field of education, as well as with notions of the 'common good'. The notion of the 'common good', or responsibility for others, appears in both religious teachings and Aristotelian philosophy as a key aspect of justice, but, as with the concept of justice itself, it is a term which is open to interpretation. MacIntyre discussed at length the relationship of philosophic morality to that of Christianity (1981: 154/168), and the notion of common good is an example which may be observed in a range of examples from each tradition. These include the writings of Aristotle, who argues that 'the greatest good . . . is justice, in other words, the common interest' (Aristotle *Politics* III, II. 1282b15), the letters of St Paul (1 Cor. 12:7) and the work of the philosopher David Hume (1740: 318), who argued that '[I]t'was therefore a concern for our own, and the public interest, which made us establish the laws of justice'. More recently, Morwenna Griffiths (2003: 54) has argued that social justice is 'a dynamic state of affairs that is good for the common interest, where that is taken to include both the good of each and the good of all'.

In relation to this, MacIntyre (1981: 227/232) also rehearses a number of arguments about why people are affluent or needy relative to the rest of society. In doing so, he considers notions of desert and reciprocity in terms of the distribution of material wealth and the extent to which a person can 'earn' or 'deserve' such goods, as well as the extent to which that material wealth could or should be redistributed among the 'needy'. Such arguments have been debated by many writers across time and include works such as St Paul's letter to the Thessalonians, Hume (1740: III ii 2: 318), and Minogue (1998: 258). While not addressing reciprocity directly, Rawls (1999: 301/308) debates the concept of 'fairness', which has some parallels with MacIntyre's discussion, as well as with concepts of reciprocity. Reflecting the 'slippery' nature of these notions, alternative conceptions of reciprocity and social justice – those from a political/ideological perspective – can be found in education policy internationally, particularly where these are concerned with the education of young people and adults (e.g. see OECD, 2018; DfES, 2003a, 2003b, 2006) and those from marginalized communities. In the context of such policy, educational opportunities such as skills-based training are made available to young people in return for the increased economic contribution it is assumed they will make as a result of having particular skills or credentials. In the UK, this was first given prominence in the rights and responsibilities agenda of New Labour's 'Third Way' and can be traced through the more recent policies of the Coalition and Conservative administrations (e.g. DfES, 2005: 10; 2006: 1; DfE, 2011: 1). Similar policy initiatives and ideologies can be seen internationally, with Machin (2006) noting that in 2005, OECD social policy ministers made a move from 'remedial approaches' to 'making work pay', leading to greater concern with learning experiences which might result in integration in the labour market, something also regarded as supporting the 'traditional goal of social justice'.

However, these ideologies, despite the discourses they use, derive not from conceptions of social justice or equity but rather from neo-liberal conceptions of human capital, in which individuals are positioned either as a problem or as a resource (e.g. see Ade-Ojo and Duckworth, 2015; Atkins, 2016a; Billet et al. 2010) and where, if they are unable to engage with the opportunities presented to them, they are placed within a deficit model, characterized by state discourses as failing to meet their civic responsibility of engaging with lifelong learning. Such discourses effectively transfer responsibility from the state to the individual for this perceived failure (Ainley and Corney, 1990: 94/95). In doing so, they divert attention from any critical consideration of economic and education systems, since they obscure 'the existence of systemic and structural failures which confine people to an allotted place in life, constrain individual agency and replicate social class and other social inequities' (Atkins, 2009: 144), an action which in and of itself is contrary to social justice. This implies that the role of socially just educational research is to illuminate and work to address some of the inequities and inequalities which are evident in the education system. Further, because education is so bound up with social justice, not only as a means to promote a more equitable and socially just society but also as a structure which reproduces marginalization, it is all the more essential that research and its methods which claim social justice as part of its *purpose* can be seen to be doing social justice in the context of its *process*. For example, critical educational research is a form of principle research that unites purpose and process. It is designed in its methodology not just to explain or understand social/educational reality but importantly to unsettle the status quo and change it. Duckworth and Smith (2018c) identify that the moral driver of critical research is underpinned by human emancipation and social justice. Their critical research (highlighted in Chapter 6) aims to firmly establish and maintain conditions which empower the often silenced and disadvantaged communities. A way to address this was in the development and implementation of the methodology whereby a strong emphasis was placed and driven on the democratizing of the relations between researchers and researched. This shifted from a privileging of the researcher's view of reality to a method that supports shared understandings or 'dialogic conversations'.

Such forms of critical methodology have become increasingly prominent over the past generation, by increasing numbers of scholars taking a more critical standpoint in their research and theory-making, which positions them as influencers of policy, with the aim being to redress historical inequities and 'make' social justice (Denzin and Lincoln, 2013: 580). This move towards social justice as a form of critical inquiry implies activism as well as philosophy – to quote Denzin and Lincoln (2013: 194) 'getting mad is no longer enough', and also suggests that social justice can be constructed as a form of politics, encompassing both action and value. Therefore, in the context of critical educational inquiry, both these aspects of social justice are critical in guiding the design and methodological and theoretical frameworks.

Social justice as a value

Educational Research has been conceptualized as a value-led form of inquiry and this is reflected across a broad range of scholarship, including, for example, works by Griffiths (1998, 2003), Christians (2013) and also Stenhouse (1975). Indeed, Carr (1995) considered that the educational research would not be possible unless it was value laden:

1.   *Values are so vital an ingredient in educational research that their elimination is impossible save by eliminating the research enterprise itself. Those educational researchers who claim that they are adopting a 'disinterested' stance are, therefore, simply failing to recognize certain features of their work.*

2. *The reason why educational research is always so value laden is because educational research methods always entail a commitment to some educational philosophy. 'Educational research' and 'educational philosophy' are not, therefore, as independent as is usually thought, and any separation of the two represents a historically contingent division of labour rather than any clear-cut differences in purpose.*

3. *To accept that philosophy and values cannot be expunged from educational research is not to concede that educational research cannot be a scientific pursuit. On the contrary, any coherent account of an educational science requires that the relationship between philosophy, values and educational research be formulated in a way that renders them compatible rather than antithetical* (Carr 1995: 88/89).

We also see Nind et al.'s observation (2016: 32, citing Alexander, 2009) that, while all too often neglected, values 'spill out untidily' from the analysis of pedagogy. It is worth noting that the values which underpin social justice are personal to each one of us and often related to ideological perspectives. Thus, it is not possible to argue that research and the methods employed for social justice are, or should be, in any way objective or value-neutral. Rather, we need to foreground the personal values and positioning which inform our commitment to social justice, because 'unless [we] can critically engage in examining [our] own practice, [we] cannot critically examine others' claims to knowledge' (Duckworth, 2013) and our 'research practice is immoral if [we] do not own [our] involvement in the process and if [we] claim value neutrality' (Sikes and Goodson, 2003: 48).

Social justice and power

Given the concern that social justice and equity have with in/equalities in society, this means that a key issue to be addressed in any research which claims to utilize socially just philosophies and/or methods is how to respond to issues of power and positioning, particularly where we, as researchers, claim to be representing the voice of the marginalized. These are significant ethical issues and are explored in more depth in Chapter 3.

In terms of considering issues of power and relationships in our research, we first need to acknowledge their implications. Yet, as Fine (1994: 22) has suggested, 'Social research cast through voices typically involves carving out pieces of narrative evidence that we select, edit, and deploy to border our arguments. The problem is not that we tailor, but that so few qualitative researchers reveal that we *do* this work, much less *how* we do this work.' Fine's argument is particularly significant in the context of educational research that claims to promote social justice and equity. Therefore, within the context of any educational research, consideration of the power relations within the study is essential. This consideration should be given within both the context of social justice and other values that underpin it and also in the context of the ethical issues appertaining to research with marginalized groups. Much of this work seeks to take a collaborative or participatory approach – indeed, Nixon et al. (2003: 94) have acknowledged that 'collaboration [in educational research] is . . . ethically desirable' – providing a third dimension for consideration of power relations, whilst Griffiths (1998: 57) has stated that meanings and interpretations are developed in social groups that are themselves structured by sociopolitical power relations. She goes on to argue that since knowledge depends on human interpretation and values, research methods need to take account of the unequal power of different social groups.

Expectations that qualitative research is inherently socially just or better suited to the study of marginalized and often silenced communities than other methodological approaches are inadvisable. We suggest that careful consideration on the ways that researchers may conduct qualitative research in a socially just manner is needed. Qualitative approaches can offer a driver by which socially just methods can be enacted when researchers are conscious of, and considered about, their intentions and the implications that may arise in the research journey. Socially just analysis and interpretation include truly representing the perspectives of study participants thereby promoting the quality of qualitative research. Of course, interest in engaging in socially just qualitative research practices will vary with researchers' and participants' context and experience.

Key aspects to consider include:

- Planning and preparation
- Questioning what it means to be a socially just researcher.

We would suggest that socially just researchers approach the conceptualization of the project, including research question development and other design undertakings, as an opportunity to commence forging and building a collaborative relationship with the community being studied.

Questions to ask yourself may include:

- How are you going to establish relationships in the community of research prior to data collection?
- Do you need to work closely with a gatekeeper?
- Are there other groups you need to involve, for example, who are the stakeholders?
- In relation to the research design who will be involved in the process and why?
- What might be the potential impact of the research on the community? Are you building in praxis?
- Who will the research team involve and what do they bring that will strengthen the socially just drivers of the research?

It is important to note that any educational research involving children or vulnerable adults and their communities necessarily includes individuals who are likely to have less powerful positioning than dominant groups in society, or indeed, their own community. It would be inexcusable to conduct research which purported to make any explanations in terms of such a group and to do that without attempting to redress issues of power. Such an activity would objectify the researched and fail to demonstrate the respect inherent in recognizing and respecting them as individuals; further, such an approach would be contrary to the concerns of social justice with structural inequity. Drawing on participatory and collaborative research methods (see Chapter 8) can form part of a response to these concerns, but does not in itself address issues of social justice, human value or power relations, and the consideration of these issues is of critical importance. Should a study pay lip service to notions of dialogue, equality and collaboration or should it try to find a means to negotiate the issues arising from the research with the participants in the context of an equitable relationship? This implies debates about the extent to which any research is truly collaborative and the extent to which power and control were actually vested in the researcher. Discussions around these issues address questions such as, for example, were the methods developed by the researcher or as part of a collaborative endeavour? And was the *choice* of method vested in the researcher or in the researched? What are the difficulties arising from this (e.g. such as limited understanding of research processes among young children) and how can they be addressed? To what extent does the research process remain in the control of the researcher rather than the researched? How is knowledge made and to whom does it belong? Who decides what counts as legitimate knowledge arising from the study? Gitlin (1994: 2) addresses this latter issue in his exploration of Power and political activism in educational research and with echoes of Fine's argument (1994: 2) reasons that 'attention to issues of power, to how research influences identified aims, relationships, and forms of legitimate knowledge . . . has been largely missing from methodological debates'. These are significant questions which should be addressed by any researcher investigating issues in education, but particularly by those who purport to utilize a social justice theoretical framework and socially just and equitable models.

However, in relation to power, it is not sufficient to consider the methodological implications we have briefly outlined above. Other significant issues which relate to Power, as well as to ethics and the methodological decisions taken in the research, are those of institutional and cultural context and the individual positioning of both the researcher and the researched in relation to issues of intersectionality such as class, gender, race and ability. Thus, two parallel studies with identical aims, methods and protocols exploring resilience and vulnerability among primary aged children in two different schools will raise different Power issues according to, for example, gender of the researcher, researcher's relationship with the school, whether or not the researcher has previously worked as a teacher in the sector and, if so, at what level. And this is before consideration is given to, for example, the range of ethnic and cultural groups, the dominant socio-economic groupings, the perceptions of the value of research among the teachers and the children, the relative level of ability of individual children or whether one or more is particularly dominant in the context of data collection. Any of those issues – plus many others – will create subtle differences in the power relations within the study, causing different responses and raising different methodological and ethical problems.

Related to this are questions about issues such as respect for individuals. This goes beyond issues such as acknowledging difference and recognizing individuality, although this is a significant aspect of respect. In Liz's research with low-attaining young people, for example, the participants gave her college work they had completed in order to help with her research. Liz made the decision to utilize the college work as data, rather than disregarding it, as a means of demonstrating respect for the young people. However, that decision left the study open to criticisms that it had been inconsistent in its approach, implying a lack of rigour, which had to be addressed as part of a methodological discussion encompassing social justice, respect and power relations as well as the methodological implications of the decision. Related to issues of power and ethics, this study, like others involving children, young people and marginalized groups, also raised questions about the nature of informed consent and the extent to which consent can be truly informed when given by an individual who does not fully comprehend the possible implications of educational research, in terms of potential ethical issues, power relations and the relationship issues associated with research which utilizes ethnographic methods.

Understanding social justice and equity

Most people involved with the study and research of education will claim that social justice is fundamental to broad understandings of education. Ideologically, as we have outlined above, governments of different political hue claim that achieving social justice is a key aim and outcome of their education policies. We have acknowledged in our own writing that social justice is a term which has multiple definitions (e.g. see Atkins, 2009; Duckworth, 2013, Ade-Ojo and Duckworth, 2015). However, recent research we have undertaken (see Atkins and Duckworth, 2016), exploring trainee teachers' conceptions of social justice, offers a more complex – and potentially concerning – picture. We expected our participants to provide us with different definitions: the fact that over half believed that social justice was the same as equality of opportunity we found worrying, in terms of the naivety of response among trainees who were midway through their programmes. Few of these grasped the significant difference between equality and equity. However, of greater concern were the significant minority who believed that social justice related to 'the rule of law', 'British Values' and the participant who admitted, 'I have never heard this term before'. We are continuing to develop our work in this area, but believe that it implies that Initial Teacher Education, in England and Wales at least, is failing to address key philosophical and sociological issues associated with education. How can teachers promote and engage with a more socially just system if their understandings of the term are so naïve? How can they undertake research which addresses the complex issues of social justice and marginality in our classrooms? In terms of our conception of social justice, which underpins our discussions throughout this book, we believe it to be a concept concerned with morality, as argued by the early philosophers, and would define it as a concept which supports

> Societal structures that facilitate each individual to achieve their potential in each area of their life, underpinned by an equal respect for each individual arising from their status as a person, which recognised and valued fundamental differences in terms of interest, aptitude and ambition but which is not associated with any material, intellectual or other perceived benefits and advantages, and which are concerned with issues of equity, fairness, and right.
>
> (Drawing on Atkins, 2009: 45)

Such societal structures could encompass areas including, for example, access to work, health, housing or leisure activity, but for the purpose of this book the definition is considered with particular reference to education. Within such educational structures, all children, young people and adults would be able to access a critical and democratic curriculum which prepared them for lives as active citizens. Our concept of social justice is one in which the concept of equity is both explicit and implicit: it assumes that equity should be enacted within an educational context as well as underpinning a philosophy of, and a commitment to, social justice. Equity is a word which has its origins in the Latin *aequitas*, from *aequus*, meaning 'equal' (OECD, 2003: 369), but which has evolved to have a close relationship with conceptions of social justice and to imply *fairness*, a concept which is not necessarily the same as *equality* of its original meaning. For example, Rawls (1971: 237/238) suggests that equity arises when 'an exception is . . . made when the established rule works an unexpected hardship'. A more comprehensive definition comes from Falk et al. (1993: 2) who argue that:

> Equity derives from a concept of social justice. It represents a belief that there are some things which people should have, that there are basic needs that should be fulfilled, that burdens and rewards should not be spread too divergently across the community, and that policy should be redirected with impartiality, fairness and justice towards these ends.

This concept of fairness and equity is also grounded in international law. The preamble to the Universal Declaration of Human Rights (United Nations, 1948/2018) begins with the statement that 'recognition of the inherent dignity and of the equal and inalienable rights of all members of the human family is the foundation of freedom, justice and peace in the world', a statement which emphasizes the respect for each individual's humanity which we regard as fundamental to our own understanding of social justice. In terms of education, Article 26.2 of the declaration emphasizes the need for education to promote tolerance and understanding and to aim for the 'full development of the human personality' in order to achieve this. Given that the broad aim of all educational research must be to improve or better understand education in some way, it follows that the intent behind the UN Declaration should underpin educational research as well as education itself. Indeed, Atkins and Wallace (2012: 30) have argued that the values of educational research are the same as those underpinning education. Thus, notions of equity and social justice may be argued to be fundamental to all educational research and not just that which claims to be conducted within a social justice theoretical framework.

Social justice as a theoretical framework

Over the past generation, social justice has emerged as a theoretical framework in its own right (e.g. see Griffiths (1998) for an early discussion, and 2003). However, it is one which draws heavily on a range of methodologies, philosophies and theoretical perspectives. In her paper arguing for a theoretical framework which would facilitate the understanding of social justice in educational practice, Griffiths (1998: 176) articulates her own methodological framework as being 'rooted in the multi-disciplinary and plural approaches to be found in new developments in feminist epistemology and cultural studies which take account of epistemological standpoints, and dynamic models of identity underpinning them.' Griffiths illustrates here the plurality of perspectives that socially just research might draw on. Obvious among these are perspectives such as, for example, Marxist and feminist theory or critical race theory as well as a wide range of other perspectives. For example, Mark Vicars's work, undertaken in Australia, Asia and the UK, explores issues in teacher education and has an explicit commitment to social justice but draws primarily on Queer Theory (e.g. see McKenna et al., 2013; Vicars, 2016). Also in Australia, Trace Ollis's work with marginalized communities leads her to have a commitment to social justice enacted through collaborative research; the theoretical perspective for her work draws on Freirean notions of critical pedagogy as a means to achieving justice (e.g. Ollis et al., 2014). Melanie Walker (e.g. 2003) has drawn on Nussbaum and Sen to consider what the capabilities approach can contribute to social justice in education. Liz (see Atkins, 2009) drew on a range of philosophical perspectives to develop a theoretical framework contextualized by social justice. A range of different perspectives are also reflected in Dover's (2013) work about teaching for social justice which argues that the conceptual and pedagogical foundations of social justice teaching may be drawn from a range of educational, philosophical and political movements, including democratic education, social justice education, critical pedagogy, multi-cultural education and culturally responsive education. Dover's analysis implies the importance of acknowledging institutional and cultural context, as well as recognizing issues of oppression and in/equality related to characteristics such as class, gender, race or ability which impact on moves to develop a more socially just context for education, as well as on practical methodological decisions taken by researchers working within a socially just framework. This is made more explicit in Griffiths's (2003) statement illustrating how social justice can be understood:

1. Social justice is a verb; that is, it is a dynamic state of affairs in that it is never – could never be – achieved once and for all. It is always subject to revision.

2. The good for each person both affects and depends on the good for all – where 'all' can be understood as being small face-to-face groups, structural groups (constructed both by positioning and by self-identification) and the society as a whole. How these groupings are made up is never fixed.

3. Social justice depends on both 'recognition' and 'redistribution'.

4. The issues need to be understood in terms both of 'little stories' and of 'grand narratives'; that is, both localized issues and large-scale theorizing about them.

(Griffiths, 2003: 55)

Other work draws on more established theoretical perspectives in order to address issues of social justice. For example, Vicky drew on Feminist Standpoint Theory in work which was seeking to rupture the ties of masculine domination perpetuated within what she saw as androcentric epistemologies. Thus, this work (Duckworth, 2013), while addressing issues of male domination, seeks a more equitable state of society and utilized a collaborative approach to research with women and men which reflected a conscious move away from more positivist approaches. Her research sought to build and sustain alternative frameworks which could challenge the current societal status quo in which many women's voices are not heard and the perspective of men is viewed as 'universal' (Cohen et al., 2007). Feminist epistemology has evolved through a number of stages, which include feminist empiricism, feminist postmodernism and Standpoint epistemology (Harding, 1987; see also Maynard and Purvis, 1995) and which, like the Social Justice theory which draws on feminist theory, have a plurality of perspectives. For example, Standpoint theory recognizes women's narratives as a means to place their voices within a wider theory of their positioning in society (see Lawthom 2004; Smith, 1987, 1997). However, it is not without criticism; some feminists argue that it fails to address the multiple perspectives of women, which include experiences of class and ethnicity, instead claiming a single 'universal woman' (see Narayan, 1989). The contention between essentialism and difference, and relativism and objectivism, has resulted in feminists adopting various approaches which include Stanley and Wise's (1993) move towards 'fractured foundationalism'. However, it may be argued that its strength lies in the recognition that 'feminist struggle can begin wherever an individual woman is; we create a movement that focuses on our collective experience, a movement that is continually mass-based' (see hooks, 1994: 29). Inequality and inequity are thus addressed at a collective structural level, challenging what is considered the normative culture grounded in ontological assumptions that pathologize gender and class (see Skeggs, 2002).

In addition to drawing on Feminist theory, much work concerned with issues of inequality, like that of Skeggs (see also McDonald and Marsh, 2005; Willis, 1977), draws on Marxist and neo-Marxist theory. Marxist theory is concerned with political economy and power, how it is located with those who control the 'means of production' and is drawn on and variously interpreted in epistemological terms, as well as in diverse fields such as ethics and theoretical psychology. Neo-Marxist approaches move beyond classical Marxist theories, incorporating other sociological views to provide a more holistic view of social class structures and dynamics with a focus more on society than on the economic system alone. A key contemporary proponent of utilizing Marxist and neo-Marxist theory as a means of exploring educational issues in a social justice context is James Avis.

Avis's work covers a wide area but is concerned with the relationship between education and labour markets and the (negative) implications this has for the working classes. He advocates a move towards a more social democratic form of politics as a means of working towards a more equitable and Socially Just society (e.g. see Avis, 2016). Similarly with other authors whose work is concerned with issues of Social Justice, Avis draws on Pierre Bourdieu's overarching 'theory of practice', or inequality, first propounded in 1972, which is predicated on a range of concepts but most specifically field and habitus. Bourdieu, whose work owes much to Marxist philosophy, argues that society is structured to reproduce privilege, which is located with a small elite, as a result of the constraints of habitus and the individual's location in the field. Bourdieu defines the field as 'a configuration of relations between positions objectively defined, in their existence and in the determinations they impose upon the occupants, agents or institutions' (1996/1992: 72/73) using football as an analogy. He explains that a footballer is able to anticipate what happens next due to their 'feeling' for the game. Similarly, he argues that individuals are 'born into' social fields (e.g. particular cultures or social classes) and learn the 'symbolic capital' of that field – unwritten rules, cultural beliefs and practices, language – necessary to survive and succeed in that field. The related concept of habitus recognizes that people are born into different circumstances, for example, into wealth and poverty. This generates their primary knowledge of their life and situation and reflects their 'inheritance of the accumulated experiences of their antecedents' (Robbins, 1998: 35). It is demonstrated in everyday human behaviour such as 'blowing of the nose', gait and attitudes. On a symbolic level it is visible in, for example, the way a person speaks and dresses. It also relates to ways in which access to different forms of capital and the ability to mobilize those capitals shape learners' lives. Bourdieu (1997) argues that the combination of economic, social, cultural and symbolic capital constitutes a habitus. Different classes, he argues, have different habitus and therefore different perceptions, aspirations, dispositions, tastes and cultural values. Thus, the ways in which individuals think and behave may be explained by the concept of habitus. The theory has been argued to be deterministic, but, as Hodkinson (2008) argues, 'neither positional factors nor the forces interacting in the field are deterministic', implying that habitus cannot be deterministic since it is mediated by these factors, something which we have both observed in our own research (e.g. see Atkins, 2016a; Duckworth, 2013; Duckworth and Smith, 2018d).

This idea that the forces interacting in the field are not deterministic implies that where education is transformative, this can contribute to addressing issues of inequality, highlighting the importance of research which seeks to do social justice by understanding better what *makes* education transformative, as well as research which seeks to do social justice by understanding the conditions which lead to inequality. This book seeks to provide guidance for ways in which the aims and process of educational research, as well as its conceptual and theoretical basis, can be seen to be socially just. In short, it offers ways in which educational researchers can 'walk the walk' as well as 'talk the talk', supporting socially just research as a form of activism and a form of action. We believe that underpinning our research with a social justice philosophy imposes a moral imperative on us to act in accordance with the expressed values of that philosophy. This imperative to respond is emphasized by Griffiths' argument (above) that 'Social Justice is a verb' and by Walker (see Griffiths, 2003: 125) who also emphasizes the active in her argument that 'only through doing justice can we make justice'. Walker's argument also implies that actions and processes may differ across different contexts and with different people, illustrating the nature of social justice as not merely a theory but a journey. Social justice as a journey also suggests that understandings of it may change over time. Significantly, in her 1998 paper, as well as in her 2003 book *Action for Social Justice in Education*, Griffiths argued for a revisable theory. This notion now seems prescient given its particular relevance for contemporary research addressing diverse educational issues in a dynamic, rapidly changing global, political and economic context which is witnessing increasing inequality across a wide spectrum, of which education is only one component. Below, Katerina Matziari presents a case example illustrating her research and discussing how social justice was theorized and enacted during the project.

Case example

Leadership and a vision for inclusion
Katerina Matziari
Manchester Metropolitan University, UK

This case example presents the methodological rationale for addressing social justice considerations of a research project that aimed to explore the notion and function of school leaders' vision for inclusion in education. More specifically, the research project employed life history methods, and the knowledge claims made were generated through narratives based on interviews with six head-teachers of primary schools in Greece.

Theorizing social justice

In my project, I adopted a view of inclusive education as a social reform movement with the relevant discussion to be framed within a social justice framework. The emphasis of the relevant discussion is developed around the demand for a move from the existent exclusive education system to a more inclusive one (Slee, 2006). Keeping this notion of inclusion as a reform movement, Nilholm (2006: 436) suggests that *inclusion* 'connoted changes with regard to the system rather than to its parts'. Such a reform process tries to reveal the sociocultural and context-dependent process of students' categorization practices. Within that framework, inclusion appears rather to be a process for change than an outcome (Ballard, 1999; Sebba and Ainscow, 1996).

Within that conceptualization of inclusive education, the essential role of leadership is emphasized, and school leaders appear to act as change agents capable of implanting inclusive ideals in the school community and promoting inclusion as social value commitment (see Ainscow and Sandill, 2010; Coleman, 2012; Guzmán, 1997; Kugelmass and Ainscow, 2004; Leo and Barton, 2006; Lumby and Morrison, 2010; Rayner, 2009; Riehl, 2000). From that perspective, leadership was conceptualized as a social practice and leaders as social actors. However, school leaders' practice is developed and actualized within a space of several contradictions as it is shaped by policy demands for performativity and accountability that characterize the neo-liberal Western societies, different definitions of inclusive education and an interplay of enacted personal, professional and organizational values. The research project focused on that conceptual space that permits social agents to participate in the change process by attributing their own meaning to the concept of inclusion, practice and the policy content. From that view, the elements of personal interpretation and values were placed at the centre of the research exploration by utilizing the concept of vision.

Enacting social justice

A connection of my project with social justice rhetoric can be seen in the articulated research purposes. The notion of inclusion and/or exclusion has been widely recognized as a social justice concern in education (see Griffiths, 1998). As discussed elsewhere in this chapter, one of the aims of social justice research is to explore and reveal 'what *makes* education transformative'. My project organized its research aims around that aspect of inclusive education by inviting head-teachers to share their life stories with the view to explore the process and content of their vision in the *transformative* process of their schools.

However, an aspect that was of a great importance for me to develop within a social justice view was that of the process of the research and my practice as a researcher within that field. Reflecting upon the work of Griffiths who suggested that a theoretical framework for research for social justice should develop its philosophy as 'a co-construction, made with the co-operation of, and in collaboration with, practitioners' (Griffiths, 1998: 175), I tried to be very explicit with regard to the notion of co-construction of the research in a life-history research design. As Lieblich et al. (1998: 8) explain, 'the particular life story is one instance of the polychromic versions of the possible constructions or presentations of people's selves and lives, which they use according to specific momentary influences', and the relationship formed between the interviewee and interviewer influences the way that the narration is built.

The acknowledgement of the active participation of the participants in the research conduct is not to hinder the power relationship between the researcher and the informants. Despite the quality of interaction with the participants and the degree of collaboration that the researcher and the research design allow in the research conduct, the responsibility of the research conduct and research account rests with the researcher (Denzin, 2009). Usually, the interpretation, analysis and use of the data are territories that informants have limited, if any, participation. In my attempts to address these aspects of the research process, I involved participants in the research process and after the stage of data collection by sharing with them the life history narratives I produced and the concomitant part of the analytical discussion.

My desire to develop an explicit relationship of integrity between my epistemological stance and my practical research approach was informed by Slee's (2006: 116) powerful prompting for 'a fundamental analysis of the relationships between ontology, epistemology, language and action' in the research for inclusive education. Slee (2006) emphasized that for inclusive education to succeed as a reform movement, we have to be clear about our own foundations and motives. Kvale and Brinkmann (2009: 315) contend that such a stance in the research conduct does not involve 'just self-analysis, but also practical social-practice analysis is required' in terms of how the researcher conceives knowledge production and what 'presupposes about the human reality, and how it affects human reality'. In my practice as a researcher, I argued that by being explicit on how these issues are addressed within the inclusion rhetoric, the connection between the theory and practice will be clear. Especially for the researcher who works with a view to the educational change – to describe, understand, secure or promote it – the dimension of practice as enacted praxis is of a great significance.

Ethics, power and positioning

As one of my guiding research aspirations was to keep an integrity between my epistemological stance, the methodological choices and the descriptive language used in my research approach, I wanted to make sure that my positionality and theoretical stance with regard to any issues of power was 'visible' in my claim to represent the voices of my participants. In my project, the issues of power were mainly revealed and/or hidden within underlying claims of agency attributed to my participants in the change process of education towards a more just society.

Gunter (2005: 173) emphasizes that underneath the debates around the agency of the head-teachers on the process of change 'are epistemological divergences regarding what constitutes knowledge and knowing, and who are regarded as the knowers'. My interpretative approach did not employ a comprehensive explanatory theory that could give a straightforward explanation of the structure of the systems of power in social world. However, I did openly recognize – and opened myself to criticism – that the attributed agency to the individuals can be seen as an activity of political power 'that undertakes to conduct individuals throughout their lives by placing them under the authority of a guide responsible for what they do and for what happens to them' (Foucault, 1997: 68). I felt that such a claim was incongruous with the epistemological stance of a constructionist inquiry that places at the centre of its interest the active construction of knowledge by human agents that shape action, as it is the praxis that is the ultimate interest for the constructionist researcher (Lincoln and Guba, 2005) and also consistent with my theoretical framework.

Hence, the most important challenge that I felt needed to be addressed for my project was for me to consciously accept my own epistemological and philosophical claims and reveal how they shaped my *praxis* as a social researcher in the field of social justice research.

The ethical approach of my project was conceived not as a separate part of my research practice but as an indivisible constituent of the research process which pervaded all the different stages of the research from the research design to the practicalities of the fieldwork until the use of the data. As Shaw suggested, doing otherwise 'risks compartmentalizing ethical aspects of research, and shutting them off into a preamble to research' (2008: 400). A main ethical concern was to keep the voice of my participants 'alive' in the interplay of their narrated experiences and my interpretation. The way that I tried to address that was through being explicit about my analytical stance by employing multiple narrative styles for presenting my data and finally by sharing my – and/or their (?) – narratives with my participants.

Conclusion: Positioning ourselves, positioning social justice

The debates that we have explored in this chapter imply that social justice is a form of politics, a form of critical inquiry, but also a guiding philosophy, so it behoves us to discuss our own stance in relation to social justice and equity at this point. We see the world, especially the educational world, as being structurally unequal. We believe that the inequities and inequalities we strive to redress are shaped by cultural, social, gendered and political values – among others – into forms of alternative reality, which can be deterministic but which are also amenable to change (e.g. see Bourdieu and Passeron, 1990; Rawls, 1999). We consider that 'the common good is accessible to us only in personal form; it has its ground and inspiration in a social ontology of the human' (Christians, 2013: 155). Our values and philosophy are informed by that ontological perspective, committing us to critical exploration of the underlying causal mechanisms of structural inequalities in education, through teaching, research and activism. Of course, others may have entirely different perspectives, but still frame their research within a social justice philosophy. We are also influenced by a belief that education can be transformative in addressing issues of social justice, acknowledging Carr's (1995: 90) argument that 'Any particular [educational] research methodology always incorporates a particular educational philosophy.' Thus, it follows from this discussion that social justice is, indeed, a philosophy. However, it may be argued to differ from other philosophies in terms of its imperative for action, which may be argued to make it a form of political endeavour as well as a philosophy. This is a critical point. The imperative for action, and conceptualization of social justice as political endeavour as well as a philosophy, means that it does not merely provide the lens through which we interpret the world or, indeed, our data. It also requires us to *enact* social justice as part of the research process addressing questions such as 'how does/can my research enact social justice and reflect the values of social justice in its purpose and its process? How does/can it promote equity and justice?' It resides, therefore, not only in the philosophy of the researcher but also in her actions, from her initial idea, through the design and process of the research to the selection and interpretation of the data. Throughout all this, each action and decision taken is mindful of the researcher's responsibility *for*, as well as *to*, others. Thus, it is indivisible from notions of ethics and of reflexivity and resides equally in method, methodology and theoretical positioning. It follows that we cannot consider research to be socially just unless it can be seen in its aims and methods to be *doing* social justice and to be considering the implications of reciprocity, care for others, for the community and the common good more broadly of each aspect of the study. And importantly, as researchers we are aware of our privilege and that awareness is importance – we firmly believe that it will not be until a more just society is in place that we can truthfully know and realize what research for social justice looks like.

Further reading

Ade-Ojo, G., and Duckworth, V. (2015), *Adult Literacy Policy and Practice: From Intrinsic Values to Instrumentalism*, London: Palgrave Macmillan Pivotal.

Aristotle (1988), *The Politics* (editor Stephen Everson), Cambridge: Cambridge University Press.

Carr, W. (1995), *For Education*, Buckingham: Open University Press.

Hume, D. (1740/2000), *A Treatise of Human Nature* (editors David Fate Norton and Mary J. Norton), Oxford: Oxford University Press.

Minogue, K. (1998), 'Social justice in theory and practice', in D. Boucher and P. Kelly (eds), *Social Justice from Hume to Walzer*, London: Routledge.

Nixon, J., Walker, M., and Clough, P. (2003), 'Research as thoughtful practice', in P. Sikes, J. Nixon and W. Carr (eds), *The Moral Foundations of Educational research: Knowledge, Inquiry and Values*, Maidenhead: Open University Press.

Rawls, J. (1999), *A Theory of Justice Revised Edition*, Oxford: Oxford University Press.

CHAPTER TWO

Research methods for social justice and equity in context

Introduction

In this chapter we address some of the issues in society and education which compel us to undertake our research using philosophies, approaches and methods which can be described as socially just. While much of the work of researchers committed to social justice is undertaken in and with marginalized communities, research in this area encompasses a wide range of the theoretical and empirical. This encompasses theoretical critiques of the social and educational impacts of globalization and neo-liberalism (e.g. see Avis, 2016; Ball, 2012; Reay, 2004, 2006) as well as activist work addressing local and global inequalities (e.g. see Duckworth and Smith, 2018a; Mishra and Raveendran, 2011; Smith et al., 2016). Other examples of such work include that using specific theoretical approaches to address issues of social justice, such as, for example, Melanie Walker's work on social justice and capability theory (e.g. see Cin and Walker, 2016; Otto et al., 2017; Walker, 2017). What is common to those researchers who are driven by a commitment to social justice is that they are transparent about the values that researchers should adhere to, most notably, democratic values: demonstrate concern for marginalized and minority rights and dignity, show commitment to the common good, have conviction in the power of people to enact individual and collective agency and have a belief in the importance of dialogic engagement and the transparent stream of ideas, reflexivity and the central premise of individual and collective responsibility for others and their communities. This requires engagement with critical pedagogy, research and theory, which are based on a set of assumptions about the world articulated by Kincheloe et al. (2013: 341) as follows:

- All thought is fundamentally mediated by power relations that are socially and historically constituted.

- Facts can never be isolated from the domain of values or removed from some form of ideological inscription.

- The relationship between concept and object and between signifier and signified is never stable or fixed and is often mediated by the social relations of capitalist production and consumption.

- Language is central to the formation of subjectivity (conscious and unconscious awareness).

- Certain groups in any society and particular societies are privileged over others and, although the reasons for this privileging may vary widely, the oppression that characterizes contemporary societies is most forcefully reproduced when subordinates accept their social status as natural, necessary or inevitable.

- Oppression has many faces and focusing on only one at the expense of others (e.g. class oppression vs racism) often elides the interconnections among them.

- Mainstream research practices are generally, although most often unwittingly, implicated in the reproduction of systems of class, race, and gender oppression (De Lissovoy and McClaren, 2003; Gresson, 2006; Kincheloe and Steinberg, 1997; Rodriguez and Villaverde, 2000; Steinberg, 2009; Villaverde, 2007; Watts, 2008, 2009).

These assumptions are significant in addressing issues of social justice in a meaningful and rigorous manner, producing work which can 'talk truth to power' and influence governments and policymakers to use the outcomes to inform more socially just approaches to policy. While this is a key aim of socially just research, it is recent in origin and associated with developing scholarship around social justice in respect of critical theory, pedagogy and methodology.

The social justice turn

In recent years, social justice has become a buzzword, bandied about by policymakers and politicians from both ends of the political spectrum (e.g. see DFES, 2005: 10; 2006: 1; DfE, 2011: 1). This means that it has multiple connotations, which can be problematic in a research context. Buzzword status also seems to imply that it is, in some way, 'easy' and merely associated with uncritical activism or political ideology. For example, Duckworth and Ade-Ojo (2015) highlight how fastidious adherence to specific ideologies have been informed by the different philosophical positions of succeeding governments and question whether the discourse around notions of *social justice* can be separated from the ideologues of the government espousing it.

Socially just research demands engagement with political discourses, critical theories, methodologies and pedagogies in order to enable us to understand and address the challenges facing our world in both an educational and wider social context. Social issues and their impact are of interest to all social justice scholars, given the ways in which structural social inequalities, such as class, race and gender, shape educational access and opportunities. These concerns do have a relatively recent history, and the concept of education for social justice might be argued to have its roots in alternative, rather than mandatory, education. While universal education in England and Wales (which was used as a model in many international contexts) was developed largely along class lines via the Clarendon, Taunton and Newcastle reports (e.g. see McCulloch, 1991, 1998) – something which itself has led to differential opportunities for different social classes – the education offered by the technical institutes (forerunners of today's further education colleges) in England provided opportunities for those who require more advanced skills to deal with the rapid technological advances of the new industrial age (Walker, 2016). This gave rise to organizations such as the Workers Education Association (founded in 1903) which remains 'committed to adult education for social purpose and to achieve social justice' (WEA, 2017). Internationally, other movements were concerned with adult education, such as that inspired by Paulo Freire, whose approach to education linked 'the identification of issues to positive action for change and development' (Freire Institute, 2017). Concerns about social justice among education theorists in the mid-twentieth century were largely confined to social class, including race and gender, during the 1970s and 1980s (Griffiths, 2003: 41). As Griffiths goes on to point out, it was only subsequent to this that the education research community experienced a realization that these issues could not be addressed in isolation from one another, but also that research and scholarship around intersectionality presented a whole new set of challenges. These understandings of the historical and social structural inequalities which contribute to oppression and marginalization may have only been explored relatively recently but have resulted in the utilization of social justice research as a form of activism, reflected in Lincoln and Denzin's observation (2013: 580) that:

> A mere two decades ago, only a handful of scholars were talking about the impact of their work on issues of social justice, by which they meant the ability of social science to be put to policy objectives with the purpose of redressing a variety of historically reified oppressions in modern life: racism, economic injustice, the "hidden injuries of class", discrimination in the legal system, gender inequities, and the new oppressions resulting from the restructuring of the social welfare system to "workfare". Today, many scholars, positivists and interpretivists alike, purposefully direct their own research toward uncovering such injustices, exposing how historic social structures reify and reinvent discriminatory practices, and proposing new forms of social structures that are less oppressive. The turn toward social justice, of course, is directly linked with the turn toward more critical stances in interpretation and representation (Cannella and Lincoln, 2009; Denzin, 2009; 2010; Denzin and Giardina, 2006, 2007, 2008, 2009).

The American social justice turn ran parallel to similar developments in the UK. By the early 1980s British sociologists of education were modifying class analysis to incorporate gender inequality. A number of influential anthologies were published in this decade that included both empirical studies and theoretical analyses of gender (e.g. see Arnot and Weiner, 1987). A decade later Skeggs (1997) published her longitudinal, ethnographic study of eighty-three white working-class women in the North of England. In it she explores gendered production of subjectivity, trajectories and notions of *respectability*, a theme Vicky builds on in relation to adult literacy learners. Griffiths's work on social justice (1998, 2003) was published around the same time, and work in this genre has continued to challenge assumptions and inequalities based on dominant discourses of privileged groupings. Despite this, there are multiple examples of the types of 'modern oppressions' that Denzin and Lincoln refer to. The English education system offers a historically situated example of gender inequality. Universal primary education entered statute in 1870. Female teachers were all single women who were legally forbidden to marry until the Sex Disqualification Removal Act of 1919. However, social pressures due to large numbers of unemployed men following the end of the First World War (and also arising from long-standing cultural practices) meant that the situation remained largely unchanged. Women were unable to access higher education (HE) until the twentieth century, and Cambridge University conferred degrees on women only as recently as 1947; so, as was common among the few women in the workforce, these early teachers had low levels of education and limited training. This historical background, women's perceived role as caregivers, and their traditional economic dependence on men mean that the struggle for equality in the workplace continues. In terms of HE in England, in 2017, fewer than 25 per cent of professors are women. However, achieving that status is an even more challenging and difficult journey for women of colour. At the time of writing, as Emejulu pointed out in her call for a bespoke strategy to increase the numbers of British, Black and Minority Ethnic (BME) women in HE in the UK, only 30 women of colour form part of that (nearly) 25 per cent (Grove, 2017). The difference is even starker in Science, Technology, Engineering, Mathematics and Medicine (STEMM) departments where, in 2016, only '1.1% of BME female respondents were the head of their school, division or department, compared with 3.1% of white female respondents, 6.6% of BME male respondents and 7.0% of white male respondents' (ECU, 2017). Intersectional issues such as this are reflective of the ways in which societal perception and positioning also become part of the embodied habitus of individuals determining and reproducing how they think and behave and, as such, are 'constitutive of, rather than determined by, social structures' (Reay, 1998: 61). It is not merely traditional societal structures and positioning which reinforce traditional positioning and in/equalities. In the past decade, as we have entered a 'post-truth society' with 24/7 access to news and (uncritical) opinion, news and social media can have a significant impact on identities and the ways in which they are represented. Consider, for example, how different forms of family – characterized as 'good' and 'deserving' or 'bad' and 'undeserving' – are depicted in the media.

Bourdieu places the family at the centre of social capital (Bourdieu, 1986) and yet the field of family is not homogenous. The notion of 'family' and what a family constitutes has different meanings depending on the lens through which it is viewed. When viewing notions of the family from the dominant middle-class lens, the symbolic power of a two-parent family is vastly different to that of the pathologized single teenage mother represented by the media (e.g. see Sales, 2017). Sales critiques the American TV show SMILF which represents single mothers as promiscuous, idle and uncaring (see also McRobbie's (2006) comments about the way the internet site 'Popbitch' characterizes young mothers). Similarly, we might consider how refugees are constructed in the media and social media – as 'deserving' refugees and 'undeserving' migrants (Holmes and Casteneda, 2016) – or the dichotomous way in which young people are represented, for example, as being involved with violent crime or belonging to gangs, whereas the 'positive' stories generally relate to overcoming disadvantage of some sort, thus still implying a deficit model of youth, and government policy characterizes them as potential human capital. These perceptions are evident on a global scale and reflected in education policy internationally (e.g. Atkins, 2016a; Billett et al., 2010). Binary views also relate to how we perceive other groups: the vulnerable, needy, disabled person, for example, or the Paralympic champion. Such representations are seen and absorbed and come to form part of the way in which we perceive the other and, indeed, perceive ourselves. It is important to note that they extend well beyond social media, with online and computer games adding to existing, paper-based stereotypical representations of the other. As Higgin (2009: 3/11, cited Rose, 2016) has eloquently argued in relation to his work on computer gaming:

When one sees a race called 'human' within a MMORPG and it is westernized as well as White with different shades of color for diversity (but nothing too Black), a powerful assertion is made. This assertion is that humanity will only be understood within the fantasy world if it is primarily coded White . . . because video games both model and shape culture, there is a growing danger and anxiety that some games are functioning as stewards of White masculine hegemony. (Higgin, 2009: 3/11)

These few 'broad-brush' examples are illustrative of the fact that within all contemporary societies there are groups that struggle to gain equality of opportunity and social justice in national educational systems. More than this, those who are responsible for the education of young people – whether marginalized or not – hold their own, unconscious, perceptions of the other, something we see resulting in structural forms of discrimination. This includes statistics such as that in England, boys are over three times as likely to receive a permanent exclusion than girls, black Caribbean pupils are more than three times as likely to be permanently excluded from school as white pupils, while the highest permanent exclusion rates are found among Gypsy/Roma and Irish Traveller groups (DfE, 2017).

Key reasons for such disparities between groups with different characteristics are disturbing. We cannot, based on statistical information, have an understanding of the individual stories that led to these issues, but the disparities should give us cause for concern in terms of the ways in which we ascribe particular characterizations to individuals based on our personal perceptions of, for example, racialized or gendered identities, how that relates to our own position of privilege and power, and the implications for the positioning and voice of those we other in this way.

Francis Farrell is a teacher educator specializing in religious education (RE). Before entering HE as a Postgraduate Certificate in Education (PGCE) course leader, Francis worked in secondary schools in the north of England teaching RE, history and citizenship. His research interests include gender and education, particularly masculinities and education, education policy, teacher and pupil identities. Some of these issues are addressed in Francis' discussion of his research into teenage boys' masculinities.

Case example

Boys and voice
Francis Farrell

Moral panics about failing boys have dominated education policy discourse since the introduction of league tables in the 1990s when gender differentials between boys' and girls' educational outcomes became a major focus for policymakers and practitioners alike. As a former secondary school teacher, my research is concerned with the relationship between young masculine identities and secondary education as the social site for the performance of masculine identity. So, there is a strong reflexive dimension to my research where I am highly situated, as a man and as an educator working in the competitive, performative environment of the British education system, a masculinist system that I interrogate and trouble through my critical investigation of the gendered power relations it brings into play. My doctoral research and subsequent empirical studies have focused upon the ways that boys engage with education and the gendered meanings boy's attribute to subject choices (Farrell 2014). Further studies have explored year 6 (ages 10–11) and year 9 (ages 13–14) boys' constructs of masculinity and how these constructs affected their educational and work aspirations and their notions of the kind of men they wanted to become (Farrell, 2016a).

What unites these projects is an overarching concern with the social construction of masculine identity and the ways in which secondary schools could be said to operate as discursive sites for the reproduction of dominant masculinities (Connell, 2000; Mac an Ghaill, 1994; Martino, 1999). Broadly speaking, my research has addressed these key questions focusing on the relationship between masculinity and schools as 'masculinizing' social machines:

- In what ways do boys perform their masculine identities?
- Are boys able to extract a dividend from this gendered performance?
- Do boys resist, disrupt or trouble dominant discourses of masculinity?
- What contribution can educational interventions make to the critical de-construction of hegemonic or oppressive forms of masculinity?

My methodological perspectives are informed by a concern with gender and power relations. Drawing from critical pro-feminist masculinities scholarship, my empirical work belongs to a sociological tradition that theorizes schools as disciplinary spaces that sustain the gender order that esteems heteronormative masculinity at a cost to women, girls and 'other' men and boys. Masculinities scholarship has been developed by feminist and pro-feminist theorists whose political, moral and scholarly activities are informed by a concern to interrogate the practices and policies that sustain systemic gender inequities. In respect of my focus on school boy masculinity, Connell (2000: 5) neatly captures the social justice underpinnings of critical work on gender and education:

> How we understand men and gender . . . what we know (or think we know) about the development of boys, may have large effects- for good or ill- in therapy, education, health services, violence prevention, policing and social services. It matters therefore to get our understanding of these issues straight.

In this analysis, critical work on the social construction of young masculinities has implications not only for practitioners and policymakers but, more significantly, also for the women, girls and men and the communities that these boys will live in. In education, masculinities methodologies offer researchers the critical tools to work towards an equitable experience for all:

> How would *both* boys' and girls' development as learner-citizens be enhanced by a curriculum which fore grounded the values of caring in both public and private life? (Foster, et al. 2001: 11)

Connell's ground-breaking work on hegemonic masculinity has been fundamental to my methodological perspective. Significantly, Connell's key insight is a recognition that masculinity is a social construction which enables male bodies to benefit from a patriarchal dividend and maintain the gender order which sustains male privilege – a discourse of 'natural superiority' (Ramazanoglu, 2002). More recently, it is the work of scholars influenced by post-structuralist third-wave feminism, such as Butler (2007), Skelton and Francis (2009), Martino (1999, 2000) and Whitehead (2002), which has shaped my methodology. In this analysis, there is no pre-discursive masculine subject that exists separately from language, culture and the social codes which stratify, normalize and discipline the gendered bodies of men and boys. From a social justice perspective, this rejection of the 'metaphysics of substance' at the core of the masculinist meta-narrative has significant implications. In Butler's analysis, social construction is the site of agency:

> As an on-going discursive practice it is open to intervention and resignification (Butler, 2007: 45). In Butler's work the construction of masculinity is shown to be a performance, ontologically fragile, and in need of continuous work and iteration. As Donaldson argues, masculinity is pseudo-tough, pseudo-natural, but it constitutes the most dangerous thing we live with (Donaldson, 1993).

Research on masculinities in education

In this section I wish to provide a short example of how these methodological 'tools' can be utilized and applied in empirical work, particularly the post-structuralist perspectives. This example is a study that set out to critically investigate year 6 and year 9 boys' constructions of masculinity in the light of new theories of inclusive masculinity (Anderson, 2012; McCormack, 2012) and to consider the implications of the findings for educational research (Farrell, 2016a). Qualitative data were collected in school settings, consisting of observations and semi-structured interviews in single-sex male groups.

As a stimulus for the primary school year 6 group interviews, the boys were shown ten pictures based on Pollack's (1999) concept of the 'boy code'. The boy code is a set of rules and social expectations that shape and discipline young masculinities. At the heart of the code is the requirement to show 'no sissy stuff'. Boys must keep emotions in check, act tough, be the stoic 'study oak', 'give 'em hell' by taking risks and be the 'big wheel' by gaining status (Pollack, 1999). The boys were invited to share their views on whether the rules shown in the pictures made it hard to be a boy. Following the group discussion the boys were shown a short excerpt from the film 'Danny the Champion of the World' which provided the focus for a group discussion about the contrasting masculine styles of the teachers Danny encounters in his school. Two of the film's characters, the authoritarian, physically brutal Captain Lancaster and the kindlier, sensitive Headmaster, were contrasted. The boys discussed which of the teachers had the best approach and which teacher they would like to teach them.

The focus of my research in the secondary school took the boys' educational and career aspirations as the site through which to explore their emergent constructs of masculinity. Data were collected through a class discussion based on an extract from David Puttnam's film about young people, class, education and aspiration, 'We are the People we've been waiting for', followed up with focus group interviews exploring the types of masculinity featured in the excerpt. The boys were invited to discuss which type of masculinity they most identified with and how masculine practices shaped their lives and aspirations.

Data analysis drew upon pro-feminist and post-structuralist theories of the gendered subject. Findings showed some evidence of inclusive forms of masculinity expressed by the year 6 boys' rejection of the 'boy code' (Pollack, 1999), through their displays of homosocial tactility in the classroom and their narratives of caring and emotional experience. However, discourses of dominant masculinity as the culturally esteemed norm persisted in both the year 6 and year 9 narratives and continue to dominate the boys' experiences. The most striking finding of the study for social justice agendas was the capacity of the educational gender work programme reported on to provide boys with the resources to problematize the social construction of masculinity. Significantly, the data suggested analysis in binary terms of inclusive or dominant masculinity fails to recognize the fuzzy educational middle ground occupied by the 'overlooked ordinary boys' (Brown, 1987; Roberts, 2012) of this study.

The practical implications of the study were that educational gender work programmes which provide boys with the resources to question dominant masculine practices enable boys to exceed the 'symbolic order' and trouble dominant gender discourse. Where the discourse of dominant masculinity can be rendered fragile, re-signification and change become possible. What this study shows is that in a neo-liberal policy context the role of gender equity programmes with the capacity to produce more reflexive masculine subjects requires reassertion within the curriculum.

Boys and voice

Farrell's work illustrates the importance not only of research for social justice but also of critical pedagogic work, informed by that research, as a means of developing a more equitable, critical and democratic education system. We believe that it is the responsibility of all teachers and researchers to engage with work of this nature, as part of our moral, collective responsibility to work for a more just and equitable society. We move on to discuss some of the theoretical and practical strategies that we have used to theorize and shed light on issues of equity and social justice. It is important at this point to make a distinction: throughout this book we are discussing research *for* and *about* social justice. This encompasses research such as Farrell's which engages critically with concerns related to social justice and also attempts to find strategies to address in/equality. We refer to this as research *for* social justice. On the other hand, there is also research – which we term socially just research – which attempts to make social justice as part of the research process, principally through collaboration with the communities and individuals who are researched. All research which claims social justice as part of its aim and/or purpose will include elements of both, and we do not privilege one above the other. However, it is important to be aware that both have implications for the selection and use of different research methods. While methods must be fit for purpose and an appropriate match to the research question(s) (Wellington, 2015: 108), in research which claims to be socially just and which is therefore concerned with respect and empowerment, greater consideration needs to be given to the implications each method has for the participants. To what extent is their role active or passive during data collection (social justice would imply a more active role)? Does the application of the method demonstrate value and respect for each individual? Is it empowering? How is this happening and in whose judgement? What is the relationship between that method, the participants and researcher(s) in the context of the overall methodological approach and ethical framework? These are difficult questions which have a moral and ethical dimension in terms of research which claims to be socially just. For this reason, we also note that addressing issues of reflexivity, acknowledging power relations and giving consideration to issues of intersectionality, in/equality and oppression are fundamental to all research which is concerned with social justice.

Collaboration, voice, power and representation

All the projects alluded to in this book are concerned with marginalized groups or those with the potential to be marginalized in the future. For example, Mark Vicars's work involves unqualified teachers and marginalized children in Myanmar, a developing country; Kay Heslop is concerned with elders and small children in intergenerational learning, while Laura Nicklin's research relates to the education of incarcerated men. Vicky Duckworth's work addresses the personal and public trajectories of female and male learners and how they navigate across the domains of their lives, which include the fields of education, work and family; Joanne Clifford-Swan's work is about those children who are 'slow to read' and Liz Atkins's focus is level 1 learners in further education. Each of these groups is characterized by different forms of social inequality and oppression which places them educationally at the bottom of a hierarchy of opportunities which are notable for their differential access. 'Slow to read' learners, for example, are located mainly in schools serving area of disadvantage, and their reading difficulties have the potential to result in significantly limited educational opportunities for them in the future; educational opportunities for prisoners – a majority of whom require basic skills support – are limited, while level 1 learners are located at the bottom of a hierarchy of low-status vocational programmes in low-status institutions which form part of a broader system in which vocational education is held in lower esteem than academic education. In addition to their educational positioning, individuals from marginalized groups are often also characterized in the context of discourses of deficit and underachievement. These discourses, based on uncritical stereotypes of marginalized groups, effectively justifies and reinforces public and policy perceptions that particular groups have homogenous learning and attitudinal deficits as well as homogenous needs. From a social justice perspective, these discourses raise questions about how it feels to be positioned and regarded in this way and challenge the researcher to consider ways in which it might be possible to undertake research which offers the possibility of empowerment and inclusion to its participants.

From a methods perspective this implies that the research methods selected have to be designed in ways which allow them not only to gather the data necessary to illuminate or address an issue but also to interact with the participant in ways which are in tension with the prevailing discourses. This would mean developing methods – possibly in collaboration with the participants – which recognize their fundamental contribution to the research as well as respecting them as individuals with valuable lives, stories and histories. In a broader context, this may also involve undertaking research in which the participants have the opportunity to reflect on their position and which informs the development of critical pedagogic interventions to address inequalities. It may also involve collaboration with the participants as a means of empowerment. Participation and collaboration can enable the voices of people who have been historically silenced to be heard and, in research terms, can be described as researching 'with' and not 'on' (Griffiths, 1998). This approach arises from moral and ethical concerns about social justice and finding a means by which the voices of marginalized groups and individuals – such as the 'ordinary boys' in Farrell's research – might be heard.

A key premise of socially just research is examining power issues within research relationships, the central aim being to ensure greater equity with the participants. This includes establishing a democratic relationship based on the sharing of power and promoting of autonomy for marginalized groups. In respect of education, there are particular challenges in terms of teaching-research and its implications for democratic relationships. Classrooms are privileged spaces, where identities are conferred on learners by those in a position of power, including teachers, peers and social workers, who use what is deemed 'legitimate' to carry out symbolic violence on those positioned as not having what Bourdieu characterized as the right 'habitus' or 'capital'. For example, those who teach or are in a position of power are able to transmit their values, their world visions, their ideologies and prejudices; this makes, for example, the teaching–learning process a non-neutral one. It is positioned by the subjectivities of those who are involved in it and by the symbolic–cultural determinations that are representative of the educational system, constructed from a privileged logic where those in a position of power (having the valued forms of capital) can determine whether the capital the learners possess are legitimate or illegitimate.

Addressing these concerns implies a pragmatic and reflexive approach. This might include, as well as transparency and sharing of the data, the co-construction of meaning between the researcher and participants. Collaborative sense-making has the potential to lead to new meanings, new interpretations and co-construction in the generation of knowledge. This approach contrasts the dominant paradigm whereby the participants are positioned as passive and researchers as the powerful experts. It is two decades since Griffiths (1998) outlined different forms of collaborative relationship in the context of socially just research, advocating 'joint theorizing and action' within the context of the power of agency and arguing that such relationships offer a means for developing empowerment and ultimately social justice. Fine (1994: 31) had earlier argued that intellectuals carry a responsibility to engage with struggles for democracy and justice. Over the intervening generation, socially just research become more widely used by scholars within and beyond education, and thus collaboration with participants through various participatory models has become standard research practice among a diverse range of theoretical perspectives (an excellent resource on this is Frankham's (2009) paper, which explores some of the challenges and questions concerned with service user involvement in research). However, this is not to say that all research which aims to promote social justice takes an actively participatory stance with all participants deeply involved with all stages of the research process. It will, however, utilize critical theories, methods and analytical approaches which acknowledge the different positioning of the researcher and the researched and will have a clear aim in terms of informing policy and/or pedagogy.

The notion of participation in contemporary social justice theory also implies that those people and communities who are the focus of a social policy – and so, by definition, subject to inequality – should participate in the shaping of that policy. This approach includes active participation within policymaking, a process which emphasizes inclusion and democracy. Whether contemporary government policy reflects such shapings is difficult to pin down. However, there are points of articulation between policy, activism and research which must continue to be exploited if social science is to act as a major force for social change. In this respect, methodologies which enact social justice and which are also forms of social activism provide opportunities to address issues of social justice and thus to 'make the invisible visible' (Dagley, 2004: 613).

Using more traditional, less participative methodologies risks replicating existing power relationships by excluding stakeholders from 'dialogue' and 'active participation', thus weakening the dialogic and participatory dimension of the research and 'decreasing the possibility that previously silenced voices will be heard' (Howe, 2004: 56/57, cited Denzin and Lincoln, 2013: 15), something which would reduce their importance as individuals (Dowse, 2009: 150). More reflexive and participative approaches, similar to those advocated by Dowse and by Denzin and Lincoln, seek to address methodological concerns around power, voice and control, while also emphasizing the 'active' and engaging in work that empowers and 'makes' social justice. A practical example is the research conducted by Duckworth and Smith (2019a and b) which was predicated on shifting from the kind of social critique motivated by paternal concern and intent on the 'diagnosis of incapacity'; rather, the methodological approach sought to be forward-looking: to validate newly established learning identities and to share in a collective imagining of future plans. Research discussions were typically informal and reciprocal, and there was a dialogic sharing of stories between the interviewer(s) and the participant.

While many researchers are engaging with these issues, there are, unfortunately, no simple approaches to empowerment, and the use of voice raises significant issues. Both Fine (1992, 1994) and Usher (2000: 34) have warned of the paradoxical effect of 'distorting and controlling' the voice of the other. Lincoln and Guba (2000: 183) make reference to the 'multi-layered problem of voice' citing Hertz (1997) who points out that 'voice has multiple dimensions: first, there is the voice of the author. Second, there the presentation of the voices of one's respondents within the text. A third appears when the self is the subject of the inquiry . . . Voice is how authors express themselves within an ethnography.' The author's voice in all this is 'rarely genuinely absent, or even hidden' (Lincoln and Guba, 2000: 183) and therefore requires a reflexive response which constitutes a 'moral voice' (Usher, 2000: 34) in the narrative of a socially just study. Reflexivity acknowledges our multiple identities and demands that we 'interrogate each of our selves regarding the ways in which research efforts are shaped and staged' (Lincoln and Guba, 2000: 183). Reflexivity also raises questions, however, such as how the researcher can respect the narrative of the participants, place them within a social and historical context and yet 'not collude' with the social science fixation with the working class (Fine et al., 2000: 120). As Fine et al. acknowledge, there are no easy answers to this problem. However, as identified in Duckworth's (2013) research, the inclusion of her own changing position in the research juxtaposed with that of the other respondents allowed the reader an insight into how the narratives were formed and a recognition that the stories told, sometimes of pain, are separate stories, even if they are linked and allow us to make connections (and see Ahmed, 2000, 2004).

Notions of truth raise other concerns in terms of socially just research and the interpretation of data where that lies with the researcher. How can data be represented as 'truth' when it is used to 'create meanings and produce identities' (Usher, 2000: 26) about particular groups which they may not recognize? This is particularly the case where research participants are from traditionally oppressed groups and where researchers make specific gendered or class-based interpretations of the research process and data. We have found that involvement of participants in the processes of interpretation and taking a critically reflexive approach to our work are two key strategies in addressing these concerns.

'Doing' reflexivity

In order to achieve a more participative and dialogical approach to our research, we have both always attempted to question our own assumptions and behaviour at each point in the process, in order to achieve a degree of 'reflexivity' or 'introspection and self-examination' (Wellington, 2015: 344). This involves a consideration of our own positionality in relation to the researched group and how that may influence the design of the study, the collection and interpretation of data and relationships with other participants in the research. It is important to note here that this is an approach which cannot be disentangled from undertaking research which is moral and ethical. Sikes and Goodson (2003: 48) have argued for the use of 'interior reflexivity', suggesting that this is a better 'anchor for moral practice' than any external guidelines (such as the somewhat instrumental university processes that all involved in HE have to respond to), and we have used this approach while undertaking research for social justice, using it to attempt to understand and clarify the relationship between our own values, assumptions and experiences and our research practice.

Supporting this, Grenfell and James (2004: 507) have argued that radically reflexive research methodology 'has the capacity to found a critically effective discourse', and in her early work on research for social justice, Griffiths (1998: 96/97) also advocated that the researcher should demonstrate reflexivity about their own position and interests and reflexivity about their own understanding and values, arguing that this approach is designed to emphasize to researchers the need to take responsibility for their own practices. However, she does sound a note of caution in her suggestion that researchers need clarity about what types of responsibility they are, in fact, able to exercise, either as an individual or a group, pointing out that 'no-one is responsible for everything'.

Methods

Most methods and methodologies utilized in research for social justice are drawn from the qualitative paradigm. Quantitative approaches do not offer the same opportunities for collaboration with, and participation by, researched communities, thus limiting the possibilities for empowerment and making voices heard. Similar arguments can be made in respect of some approaches to mixed methods, as Denzin and Lincoln (2013: 15, citing Howe, and Teddlie and Tashakkori) have noted:

> The traditional mixed methods movement takes qualitative methods out of their natural home, which is within the critical interpretive framework (Howe, 2004, p.54; but see Teddlie & Tashakkori, 2003a, p.15). It divides inquiry into dichotomous categories, exploration versus confirmation. Qualitative work is assigned to the first category, quantitative research to the second (Teddlie and Tashakkori, 2003a, p. 15). Like the classic experimental model, this movement excludes stakeholders

from dialogue and active participation in the research process. Doing so weakens its democratic and dialogical dimensions and decreases the likelihood that previously silenced voices will be heard. (Howe, 2004, pp. 56–57)

Ways of avoiding the risk of silencing voices lie not only in the method used but also in the research relationships: a socially just approach will always involve a re-thinking of the relationship with the participants in the research and consideration of ways in which more collaborative and empowering relationships might be engendered, such as developing the more dialogical process advocated by Gitlin and Russell (1994: 184), something which is argued by Fielding (2004: 306) to have considerable promise for transformation. It is these relationships that are core to all socially just research, although within the qualitative paradigm there may be significant differences between, for example, research undertaken from a Critical Race Theory perspective and that undertaken from a Queer Theory perspective. However, it is important to note that 'each practice makes the world visible in a different way. Hence, there is frequently a commitment to using more than one interpretive practice in any study' (Denzin and Lincoln, 2013: 7) and thus that all these perspectives offer important, if different, insights, meaning that no single perspective should be privileged above another.

Moving from methodological approach to method, this is a creative as well as a critical process; thus, the use of particular methods is constrained and enabled by context, rather than adherence to any particular paradigmatic dogma. If you are engaged with participative research, then the other participants may have some ideas about how they wish to be researched. We are always troubled by the limited and limiting approach that many of our students take to data collection; irrespective of the nature of the inquiry, many students will plan a study which involves questionnaires and interviews as sole data-gathering instruments. Notwithstanding issues around sample size, questionnaires concern us in a socially just context given the assumption that all participants will have a level of literacy which permits full engagement and given that they are invariably constructed by the researcher and as such likely to reflect particular gendered and cultural assumptions. These issues are likely to result in voices which are distorted and controlled (Usher, 2000: 34). Interviews are a dominant method in educational research and there are multiple texts offering guidance on how to undertake them (e.g. see Atkins and Wallace, 2012; Wellington, 2015). Much guidance is procedural, such as whether to use a structured, unstructured or semi-structured approach, whether to use individual or group interviews and the importance of eliminating ambiguous, confusing or insensitive questions. However, there are also significant ethical and methodological considerations to be addressed in the use of interviews. These include the issues of power relations and use and mediation of voice as discussed in this chapter, as well as 'reducibility', or the problems associated with retaining the 'life and texture of the original source' in interview transcripts (Roizen and Jepson, 1985: 11, cited Wellington, 2001/2015). The notion of reducibility is also an issue in paper-based observation records, as are strategies for interpretation. From a critical perspective it is also necessary to give reflexive consideration not only to your own relationships and impact on and with the research but also to your position in the context of each observation. Wellington's (2000/2015) spectrum of observation can be helpful in informing this.

There is a broad spectrum of other methods which socially just educational research might draw upon, and each offers different challenges and opportunities. For example, the use of visual methods – the rigorous and critical interpretation of texts, pictures, photographs and film for example – can be helpful in terms of 'visualizing social difference' (Rose, 2016) but can present challenges in terms of interpretation and ownership. If images are data, to whom do they belong? The producer of the image or the researcher? Discussions around these issues can be found in a wide range of literature, including, for example, BERA Ethical Guidelines (2018), Cheek (2000), Kozinets (2015), Rose (2016). Ownership of data is a tricky problem which also arises with the use of some digital methods, which can involve either using computer-mediated communication (CMC) as a means of generating and analysing data or researching the social, cultural and educational dimensions of CMC itself. Diaries can potentially provide a rich source of data to triangulate with interviews, observations and other forms of data but require time, discipline and advanced literacy skills, presenting challenges which may outweigh their potential for data. Similarly to some digital and visual methods, they also present challenges in terms of ownership. Who actually 'owns' the diary? The participant or the researcher?

Field notes can be critical in generating data and supporting interpretation. However, they also serve an important function in terms of reflexivity, providing the opportunity to record feelings and perceptions at the time and then to return to these and reflect on them more critically. Spradley (1979, cited Silverman, 2009) suggested keeping four separate sets of field notes:

- Short notes made at the time
- Expanded notes made as soon as possible after each field session
- A fieldwork journal to record problems and ideas that arise during each stage of fieldwork
- A provisional running record of analysis and interpretation

In this context, the journal could make a potentially valuable contribution to ongoing acts of reflexivity.

Irrespective of which methods you choose – and those mentioned here form a far from comprehensive list – the importance of using those is in ways which demonstrate respect for other participants and are framed in ways which can be argued to promote social justice. Finally, once research for social justice is written, much of it relies on narrative forms of presentation. This is partly a response to problems of voice and also serves to illuminate particular aspects of educational inequality. Representation of the other and mediation of voice are, clearly, particular challenges in the writing of narratives. However, narratives also raise broader issues. They are personal stories that have arisen in a particular educational, social, political and cultural context. How does the research address those issues beyond the scope of individual experience?

Exploring individuals and communities using socially just research methods

In order to illustrate how socially just research can support people's ability to consciously act to change their social circumstances where this is constrained by various forms of structural inequality, we draw on two examples from the work of Walker and Loots in South Africa, a country with a historical legacy of deep inequality, in which young people, born into the attitudes and culture of past generations, are tasked with building a fairer and more democratic society. Walker and Loots's work with undergraduate university students forms a response to this and is an attempt to find ways of enabling young people to understand and actively engage with issues of inequality and social in/justice. Their work does, however, also illustrate the challenges of making structural, rather than individual, change for social justice.

Walker and Loots (2014) report on a study exploring the impact of a student leadership project at a university which was formerly white and 'advantaged' and which now has a majority black student body. In common with other South African universities, it faced entrenched problems associated with racism, prejudice and exclusion. The project involved a funded exchange trip to the United States, where students were exposed to different cultural mores (e.g. tolerance of same-sex relationships), some of which challenged their own attitudes and beliefs. The programme required regular conversations between its participants, drawing on Dewey's (1916) concept of a pedagogy of doing democracy to learn democracy. Walker and Loots note the uncomfortable nature of some of these discussions, such as when issues around Apartheid were raised. Two years after the programme, most participants recognized sustainable change in their approach to citizenship. Walker and Loots conclude that the programme 'supports the importance of universities as spaces for the formation of individual citizenship capabilities and functioning and democratic citizenship values [pointing to] critical possibilities for change and for citizenship formation through opportunities afforded at university' (Walker and Loots, 2014).

In a second project, this time aiming to generate changes in gender awareness and practices among university students who all came from rural communities with deeply ingrained gender inequalities, Walker and Loots (2017) engaged in a participatory process with thirteen undergraduate students. The project involved several participatory workshops over eight months, beginning with one in which participants worked to develop aims, research questions, structure and potential outcomes around the broad theme of the project. A range of methods were used, including 'Visual representations of gender identities and norms, using a problem – tree exercise to explore causes and effects of gender inequalities, and discussing different types and manifestations of power'. This provided the basis for discussions and reflections in later workshops, which led to the students considering 'policy goals and broader structural interventions'. The project did raise awareness, but frustratingly for Walker, Loots and their participants, no structural change has yet taken place. However, the participants have demonstrated sustainable 'personal development and personal commitments to gender equity'. Walker and Loots conclude by arguing that while projects for change can lead to more justice, they are limited by being research projects rather than political change projects, as well as by an absence of 'powerful advocates and organised political struggles for transformative change'; despite this, they offer a 'productive place' to start work and highlight the importance of productive relationships with those who have the power to bring about change (Walker and Loots, 2017).

As Walker and Loots have noted, making change can be difficult. This reflects the time taken to make the cultural and attitudinal changes necessary to address structural inequalities. Illustrating this point, neither project can point to major structural change, but both provide empirical evidence of cultural change among the participating students, pointing to the possibility of wider societal change in these areas over time.

Conclusion

In this chapter we have offered an overview of some of the theoretical and practical ways in which it is possible to engage with research for social justice and equity. While much of this is participative (such as the examples from Melanie Walker and Sonja Loots's work), much else is not (such as Francis Farrell's case example) but aims to generate understandings about in/equalities which can inform policy and pedagogy. Both are critical in a context which demands ever greater engagement with scholarship as a key strategy for informing more socially just policy and pedagogy at macro, meso and micro levels.

As is apparent from this chapter and other chapters in this book, educational research and social justice are, or should be, indivisible from one another. Education is a key responsibility of every society to its youth, to ensure that that society and all its members can flourish. For this to happen, every child and young person has to have an equitable chance of an education, in order to move towards a situation where we have more meritocratic and socially just communities. And yet, our education systems internationally remain 'divided and divisive' (Reay, 2017; Tomlinson, 1997): class bound in Great Britain, divided on religious lines in Northern Ireland, by access to money in Uganda and by gender in Nigeria and Pakistan, both countries where girls have particularly limited access to an education. Other examples include a system which is heavily racialized in America, and in Australia where Indigenous youth have substantially worse educational outcomes than white Australian youth. Within each of these examples there are multilayered complexities and issues of intersectionality concerned with, but not limited to, poverty, class, race, culture and geography influencing each individual's personal opportunities for educational – and hence social – inclusion. As scholars concerned with education and social justice, we have a moral responsibility to address these issues through the media of critical research and pedagogy. This can enable us to help education move towards a position of greater social justice one step at a time, by working with individuals and groups, but collectively, it can enable us to influence policymaking in education for the greater good of future generations.

Further reading

Farrell, F. (2016a), '"Learning to listen": Boys' gender narratives – implications for theory and practice', *Education + Training*, 58(3): 283–97.

Fielding, M. (2004), 'Transformative approaches to student voice: Theoretical underpinnings, recalcitrant realities', *British Educational Research Journal*, 30(2): 295–311.

Holmes, S. M., and Casteneda, H. (2016), 'Representing the "European refugee crisis" in Germany and beyond: Deservingness and difference, life and death', *American Ethnologist*, 43(1): 12–24.

Kincheloe, J., McLaren, P., and Steinberg, S. (2013), 'Critical pedagogy and qualitative research: Moving to the bricolage', in N. Denzin and Y. Lincoln (eds) *Landscape of Qualitative Research*, 4th edn, pp. 339–70, Los Angeles: Sage.

CHAPTER THREE

Socially just research as ethical endeavour

Introduction

As we have discussed earlier, we view research for social justice, and socially just research, as being fundamentally concerned with ethics and morality. All research, of course, has a concern with ethics: indeed, Wellington (2015: 113) argues that 'the *main criterion* for educational research is that it should be ethical' (original emphasis). In research for social justice the ethical dimension is fundamental to all aspects of a study, going way beyond contemporary ethical approval processes, and it is these wider ethical issues and the challenges and opportunities they present that we address in this chapter. Such challenges can be daunting for researchers, especially those committed to using research to create a more just and equitable society. Indeed, for us knowledge generation through our research has involved both opportunities and barriers. Our emotional engagement and political positioning has been an explicit part of the process and a driver of our own research.

In addition to ethics, we address the moral dimensions of research. Ethics and morality are terms that have slightly different meanings and which generate considerable debate. In the context of this book, we regard morality as part of a wider belief system (which will be informed by individual values, culture and habitus among other influences) and ethics as the application of morality. Therefore, where research is moral, it follows that it will also be ethical. Fundamental to this are the ways in which individuals understand and distinguish between the binary notions of right and wrong. Although most of us establish a compass of right and wrong during childhood, moral development occurs throughout our lifetime (Kohlberg and Kramer, 1969) and is shaped and re-shaped throughout our lifetime as we pass through different stages of growth and mature to adulthood. For example, consider how your morals have been shaped and enacted in early childhood compared to teenage years and then in your thirties. The ethical norms for all cultures and societies – in life and in research – are so embedded that individuals might be drawn to regard them as simple commonsense without giving consideration to their wider implications. For example, is what is considered ethical in one culture similarly regarded in another? What are the implications of such questions for international studies, particularly where they include traditionally oppressed groups (such as indigenous peoples)?

Clearly then, notions of morality and ethics are complex and have particular resonance in research for social justice which is predicated on ideas of a more equitable (and thus more moral and ethical) approach to society. A significant aspect of this and an essential part of the responsible conduct of research is social responsibility. Recognizing one's social responsibilities as a researcher is a vital first step towards exercising social responsibility, but it is only the beginning, since you may confront difficult value questions when deciding how to act in a responsible and socially just manner. Therefore, acknowledging our social responsibilities is only the start of dealing with the value implications of research, since responsibility requires us to address the moral, political, social and policy issues at stake.

There are codes, policies and principles that are both important and useful in shaping our research (e.g. see BERA, 2018). However, like any set of rules, they are not exhaustive and do not cover every situation; indeed, they often conflict, and their application requires significant consideration and interpretation. Such codes, policies and principles also bring with them their own challenges and dilemmas. For example, in contemporary times, all universities have internal processes for ethical approval for research, which will include a set of ethical guidelines. This was not always the case, and in an increasingly litigious age, it could be argued that concern about the risk of litigation, rather than morality, is a key driving force behind many such procedures. While we acknowledge the importance of such codes and procedures, we still have concerns about their instrumentality as we believe that, too often, they fail to create the necessary space for reflection and reflexivity essential to ensuring that the whole research process is ethical. This perspective was eloquently argued by Greenbank (2003, citing Glen, 2000) who considers that 'simple adherence to ethical codes or rules discourages researchers from reflecting upon the morality of their actions and working out for themselves what they need to do in particular circumstances', something we both have experienced with students undertaking research assessments. Similarly, Hammersley (2009) has described ethical approval processes as being unethical in and of themselves; Nutbrown (2011) has questioned the impact of some contemporary 'ethical' conventions in research with young children which, in her view, represent a 'crisis of representation' which result in the 'Othering' of the children concerned; and Sikes and Piper (2010) in the editorial to a special edition addressing these concerns highlight many of the issues and tensions arising from contemporary approaches to ethics review processes. That said, most educational researchers (e.g. see Atkins and Wallace; 2012: 30/31; Tummons and Duckworth, 2012; Wellington, 2015: 113) do acknowledge the need for a universal code on research ethics which should not be violated. Internationally, Educational Research Associations – which operate at national and supra-national levels – have developed their own codes of ethics. While articulated slightly differently, these all conform to the same core principles and values. For example, the Australian Association for Research in Education (AARE), the American Educational Research Association (AERA) and the European Educational Research Association (EERA) all address common concerns around issues such as protection from harm and informed consent. Codes of ethical practice can be dated back to the Nuremberg Nazi war crimes trials post the Second World War (Sikes and Piper, 2010), but took time to become more formalized. The British Educational Research Association (BERA) first published such a set of guidelines in 1992 (most recently updated in 2018). The key principle underpinning the guidelines is that all educational research should be 'conducted within an ethic of respect' (2018: 6) for the person, taking into consideration their social and cultural positioning, as well as characteristics associated with intersectionality and the structural inequalities arising from those characteristics.

While such guidelines are clearly consistent with socially just research, it is not sufficient – indeed, it is unethical – to address them at a superficial level. Without giving reflexive consideration to the research process throughout, the researcher can run the risk of unethical behaviour throughout the research process. As Wellington (2015) reminds us, educational research can be unethical at all stages of the process from design to findings and including all stages in between.

However, where research claims social justice as part of its purpose this means that if it is about empowerment and social change, the research *itself* forms an ethical endeavour. This is significant, since it requires acknowledgement of the value-laden nature of research and generates another dimension of ethical issues which the researcher needs to acknowledge and respond to in the context of taking a moral and reflexive approach to their work. This approach sits within the context of critical, feminist and participatory forms of research which, rather than conforming to a set of principles on which all parties agree, draws on conceptions of social ethics. In doing so, it takes a complex view of moral judgements which are seen as integrated into everyday experiences, beliefs, feelings and understandings of right and wrong in terms of social structures and human relations (Christians, 2013: 142). Similarly, Cannella and Lincoln (2013: 172) have argued that 'An ethical perspective that would always address human suffering and life conditions, align with politics of the oppressed, and move to reclaim multiple knowledges and ways of being certainly involves complexity, openness to uncertainty, fluidity and continued reflexive insight', both texts consistent with Aristotle's early definition that Ethics must 'aim at . . . the good of man' (Aristotle, 1911/1998).

It is therefore essential that as researchers we are confident in interpreting, assessing and applying various research rules (including, e.g. our application of theoretical frameworks) so that we make effective decisions and act ethically in different situations. We must also be mindful that the unexpected often occurs in research, and in that situation we are under an imperative to take a situated, moral and ethical approach to the dilemmas that confront us. These can be many: for example, promoting a participative approach and autonomy for your participants if they are characterized as 'vulnerable' in any way, understanding what is meant by informed consent and the extent to which your participants are truly informed, or being presented with a disclosure of abuse/criminal activity during the research process. Similarly, there are significant issues around the use and mediation of Voice in relation to marginalized communities, as well as those related to power relations. Where these arise unexpectedly, as in the following example from Liz's research, they can be particularly difficult to address.

Ethical dilemma

Keira, a level 1 Health and Social Care student, presented a particular ethical challenge during a group interview which required an immediate and situated response. Prior to the interview, the class tutor stated that Keira had carer responsibilities for her mother, but that the college was unaware of the nature or extent of these responsibilities – Keira would not discuss her home situation. She was interviewed with three friends and throughout the interview process sat holding hands with one of these friends. She spoke quietly and in monosyllables in response to questions and was much less forthcoming than her peers, who were all very keen to contribute. When asked what her family thought about her course, Keira became visibly anxious and did not respond. Another group member, Brady, volunteered that Keira's mum was disabled and 'she can't talk to her about it'. Subsequently, as the group explored issues around family support for future study, Keira began to cry and was comforted by her friends. All four rejected a suggestion that the interview should be discontinued. They had all recently completed a unit on their learning programme covering confidentiality in care settings, but had developed an imperfect understanding of the term, the other students suggesting that Keira disclosed her circumstances in the interview, one reassuring her that 'all this is confidential and she won't say anything to anyone, ever'.

Inevitably, this created some immediate ethical dilemmas. Should the interview be continued as requested by Keira and her friends or discontinued in view of her distress? Should that distress (and any of Keira's confidences) be disclosed to her tutor, in view of her apparently significant home difficulties, and breach the trust and understanding of the group? What was the right course of action in terms of valuing and respecting the individual? Ultimately, Liz decided to carry on, despite Keira's distress, because she and her friends were adamant that this should happen, but suggested that she talked these issues through with her tutor. In doing so, she was uncomfortably aware that she had crossed the line between 'researcher' and 'pastoral support', but felt that such a response was both necessary and appropriate given Keira's level of distress and vulnerability. After the interview, supported by her friends, Keira did ask to speak to her tutor and disclosed the extent of her responsibilities, which involved being the sole carer for a terminally ill, bedridden mother. The day before, her mother had been admitted to the local hospice for respite care. As a result of this disclosure, Keira was provided with ongoing support by the college support team.

Reflecting on this issue, with the passage of time, it continues to raise unanswered questions in an ethical context. Were the actions taken at the time moral and ethical? Did they contribute to or diminish the intention to undertake research which was socially just? What are the ethical issues surrounding dissemination of this case, in the thesis and now, as an exemplar in this chapter? These are challenging questions which bring into question every action and every decision in educational research, particularly where that research, as in this case, claims social justice as aim, theoretical framework and/or underpinning value.

Reflection on the ethical and moral issues and decisions raised by this case require not just thought about right and wrong but of our own positioning in relation to the population we are studying, particularly when, as in this case, we are positioned far away from the realities of the lives of the researched. This highlights the importance of recognizing our positioning in the research and in the community as well as the culture we are studying (see Chapter 4 for insider perspective). This has been a significant, ongoing, issue for Liz – a middle-aged, middle-class, educated woman, undertaking research with low-attaining youth from socially excluded communities, whose social positioning and cultural background are very different to her own. This is an issue for many researchers concerned with social justice, themselves members of a culture endowed with 'the dominant legitimacy' (Bourdieu and Passeron, 1990: 23), but who research cultures which are often alienated, marginalized, othered and subject to 'symbolic violence' in consequence of this (Bourdieu and Passeron, 1990: 4). This highlights the importance of cultural awareness in its broadest context, as well as the significance of concerns around intersectionality which often disproportionately affect marginalized communities (e.g. see Strand, 2014). It is also important to recognize that we research from a position of privilege. Without a reflexive approach to the issues and dilemmas posed by research for social justice, it can be easy for a study of this nature to take the route of researching on, rather than with, participants and interpreting the data from that privileged position. There are, historically, many examples of such research.

Anthropologists, in particular, have a long history of carrying out research with minority ethnic groups. Historically, it has been supposed that those hailing from Western academic institutions had a right to engage in such cross-cultural study. Indeed, the power relations embedded in this research were not considered important enough to be reflected or commented upon. However, today the increasing political and socially just insights of minority ethnic groups have fed into vital changes in the ways in which such research is carried out. A strategy to promote greater equity and social justice would be to encourage more collaborative research. It is important that research gives voice to the interests and concerns of minority ethnic groups and indigenous peoples, especially where these groups continue to face political repression or subversion of their rights. There are considerable tensions between Western research and postcolonial and de-colonizing methodologies (Chilisa and Ntseane, 2010). Tuhiwai Smith (2012) articulates it thus:

> From the vantage point of the colonized, from which I write, and choose to privilege, the term 'research' is inextricably linked to European imperialism and colonialism. The word itself, 'research' is probably one of the dirtiest words in the indigenous world's vocabulary.

In response to such concerns, there is now an extensive body of work addressing decolonizing methodologies and the development of indigenous methods including that by Tuhiwai Smith but also including work by, among others, Chilisa (e.g. 2012) and Gloria Ladson-Billings (e.g. Ladson-Billings and Donnor, 2005). The following case example seeks to illustrate some of these challenges in a UK context.

Case example

Fundamental British values and teacher subjectivities
Francis Farrell and Vini Lander

Introduction

The US political scientist John Brenkman states that since 9/11 the 'fog of war' has enveloped the political life of Western democracies permeating policymaking with direct consequences for education policy and practice. In the British context the 'war on terror' has given rise to an epidemic of safeguarding and surveillance policies, collectively referred to as Contest. In education these policies appear to incorporate a narrative of civic nationalism centring on the requirement placed upon teachers in part 2 of the Teachers' Standards, 'to not undermine "fundamental British values" ', defined as 'democracy, the rule of law, individual liberty, and mutual respect and tolerance of those with different faiths and beliefs' (DfE, 2013: 14). In 2014, DfE guidance on spiritual, moral, social and cultural (SMSC) development went one step further, stipulating that schools are required to 'actively demonstrate' they are promoting fundamental British values (FBV; DfE, 2014: 3). However, this is a definition taken from government counterterrorism legislation and represents a major discursive shift in the cultural core of state education. In our research we aim to critically report upon the impact of these securitizing education policies on teacher subjectivities. As Brenkman argues, context and intertextuality are key to this analysis. The discourse of multicultural pluralistic education in which social and cultural difference is valorized in a vision of Britain as a community of communities has been slowly undermined by a governmental assimilatory neo-liberal narrative which seeks to replace multiculturalism with the 'muscular liberalism' and defence of 'our way of life'.

In an already over-regulated, performative system characterized by a high-stakes inspection and audit culture, education has become one of the front lines of what we characterize as the domestic war on terror. Our research and other studies show that schools have become highly politicized border zones where students and teachers surveil and are surveiled (Elton-Chalcraft et al., 2016; Farrell, 2016b; Lander, 2016). As reflexive educators committed to a critical multi- and intercultural education agenda, we seek to problematize the assertion that there is something uniquely British about FBV. We are concerned that FBV amounts to a kind of state-sanctioned national identity with the potential to exacerbate age-old racial tensions to produce suspect citizens through its 'insider–outsider' binary.

We began our research in 2015, building on earlier empirical work undertaken by Lander on primary student teachers' notions of Britishness. Our research focused on secondary teachers of religious education (RE) and was undertaken not long after Lord Nash had published his letter to local authority Standing Advisory Councils for Religious Education (SACRE) advising them of the special role RE had to play in the promotion of FBV through SMSC. Data collection took place throughout 2015 in two phases, February–March 2015 and December 2015. Our participants were all volunteers, including two Postgraduate Certificate in Education (PGCE) RE cohorts (n = 27) and in-service teachers of RE (n = 12).

Our research questions were formulated to illuminate the effects of these high-stakes policies on the teachers' subjectivities, their relationships with their students and the attendant challenges of enacting policy, as follows:

- How do the teachers understand their positioning in relation to FBV? To what extent do their narratives indicate a relationship of compliance and accommodation or is there evidence of disruption or resistance?
- As the point of its articulation, how do the teachers view the implementation of FBV in their practice?
- How do the teachers interpret, translate and enact this policy discourse?

Methodology and theoretical framework

Our research and data analysis draws upon both critical race theory (CRT) (Delgado and Stefancic, 2017) and post-structuralist critiques of the power relations operating through social institutions such as education. We argue that there are theoretical synergies between CRT and post-structuralism through their shared emphasis on interrogating the asymmetrical power relations operating through the social construction of raced binaries. CRT's rejection of essentialism and its commitment to praxis and social change also align to the activism of our other principal influence, Michel Foucault. In our recent research, our ontological orientation is largely taken from Foucault and focuses on the ways in which power relations shape subjectivity. There is no a priori pre-discursive social subject in this analysis; rather, the subject is constituted historically through power and discourse, the 'patterns that he finds in his culture . . . imposed on him by his culture, his social group' (Foucault, 1984: 11). Foucault argues that discourse is irreducible to signs, language and speech; it does 'more'; 'and it is this "more" that we must reveal and describe' (Foucault, 2002: 54). Discourse 'constitutes' and consists of 'practices that systematically form the objects of which they speak' (Foucault, 2002: 54). In our research we aim to interrogate the ways in which the discourse of FBV constitutes teacher subjects as its point of articulation, in order to reveal and describe this 'more'. We move on to explore the method and methodological approach we utilized in order to achieve this in this study.

RE student teacher positioning within a discourse of discipline and control

Here we provide an illustration of the ways in which our methodology and methods of data collection were applied in an investigation of student teachers' views of FBV (Farrell, 2016b; Lander, 2016). In this study we used qualitative group interview methods to gain insights into eleven RE student teachers' understanding of FBV. The focus on the teachers, four of whom were practising Muslims of south Asian heritage, allowed us to obtain rich data from practitioners at the sharp end of policy implementation, required to work within the statutory parameters of the Teachers' Standards and the increasingly securitized domain of school safeguarding. Our focus on classroom practice and the dilemmas experienced by new entrants to the profession enabled us to explore what Ball (1997) calls the rich empirical underlife of policy, that is, the ways teachers translate, interpret and enact policy in real classroom contexts. Our privileging of student teachers also reflected our commitment to creating a critical space for those who are minoritized and also subjugated within the disciplinary spaces of our increasingly coercive education system. In this way our work shares the values of both CRT and Foucault as outlined in his work on genealogy by creating a problematizing critical counternarrative to the official policy discourse of government.

Findings

We found that there was very little consensus about what constitutes Britishness in the student teachers' interviews. The teachers felt that there was nothing uniquely British about FBV and were very concerned that by labelling values such as democracy and tolerance as British, FBV had the capacity to alienate pupils who felt excluded by British society, thereby producing the very opposite of what FBV and Prevent purport to achieve. The teachers were concerned that FBV was creating an insider/outside binary that would produce simplistic, narrow and reified versions of Britishness likely to make some of their pupils feel they were the un-British 'suspects'. The student teachers felt that FBV sent out profoundly contradictory messages that were incompatible with the pluralistic and intercultural values of RE. One of our participants, Shazia, summed this dilemma up when she stated, 'We're not British values teachers, we're teachers of RE!'

A further key finding was that the student teachers were able to demonstrate agency through their commitment to the development of learners' moral imaginations and religious literacy. There was evidence, even at this early stage of the implementation of the policy requirement, to actively promote FBV through SMSC, the teachers were interpreting these requirements and translating them in a way that would promote debate and dialogue. They were beginning to trouble the policy and to an extent to reappropriate it.

Our subsequent work will continue to explore the themes of policy enactment and ways in which practitioners make adjustments that can accommodate and reappropriate the demands of policy.

Reflexive process

Reflecting on the process of our research and trying to understand how our values and views may shape and influence findings adds credibility to the research and should be part of any socially just method of qualitative enquiry. This process includes an explicit conscious awareness of our beliefs, in which we continually question the extent to which we are in a better position to approach the study honestly and openly. Exploration of personal beliefs makes the investigator more aware of the potential judgements that can occur during data collection, analysis and generation of knowledge based on the researcher's belief system rather than on the actual data collected from participants. This process is used to separate personal views and preconceptions from the phenomenon being investigated.

Questions we may pose to aid our reflexivity include the following:

- How has my personal history been the catalyst to my interest in this topic?

- Do I have a personal insider position and truth about the topic I am researching?

- Will my research be impacted by self-serving bias?

- How does my gender/social class/ethnicity/sexuality/culture influence my positioning in relation to this topic and my participants?

- What are my personal bias and stereotypes regarding the group I am researching?

Reflexivity, characterized by an ongoing analysis of personal involvement, helps to make the process open and transparent. Awareness of the reciprocal influence of participants and researcher on the process and outcome is a vital part of ensuring rigour in qualitative research. This awareness acknowledges one's own bias and value-position. Some writers have argued for 'value-neutrality' in research, but this is not possible in work which is concerned with individuals and communities and addressing the social and educational challenges they face, and the concept has been widely rejected in qualitative research (e.g. Christians, 2013: 127/128; Punch and Oancea, 2014). However, Greenbank (2003: 795) has warned that because emancipatory researchers aim to initiate social change (e.g. see Johnston, 2000; Lather, 1986; Troyna, 1995), they may allow their political aims to override other values relating to how they believe research should be undertaken. Indeed, Walford (1994) attempted to be objective when collecting his data on City Technology Colleges, but admits to allowing his political commitments to influence his interpretation of that information. These issues deserve careful consideration as you begin to plan your research and throughout the process. For example, Lather (1986: 270–1) advocates 'vigorous' and 'systematic self reflexivity' that demonstrates how pre-existing theoretical positions were altered by the research undertaken. This approach means continually posing questions such as those above to yourself in order to consider how your personal value positioning is affecting your research and how the research is affecting your value positioning. Significantly, you should also ask yourself 'how is all this limiting what I am seeing and what I am doing?'

Awareness of the ways in which a particular political or value position can influence our research can reduce the risk of missing something important because it does not 'fit' with our particular ontological position (view of the world). For example, Walsh (1999) discusses the need for researchers to recognize evidence that runs counter to their social values and to actively seek further insight into such evidence. How a researcher then utilizes such information may, however, create value conflict. For example, Fine et al. (2000) found that some of the women on welfare they were researching were using drugs and also neglecting their children. As they argue, 'To ignore the information is to deny the effects of poverty, racism, and abuse. To report these stories is to risk their more than likely misuse' (p. 116). In their opinion, this information could be used against the interests of these women. As a result, Fine et al. (2000) admitted, 'We have at times, consciously and deliberately left out some of these "great stories" that have the potential to become "bad data" to buttress stereotypes, reaffirm the ideology and rhetoric of the Right, and reinscribe dominant representations' (p. 117). There is, therefore, a moral dimension to the selective use of information (Greenbank, 2003), underpinned in this instance by the social values of the researchers.

Journal writing and reflexivity

An effective tool for addressing some of the dilemmas we have outlined above is the use of a journal to write, or visually record, personal reflections and field notes. As Alaszewski (2006: 33) has argued:

> Diaries provide a rich source of data for researchers who wish to explore the development of an individual life, and the activities and relationships of particular groups in society. Diaries can be used to access information within a specific society or social group and to explore the relationship between groups and even other cultures.

Luttrell (1997) describes field notes as riddled with reflective references, while Etherington (2004: 127–8) eloquently describes the power of the journaling in a reflexive context:

> Keeping a journal as part of a reflexive research can help us focus on our internal responses to being a researcher and to capture our changing and developing understanding of method and content. We reflect on our roles, on the impact of research on our personal and professional lives, on our relationship with the participants, on our perceptions of the impact we may be making on their lives and on our negative and/or positive feelings about what is happening during the research process. We can capture our dreams that might inform the research even while sleeping, or poems which reflect the essence of something barely known to us.

The use of a reflective journal by researchers has also been identified as a criterion to verify rigour in qualitative inquiry (Lincoln and Guba, 1985). This can be further enhanced by turning it into a collaborative tool which makes the knowledge and reflections visible and open to scrutiny by the research group (illustrated in Kay Heslop's case example in Chapter 8). Visual materials can also be drawn upon for reflexivity (see Davies, 2008; Pink, 2007). Indeed, 'both photographic content and the narratives photographs offer anthropologists routes to knowledge that cannot be achieved by verbal communication' (see Canal, 2004: 38).

Vicky's research (2013) explored how sixteen former literacy learners had been shaped by the public domain and the private domain of their lives. It was based on a six-year qualitative, longitudinal, ethnographic and participatory approach. The learners were all enrolled on basic skills courses at a Further Education college based in the North of England. She probed how they arrived at their current position and highlighted the learners' perception of their reality, unscrambling the links between their past, present and future while striving to highlight the intersection of class and gender on their pathways onto adult education/literacy programmes and their subsequent trajectories. While researching, Vicky found that the use of a shared written and visual journal contributed to both her personal reflexivity and the research process more broadly. On meeting with the participants, her own learners, on social occasions, the journal became a means to record everyone's voices. Vicky would take her journal on social nights out and during interviews. The sharing of these social practices was emancipatory, offering a tangible connection between the research and social life. The journal included the reflections and thoughts of the learners too. This was facilitated by sharing the ownership of, and writing in, the journal. To support this she would take the journal with her when she met participants on their own or together. Often they would write what they had been doing, how they had progressed and note any barriers they had faced. They would read her notes and share the stories of others, as they had agreed that they would all own it. When they went for meals out, the journal would be passed around the table so each member of the group could write their own account and share those of others. When they read the journal they could also see how Vicky had read their accounts, reflected on them and made comments. The participants would then discuss with Vicky whether she was gaining an understanding of the words and images they shared with her.

Photographs were used in a number of ways, which included learners offering Vicky photographs of important events in their lives (Barton et al., 2007; Barton and Hamilton, 1998). Importantly, the photography was shared, so the power of the gaze was not held in Vicky's hands alone. Photographs and videoing were also used on social nights out to record the event because they reflected the atmosphere of the event. The learners looked forward to taking photographs and sharing the images. This was particularly the case when they had made a 'special effort' and 'got dolled up'. It was as though the person they saw on the photographs was someone different to the self they knew in their daily lives. Many were convinced that they were unattractive and initially believed they were not 'good enough' to have their photo taken. The photographs were taken on a disposable camera that we all shared. The images presenting social implications of visual representations were bound to social structures and cultural meanings. Framing the images in a sociological exploration, we discussed how society is constituted, structured and reproduced and how the images reflect this, or not. The images therefore become resources for consciousness-raising by exploring the visual dimensions and how they don't just reveal structures of meanings but also practices, for example, what may be considered the socially situated gendered practice of application of make-up and getting dolled up.

Community empowerment

Research should never be merely a self-serving exercise, even (or especially) if your study is in partial requirement for an academic award. This can be achieved in various ways, from nurturing respectful and friendly relationships with our participants to forms of activism which empower them and their local and wider communities. This can mean engaging in forms of Participatory Action Research in which the research process is more equitable and, unlike conventional social science methods, which claim value neutrality, does not 'serve the ideological function of justifying the position and interests of the wealthy and powerful' (Kemmis and McTaggart, 2005: 560). This also implies that new knowledge is co-produced and therefore more meaningful in the content of the participating community. A good example of this is work by Erel et al. (2017) which uses participatory theatre methods in order to explore notions of citizenship with ethnically diverse, migrant mothers. They argue that using such methods 'create spaces for participants to enact social and personal conflicts' and that they can be socially transformative in their ability to build community and address issues of marginalization.

We have already addressed some of the ethical issues and dilemmas associated with collaborative or participatory approaches. However, one useful strategy can be to design research processes which place responsibility for action planning in the hands of community members, reflecting the importance of designing research instruments which can truly capture the experience of the groups you are studying. This involves listening to, and hearing, the voices of the participants; marginalized groups can offer us a great deal about the development of research tools and their efficacy, something which also offers us the opportunity to explore new and creative approaches to undertaking educational research. This can be challenging though: it is easy to create personal barriers to your participation and more difficult to step outside your comfort zone and be ready to commit to new experiences in ways that can benefit communities through research.

Participant voice and ethical research

The concept of voice has achieved a high profile in recent years, not only in research but also in education more broadly. Most schools and colleges, for example, now have a student council or similar body to represent student voice. Many of the arguments for undertaking collaborative research which claims social justice as an aim are framed around voice, and researchers will argue that a particular project is designed to allow the voice of a particular marginalized group to be heard. However, voice itself raises a multiplicity of ethical issues. Seminal work by Alcoff in 1992 addressed the 'problem of speaking for others', arguing that '. . . the practice of privileged persons speaking for or on behalf of less privileged persons has actually resulted (in many cases) in increasing or reinforcing the oppression of the group spoken for' an argument'. It is worth noting too that voices are always mediated by methods designed to facilitate them to be heard. For example,

Vidich and Lyman (2000: 39) argue that observations are mediated by a framework of cultural meanings and symbols arising from the observer's own life history, while Olesen (2000: 231, citing Lewin, 1991) argues that in respect of interviews, participants' voices are already mediated when they *come* to. These problems raise many questions about the ways in which voices are elicited and used. For example, where voice is represented in a research report, whose voice are we hearing? The participant's or the researcher's? What does that tell us about the power relations in the study? How do we know that the participant agreed with the interpretation of their words and the way they are woven together with others to draw particular conclusions? These are issues that most studies fail to address, but they are significant; Lincoln et al. (2013: 241) have noted that 'the issue of control is deeply embedded in the questions of voice', an issue which has been much debated over time. As early as 1994 Michelle Fine was arguing that researchers who claim to let the 'Other' speak are in fact hiding beneath 'the covers of those marginal, if now "liberated" voices" bringing into question . . . power relations'. She also suggests that where researchers do this, they are denying their 'authorial subjectivities', in other words, failing to acknowledge their value positioning and the impact this will have on their research, something we would suggest is not only unethical but which also places all control of a study in the hands of the researcher.

One of the ways in which we could address concerns about voice and power relations would be to create opportunities for participants to interpret and analyse data. Actions such as this do demonstrate respect for the people involved and can help to avoid the risk of conducting research which might be criticized as 'exploitative' or unethical. However, how to make 'voices heard without exploiting or distorting those voices is [a] vexatious question' (Olesen, 2000: 231). However collaborative the process is designed to be, it is possible that among some marginalized communities, such as young children or the low-attaining youth Liz works with, the contribution they will be able to make to the process will be limited. Further, the control of the interpretation and selection of the data to be used lies largely with the person conducting the research and as such is open to misinterpretation in a variety of ways.

Fine (1992b) has discussed different ways in which the participants' voices may be misused. These include the use of individuals' data to reflect groups, making assumptions that voices are free of power relations and failing to acknowledge the researchers' own position in relation to the voices. Such actions are clearly contrary to social justice, where we are struggling to learn from particular groups rather than 'intervene into' them (Cannella and Lincoln, 2013: 173). Cannella and Lincoln (2013) point out that voices from the margins demonstrate a whole range of knowledges, perspectives and understandings which should be foundational to our actions. How to interpret those voices in a way which generates those understandings without exerting control is problematic. As Simons (2000: 40) argues, in any act of interpretation, however hard the writer works at impartiality, the person writing the text has a stronger voice than those contributing to it. Thus, even where the text is authored with integrity, the interpretation can only ever reflect the perception of that individual. Indeed, Usher (2000: 27) has argued that 'all claims to truth are self-interested, partial and specific'.

These philosophical and ethical dilemmas associated with voice are deeply intertwined with concepts of power relations. They highlight the difficulties associated with acknowledging and acting on the need to 'listen to quiet, less powerful voices' (Griffiths, 1998: 96) and to reflect those voices in such a way as to retain the original integrity and meaning of the words. Griffiths (1998: 127) has proposed an analysis of voice and suggests that exploitation of the researched could be avoided by using an analysis of the concept of voice as a means of understanding what is, and what is not, exploitative. Using such an approach can support a reflexive approach and, while not fully addressing those 'vexatious questions' around voice, can support a moral and ethical response to issues as they arise.

In some cases, conflicts can arise between the representation of voice and other ethical issues such as anonymization. In Liz's research, the young participants wanted their names to be used in the dissemination of the study. They saw this as a moment of celebrity. However, information given by them included disclosures of criminal activity, anti-social behaviour and abuse among other sensitive topics. Therefore, Liz insisted on pseudonyms but gave the choice of those names to the participants. In this way, the voice the young people would have chosen was denied because of the conflict with other ethical principles around avoidance of harm. This raises a number of interesting questions that Liz continues to grapple with: what was the right course of action? Was the response moral and appropriate or did it fail to respect individual autonomy and deny voice? What could have been a more ethical alternative? These issues also highlight questions of power relations and empowerment as well as the 'extent to which power can be "bestowed" upon people through the medium of education or research' (Johnston, 2000: 78/79).

Funding and socially just research

Value positions are particularly significant and raise uncomfortable ethical issues when we engage with funded research. Undertaking funded research is a prerequisite of working in an increasingly marketized Higher Education sector. However, the value position of the funder will normally dictate the structure of the research as well as its focus. Many large funders are in receipt of government funding, which means that there is an ideological policy driver behind funding priorities. Further, in relation to educational research, over time, governments have moved towards an increasingly quantitative paradigm which often fails to acknowledge the voice and lived experience of marginalized groups and individuals. Government has had, at best, an ambivalent approach to social research for many years. In 2000, while arguing for ' "blue skies" research which thinks the unthinkable (GB, DFEE, 2000)' David Blunkett (2000) also argued that social science research was 'inward looking' and failed to build knowledge in a coherent way. There has also been a move towards 'evidence-based education' premised on 'evidence-based medicine': notable advocates include Hargreaves D. H. (1996, 2007) and Gorard (see Gorard and Huat See, 2017). However, 'evidence-based education' has been subject to widespread criticism on a number of grounds. These include the failure of its advocates to acknowledge unresolved problems in 'positivist' research and the problem of assuming that patterns of causation in educational questions involve 'fixed, universal relationships, rather than local, context-sensitive patterns' (Hammersley, 2007: 23). Similarly, Ball (2007: 111) argues that a focus on evidence and school effectiveness 'renders silent' other explanations concerned with social and economic context.

The particular positioning of funders dictates what is, or is not, fundable at any particular time. For example, we are keen to undertake a project exploring teachers' perceptions of social justice and its implications for their practice, but thus far have been unable to obtain funding for this. This leads us to a moral and ethical dilemma – do we bid for the research funds that are available (after all, we work for large businesses for whom income generation is critical, and we have contracts of employment requiring us to generate income) or do we persist in trying to obtain funding for important but ultimately less 'fashionable' work? Our compromise is to explore opportunities with charities and philanthropic organizations who are less influenced by political agendas. Many of these funders also have their own value positions which are more compatible with our perceptions of social justice and can facilitate us to do work that is important to communities and can make real changes to people's lives. For example, the Joseph Rowntree Foundation, originally established by the Quaker Rowntree family, is concerned with 'inspiring social change', while the Leverhulme Trust makes most of its grants in the 'responsive mode', leaving the choice of topic and research design to applicants. Inevitably, in times of austerity, these and similar organizations tend to be significantly oversubscribed.

Dissemination of ethically driven research

Part of challenging the structural oppression that marginalizes people in the first place includes the dissemination of the research and ensuring that silenced voices are heard, and taken seriously. By definition, ' "emancipatory" research should be judged by its ability to empower people – both inside and outside the actual research process. Dissemination of research findings to communities, which include those which are marginalized, requires innovative and meaningful approaches (Duckworth, 2013: 170). This means adopting a range of strategies to dissemination, which are accessible to all those who have an interest in a particular study. This might mean presenting at an academic conference, but it is more likely to involve websites, social media, local press, blogs and community meanings than more traditional forms of dissemination. Significantly, that dissemination must also be collaborative, involving the researched as well as the researcher on equal terms if the outcomes of the research are to have to impact that is hoped for. Addressing issues of voice and collaboration, facilitating participants to embed their own voice in the research has potential as an empowering mechanism. It means that participants are able to validate their experience and engage with a more egalitarian approach to the research design and process. In Duckworth's research (2013), which was disseminated through national and local media, the learners' lives and experiences were embedded into the curriculum used to develop basic literacy skills using their own narratives and poetry. For the learners in this group, who had been constrained by class, gender and ethnicity, both they and their communities benefitted from the media and specifically from the local media following their trajectories. The stories of these single mothers who had faced significant barriers prior to and while at college inspired other lone mothers in their community. The media stories allowed them to come together, to offer mutual support and to construct identities that challenged negative representations such as 'chavs' and instead validate different representations that mobilized personal agency around aspirations for educational achievement which would enable them to build a future for them and their families.

Ultimately, there are multiple approaches to dissemination, but in cases such as this, it is important to consider the particular ethical implications of dissemination. For example, did the initial consent process encompass all the forms of dissemination used? These can sometimes change over time, and there are particular sensitivities in respect of some forms of dissemination. In Duckworth's study, for example, many of the women had been victims of domestic violence. Dissemination via the media had to be done sensitively to ensure that it did not put any of these women at further risk. Further, their representation was significant, as representation within the traditional deficit models used to characterize them could only serve to reinforce those stereotypes. Dissemination is the part of a research project which can overtake the researcher (via an unexpected invitation to speak about the research on national radio, for example. Have your participants consented to this? Will it make them more visible? Under pressure, will you represent them differently or 'other' them?). This makes it even more critical that the researcher continues to work thoughtfully and reflexively throughout the dissemination process, to ensure that this part of the study maintains at all times the ethical framework and social justice philosophy underpinning it.

Further reading

Carr, W., and Kemmis, S. (1986), *Becoming Critical: Education, Knowledge and Action Research*, Lewes: Falmer Press.

Christians, C. (2013), 'Ethics and politics in qualitative research', in N. Denzin and Y. Lincoln (eds), *The Landscape of Qualitative Research*, 4th edn, Thousand Oaks: SAGE.

Greenbank, P. (2003), 'The role of values in educational research: The case for reflexivity', *British Educational Research Journal*, 29(6): 791–801.

Kemmis, S., and McTaggart, R. (2005), 'Participatory action research', in N. K. Denzin and Y. S. Lincoln (eds), *The Sage Handbook of Qualitative Research*, 3rd edn, pp 559–604, Thousand Oaks, CA: SAGE.

Sikes, P., Nixon, J., and Carr, W. (2003, eds), *The Moral Foundations of Educational Research: Knowledge, Inquiry and Values*, Maidenhead: Open University Press.

Simons, H. (2000), 'Damned if you do, damned if you don't: Ethical and political dilemmas in evaluation', in H. Simons and P. Usher (eds), *Situated Ethics in Educational Research*, London: RoutledgeFalmer.

CHAPTER FOUR

Insiders: Educators and researchers for social justice

Introduction

The dynamics between researcher and participant have become a central focus for academic attention over recent decades, and qualitative researchers have critically examined the epistemological, methodological and ethical issues related to this relationship. This chapter will explore the methods employed in socially just Insider research. When considering this it is important to recognize that the concept of validity becomes increasingly problematic because of the researcher's involvement with the subject of study. Positivists may argue that, because of this involvement, the researcher is no longer objective, and their results may be biased and distorted. This view of validity corresponds to an objective world view, derived from the early philosopher-sociologists. In contrast, methodologies adopted by critical theorists seek to avoid artificial distinctions between 'objective' and 'subjective' pointers of human action and challenge the value-neutrality stance of positivistic social science. Critical methodologies, which draw heavily on Marxist and feminist understandings, are continually evolving and seek to use critical forms of ethnography and critical inquiry as a means of engaging with social criticism and the empowerment of individuals (Canella and Lincoln, 2013). Thus, critical theory – and research – is significant in work which is argued to be socially just (implying action and social change), as well as forms of research – such as Participatory Action Research (PAR) – which claim to be critical and emancipatory (Duckworth, 2013; Freire, 1985). Action research has the potential to establish participatory ethics in the whole sense of all participants, cognitive and emotional, which we suggest is the key starting and driving force for democratized societies.

Points to consider when engaging in ethically just action research methodology:

- Ensure that the ethical positioning is explicit.

- Have a strong awareness and engagement in methodology which raises self-consciousness and self-knowledge of the subjects involved in the research project.

- Gain experience in the application of methods to assess different empowering effects during and after the research has taken place.

Importantly, PAR is viewed as one of the 'transformative framework' models in which 'disempowered groups, communities and individuals are empowered' (Kara, 2015: 45).

Critical theory is predicated on the acceptance of a certain set of epistemological and ontological assumptions. Broadly speaking, these assumptions are that all thought is fundamentally mediated by historically and socially constituted power relations, that facts cannot be separated from values and ideology, and that oppression has 'many faces' with which many research practices can be (unwittingly) complicit (Kincheloe et al., 2013: 341).

Positioning insider research

The term *insider researcher* has a number of characteristics and definitions. Insider researchers conduct research about home communities, such as one's own profession, workplace, society or culture. There are also different definitions of the positionality of an *insider*. Carrol (2009) explores the position of the 'alongsider' when examining the power relations between the researcher, clinicians, video camera and its footage in two innovative methodologies called 'video-ethnography' and 'video-reflexivity'. During video-reflexivity this process of looking 'alongside' participants included the researcher showing his/her video-ethnographic footage to clinicians, a process that she highlighted to make the researcher's gaze explicit. This draws parallels with feminist methodology which includes Harding's (1991) strong objectivity and making explicit the lens the researcher is looking through, moving to a collaborative (Kemmis and McTaggart, 1988) and self-reflective enquiry to drive forward methods that are socially just (Schostak, 2002). Insider-led, work-based projects may then be positioned as approaching from the perspective of bringing about contributions to practice that are informed by underpinning knowledge. Indeed, the success of the project may be in some part due to insider researchers' ability to negotiate around systems and practices which in Carrol's work include the alongsider element.

Milligan (2016) draws on participative techniques with final-year secondary school students in one rural community in western Kenya as an enabling tool for an outsider to both gain insider perspectives and develop a more insider role in that community by privileging and legitimating participant-driven data. Here, the notion of the 'inbetweener', whereby the researcher actively attempts to move from being an outsider to an 'inbetweener', is highlighted and also how this has the potential to have significant implications for being able to 'develop relationships built on trust and comradery, both with the students engaged in the participative research process and with the school and surrounding community more widely' (Milligan, 2016: 248).

Insider research is often aligned to emic perspectives. (Emic perspectives are those taken by a researcher who is a member of the community being studied, in contrast to Etic perspectives, which are those taken by a researcher who is an outsider to the community being studied). Thus, Insider research may also be described as the researchers and participants sharing a similar cultural, social, linguistic, ethnic, national and religious heritage. As insiders it is easy to take for granted one's social proximity and the beneficial impact this may have. Researchers have a profound moral responsibility to the participants being studied because the perspective the researcher takes impacts on the knowledge produced about the participants and can be empowering or disempowering, something which has significant implications for social justice. Indeed, Wang (1999) illuminates the importance of the emancipatory aspects of participatory research in which participants can become empowered through the process of designing, collection and analysing data.

The strength of insider research should not be underestimated. Methodologies that support insider research and from a local as well as wider reach can be of significance in generating more meaningful, nuanced and complex understandings of practices, educational experiences and processes and identities. Insider knowledge is the knowledge people have about their own experiences, gained through either practising or learning experiences. Taking and using that knowledge in robust research means being able to understand the implications of your personal positioning as an insider and being able to respond reflexively to the issues this raises. As a starting point, it can help to position yourself on an insider/outsider continuum which can help you to consider the specific methodological and ethical issues and dilemmas arising from your insider research. The continuum produced by the Teaching and Learning Research Programme (2011, cited Atkins and Wallace, 2012) is helpful here. Are you:

- a researcher who undertakes action research within his or her own classroom?

- a researcher who undertakes research within his or her own school, university or education department?

- an external researcher who is invited in to help a school by conducting some research on its behalf?

- a researcher who is conducting research on behalf of, for example, a local education authority with which a school is obliged to cooperate?

- a researcher pursuing his or her own research interests and seeks the agreement of a school to participate?

- a researcher travelling overseas to conduct some research in a community in which he or she is a complete stranger for an alien culture?

It is possible to see from this continuum that the position of the researcher in each situation is slightly different and will mean taking a nuanced and situated approach to issues such as those, for example, around power relations or blurred identity (Are you a teacher or a researcher? Where does one end and the other begin?). It is also evident that the extent of insider/outsider positioning has implications for the methodological approach utilized.

It is apparent from our own research, and that illustrated throughout the book, that different projects fill a different 'space' on a notional insider/outsider continuum. For example, Laura Nicklin's research in prisons (Chapter 4) was undertaken as a 'privileged outsider'. Kay Heslop's position (Chapter 8) might be described as privileged insider – a university lecturer undertaking research in a nursery run by one of her own students. Vicky positions herself as an insider, in the sense of her working class history, her role as researcher practitioner and the participatory and collaborative nature of the ethnographic approach to her research. The first generation in her family to gain qualifications and go to college, she was inspired by the power of adult education (which she had experienced) to transform learners' lives and opportunities. And it was this drive and commitment that drove her to become a literacy teacher in her community, working in both Further education and community settings. She does not view her health background as being separate from education; rather, she sees the crossing of disciplines to be a strength of insider research and this is reflected in her practice and research. Liz undertook research located in two settings: one where she had previously worked as a teacher, and one in which she was known as a teacher educator from the local university. She was welcomed back as an insider in the first institution and regarded (with some suspicion) as an outsider in the second. These brief anecdotes illustrate the complexity of deciding whether research is insider or outsider and the importance of determining and discussing the researcher's own position in relation to the research.

The researcher's own position in relation to her study is, however, only one aspect of being an Insider researcher that requires careful consideration. The second is the researcher's position in relation to the institution. Many people choose to research in their own institution because they are familiar with the organization and the challenges facing staff and learners. It is often also easier to negotiate access in a 'home' institution than it might be in one with whom you have no relationship. However, researching your own organization can raise practical, political and ethical issues which can lead some researchers to undertake their investigation beyond their home institution.

These issues are manifold, and some are obvious, others less so. For example, if your research highlights problems with the conduct of individuals in the organization do you use that as part of your research or address it with the individual or a manager? At which point must you cease being a researcher and take an issue further? If your research is funded by the organization (e.g. by supporting you with time or course fees if you are a student), what control does that give them over the management of the research? And how will you report your findings if they are in tension with the organizational management's perception of the situation? These are relatively straightforward questions in relation to other problems that might arise. Others are more complex. In this chapter, for example, we discuss the concept of 'shifting positionality' in relation to the participant group and how this may mean that your position as a relative insider or outsider might change. A particularly difficult and contentious problem in relation to insider/outsider research for social justice relates to questions of identity, particularly where these are associated with multiple indices of difference. Feminist theory in particular has addressed 'situated knowledges' (Haraway, 1991), which emphasizes that individuals are not just a set of characteristics, rather:

> a Black lesbian is not just a woman plus an African American plus a homosexual, but someone whose identity, experience, and knowledge are simultaneously shaped by all these attributes as they are played out in social structures where power is [often] in the hands of White, heterosexual males (Lamphere, 1994: 222).

Similarly, Olesen (2013: 268) highlights the recognition of differences among and between groups of women, recognizing that 'multiple identities and subjectivities are constructed in particular historical and social contexts'. Standpoint feminist research (e.g. see Harding, 2008) similarly sees women as specifically situated within social and racial stratification systems; Reay (1998: 61), however, drawing on Bourdieusian concepts of habitus and field, goes further, arguing that such identities are 'constitutive of, rather than determined by, social structures'.

Thus, even the insider researcher who is well embedded in their research site has difficult questions to explore in terms of researching the other. However, an extensive range of literature from different critical perspectives is available to inform the actions and decisions of the insider (and outsider) researcher working from a social justice perspective. Feminist theory, such as that outlined above, is particularly useful in this respect, given its consideration of intersectionality and ultimate aim of eliminating women's subordination (Denis, 2008: 678).

However, educational research involves people and, as such, has significant implications for human relationships. For example, how will the person with questionable conduct feel if you raise that issue? How will it affect your relationship with that individual and/ or with others? How will being a 'researcher' influence, for good or ill, the way in which you are perceived by others? In practical terms, this could be as simple as undertaking an observation in a classroom, but even if your interest is the children, this may cause discomfort to a generation of teachers who feel judged every time someone watches them. Ethically, that would require consideration, but pragmatically, it is something which could impact on relationships. Similarly, if as a researcher developing a more 'insider' understanding of a particular sub-group in an organization, this might lead to feelings of exclusion by others. These issues are far from exclusive, and subtly different variations will play out in each 'insider' context.

Insider research and action research

By virtue of the fact that much insider research is conducted by practitioners who are seeking to develop or understand their own practice, it is often associated with Action Research. McNiff and Whitehead, drawing on Stenhouse (1983), define Action Research as the 'systematic enquiry undertaken to improve a social situation and then made public' (2009: 11), while Hall (2001: 171), in relation to PAR, argues that it is an 'integrated three-pronged process of social investigation, education and action designed to support those with less power in their organisational or community settings'. In relation to these definitions, action research is considered critical because practitioners not only seek means to develop their practice within the limitations of the context they are addressing but are also change agents of those limitations and importantly of themselves. Indeed, there is recognition of the value of the researcher practitioner and the emancipatory nature of action research (Zuber-Skerritt, 1996). These arguments exemplify the notion of Action Research as political endeavour, in that it addresses inequalities in education through a democratic and emancipatory approach to research whose aim is social change. Many researchers have advocated the approach, and all have broader concerns with social justice, equity and addressing in/equalities in and through education. For example, Stenhouse (1975) was an early advocate, while notions of emancipation originate in Carr and Kemmis's work of the 1980s, which also emphasizes the collaborative nature of Action Research. The concept of PAR has its roots in the critical pedagogy developed by Paolo Friere in South America as a response to traditional forms of pedagogy in which, rather like Mr Gradgrind in Dickens's *Hard Times* (1854), teachers imparted information to passive students who were 'empty vessels' waiting to be filled. PAR developed from these ideas as a democratic means of initiating and implementing change and development in communities and groups. Despite this, like many other forms of practitioner or insider research, Action Research has been criticized for being small scale and, in many cases, lacking rigour, something which illustrates the importance of having a strong theoretical framework for your research, irrespective of the methodological approach. Some good examples of how this can be done, together with discussions of the implications and dilemmas arising from Insider Research, may be found in Sikes and Potts (2008). A final note of caution in relation to Action Research. Much Action Research (similarly to research across a range of methodologies claiming social justice as its purpose) claims to be emancipatory, but an important methodological and ethical issue is that consideration should be given to just how emancipatory it actually is. As Johnston (2000: 75) has argued, finding work for unwaged adults might be regarded as empowerment at one level, but is 'very far from broader ideas of emancipatory social change'. Goodley (2007) takes this argument further, suggesting that some practices of 'empowerment' concerning disabled people result in deficit model discourses of 'inclusion' and constructions of othered groups *requiring* 'empowerment'. In both the examples Goodley cites, action intended to 'empower' has colluded with existing oppressive systems and structures, denying agency to the oppressed group. This raises important questions for all insider researchers concerned with social justice, about the extent to which their research is truly transformational or empowering and the extent to which their own normative habitus has influenced their perception of what may or may not be empowering and emancipatory for the other.

Ethics, reflexivity and the insider researcher

Although undertaking insider research can be problematic, it is argued that researchers should be able to enter the setting with confidence, as long as the appropriate ethical boundaries are established at the outset and constantly revisited throughout the process. Ethical issues, like methodological issues, will vary according to individual positioning relative to the insider/outsider spectrum alluded to above, as well as in relation to the particular context of the research, and a reflexive approach should be taken throughout the research. Such an approach would begin with a statement of positionality and a questioning of personal assumptions which might impact on the research. Wellington (2015: 102) recommends questioning your assumptions about yourself, such as 'values, ideas, knowledge, motivation and prejudices', and their implications for the research, the assumptions 'taken- for- granted' by institutions which influence their cultures and sub-cultures. Finally, he highlights the importance of examining and questioning the language (or discourses) used in discussions about education (such as, e.g. disengaged, failing school, standards) and the implications of those for individuals.

This process of self-examination is of particular importance in Insider studies, where ease of access has to be set against other problematic issues associated with the researcher's shifting position – from teacher or colleague to researcher. Warren and Hackney (2000: 12) illustrate this in their argument that 'when researchers are already members of the settings they choose to study, entrée is unproblematic, they are already there. What may become problematic is not entrée and finding a place but rather "keeping" their place or negotiating a new one.' They illustrate this point (Hackney, 2000: 13) with reference to Back's (1993) choice of doctoral research, which is closely related to his personal experience – his ethnographic study took place in the area where he grew up and he used his working-class origins 'as a way of gaining credit for this research and thus fastidiously dissolving the division between self and other'. The fact remained, however, that Back was no longer the adolescent or a participant in the commentaries in the study. This recognition of one's changing position is vital to positioning oneself to the study and offering validity to the research process. It also raises issues about the insider/outsider dichotomy. Given the importance of personal positioning in research which is acknowledged to be Insider, the argument that that position can change over time and that there are complex subtleties and distinctions around understandings of insider/outsider research, the notion of a single continuum may be argued to be an oversimplification of a particular approach to research.

In a context where research claims social justice as part of its purpose, there are other key questions which need asking in order to address the particular ethical issues associated with social justice and its theory and philosophy. These would include, first, consideration of who the beneficiaries of the research might be and the extent to which it will 'empower or enable' them. If the purpose of the research includes addressing any personal needs or ambitions of the researcher (e.g. as a masters or doctoral study) what are the social justice and ethical implications of that? In terms of the participants who may be beneficiaries, who has determined what/how they will benefit? What does that imply about power relationships in the context of the study? In addition to these ethical and philosophical issues, there are more instrumental considerations in terms of undertaking Insider research. For example, although access may be granted and permissions given, over time the researched may forget that everything they do or say has the potential to become data. This can have significant implications for individuals who may express views or opinions they did not intend to be made public, such as, for example, an individual speaking in the heat of the moment or a manager whose words illustrate a culture of bullying and have the potential to bring an institution into disrepute. If that individual has 'forgotten' his or her position as one of the researched, should his permission be requested for the inclusion of views which reflect negatively upon himself and/or the institution? And do those data belong to the researcher or the researched? Irrespective of which side of the debate you locate yourself, it is essential that researchers taking data from persons should do so in ways which recognize those persons' initial ownership of the data and which respect them as fellow human beings who are entitled to dignity and privacy (Bassey, 1999: 74).

On a related issue, it can be more difficult to address issues of anonymization. The research will be disseminated within the institution at some level and, particularly in a small organization, anonymization may not be possible, illustrating the importance of taking a reflexive approach throughout every Insider study. This may not preclude issues such as that described here, but it will provide a firm and considered foundation for the action a researcher takes to address such a difficulty. Similarly, confidentiality can become a major issue in Insider research, simply because the researcher's location gives them privileged access to information which would not be available to an outsider – even one with a privileged position, again illustrating the importance of reflexivity and of Power Relations.

Kilgore (2001: 55) has argued that Power is a factor in 'what we know *and how* we know it' (our emphasis) suggesting that, in the critical worldview, reflecting on and challenging such knowledge is fundamental to action to 'change material and social conditions of oppressed people as well as the commonly held assumptions that reinforce their oppression' (Kilgore, 2001: 55). In contrast, Mercer (2007) has argued that for insider researchers, power relations are an issue only if the researcher is in a more senior position than the participant. However, we would argue that in research which claims social justice as part of its purpose, the researcher will always be in a position of power and, thus, has a moral and ethical responsibility to address issues of Power from a critical standpoint such as that advocated by Kilgore. The position of critical *insider* also challenges positivistic approaches to knowledge which suppose that those with distanced and 'objective' views of practice (e.g. researchers from the academy) can best understand and steer practitioners who are seen as too close to practice to embrace an accurate perception of it (Harding, 1991). We would argue that this moves to a hegemonic understanding of knowledge where as a practitioner, we cannot begin to take ownership of and understand our own practice. Therefore, knowledge is created by 'experts' beyond the domain of the school or college (Kincheloe et al., 2013: 345). This is very much a position where the institution takes control and the practitioner is positioned as passive and disempowered – not identified as a maker of knowledge but as a receiver, and it is something which must change if a 'critical reform of schooling' (Kincheloe et al., 2013: 345) is to take place.

Becoming a researcher practitioner facilitates the critical interpretation of the complexities of the education process and the interpretation of that; we would argue that unless a practitioner can critically engage in examining their own practice, they cannot position themselves as able to critically examine others' claim to knowledge. This highlights the importance of Initial Teacher Education programmes which empower trainee teachers to critically question wider education practice and facilitate them to grapple with the issues associated with undertaking socially just and critical research into their own practice. This is the focus of Alison Iredale's (2018) study in which she describes her own research journey as a 'patchwork of philosophy, reflexivity and biography'. The importance of developing teachers who are critical practitioners is also highlighted in Mark Vicars's discussion of the Monastic Education Enhancement Programme, a project he has been involved with in Myanmar. The project was funded by the Australian Government New Colombo program in partnership with Paung Daw Oo, Monastic Education Primary and High School, Myanmar, with the goal of providing mentoring in developing and delivering a child-centred curriculum in English across a range of curriculum subjects as aligned with the direction of the school in response to a direct request by the school principal. Like many other such projects, this placed the teacher at the centre of knowledge generation, incorporating elements of both teaching and research to develop a sustainable and socially just model for basic education.

Case example

Developing teacher education in Myanmar
Mark Vicars

Myanmar is a developing, Buddhist country, which does not yet have the capacity for universal education. For this reason, many children are educated through the monastic education system. This refers to basic (primary) education schools which are managed and run by monks or nuns in monasteries or nunneries. It provides education to over 275,000 children, thus providing learning opportunities for those children who are not fully served by the government system. As such, it targets marginalized children, such as those from migrant families, remote communities and conflict areas (Tin and Stenning, 2015). The Monastic Education Development Group (MEDG) is a not-for-profit independent professional organization within the monastic education system that provides technical and school development support to monastic schools across Myanmar by:

1. Taking an active and leading role in the development of national-level quality systems and the promotion of basic minimum standards for all Monastic Schools in Myanmar;
2. Networking with government, local and international non-government organizations s and donors to coordinate and mobilize support for the development of Monastic Schools;
3. Supporting the development of professional standards and training in order to promote teachers' capacity to provide creative and child-centred education;
4. Leading development of sustainable and systematic reform of Monastic Schools;
5. Prioritizing the role of schools in promoting access to quality education and responsible citizenship.

The Monastic Education Enhancement Program project focused on building the capacity of teachers within the monastic system to be able to use child-centred approaches in teaching and learning. *The objective of the program was to develop teacher education and work towards the delivery of quality basic education in Myanmar.* This was achieved by *providing mentoring and coaching in the classrooms of the Myanmar teachers.* Twenty student teachers from Melbourne were given training in coaching and mentoring and subsequently worked for three weeks with teachers at Paung Daw Oo Monastic School in Mandalay in classrooms with children who were in the English language stream. MTeach students mentored groups of Myanmar teachers in child-centred approaches to teaching and learning and contributed to their ongoing, informal, workplace education and professional development: the students also aimed to enhance their own pedagogic skills and knowledge connected to an understanding of education for Social Justice.

Paung Daw Oo Monastic School serves a local community of low socioeconomic families and hosts an orphanage for abandoned children. The project offered students the opportunity to work as teachers with untrained Myanmar teachers while reflecting on and evaluating different approaches to undertaking critical research into social justice educational issues and to co-consider solutions to teaching and learning in culturally complex classroom environments. Students worked alongside Myanmar teachers to develop skills and knowledge of child-centred learning and were asked, from their participation, to:

1. Evaluate core issues related to social justice in education;
2. Critically examine multiple perspectives related to social justice teaching and learning;
3. Formulate a conceptual and theoretical overview of contemporary issues related to social justice education.

The methods of teaching were learner focused and incorporated classroom activities such as workshops, inquiry activities and peer discourse as the basis for sharing information and experiences of and about child-centred learning. Students worked individually in the classroom teaching their curriculum specialism, and collaboratively in Learning Circles with each other and Myanmar teachers to support professional development activities. Self-managed and cooperative learning was encouraged. Students were expected to think critically and rigorously evaluate and analyse information, establish facts, use data and consider different contexts and intercultural realities when researching into their practice.

Through negotiation with a mentor, students were asked to identify a particular theoretical critical study related to Social Justice in education and articulate:

1. Evidence of a critical examination of multiple perspectives related to teaching as a praxis of social justice and develop an understanding of contemporary issues in working in culturally complex classrooms with a social justice ethos.

2.   Explanation of theoretical and conceptual framework/s chosen
     to explore the practicum and a discussion of ethical issues
     relevant to the experience and how they were managed
     (including specific reference to one or more of the key themes
     of social justice, sustainability and learning communities).
3.   Personal and professional learning that impacted on and
     deepened an understanding of social justice education in
     the work undertaken with Myanmar teachers to include a
     reflective element that considers your own stance in relation
     to the themes of ethical praxis and social justice.

Theoretical framing: Praxis inquiry

The following Praxis protocol was utilized by the students to
critically reflect and consider the work undertaken in schools and
with Myanmar colleagues.

Practice described

Pre-service teachers describe practice (cases, artefacts, anecdotes)
and identify questions. What do I wonder about when I think about
this event?

Practice explained

Pre-service teachers seek to discover professional explanations for
their practice (literature, research, mentors and colleagues, teacher
education). How can I understand this practice?

Practice theorized

Pre-service teachers consider the overriding question, Who am
I becoming as an educator as I integrate these understandings and
beliefs into my practice? Who am I becoming as a teacher?

Practice changed

Pre-service teachers plan action. How can I act to improve learning
for students and improve my capacity as an educator? What are my
new questions?

Mark Vicars's narrative is complex and raises a number of issues, not least of which is the MTeach students' multifaceted role as privileged outsiders while also being child educators and teacher educators. This is a reminder of how complex – and methodologically challenging – relationships can be in the context of Insider Research. This project illustrates the significant challenges faced by many children in accessing even a basic education and highlights the lack of ITE in many parts of the world. It also illustrates that a relatively small intervention can make a difference, if only in one school. In terms of Insider Research, many questions are posed. Did the role of the students change as the project developed? Did they, in effect, become Insiders? To what extent could the collaborative nature of the project and the co-creation of knowledge have contributed to their positioning? Ethically, did the project *promote* social justice to the same or to a greater extent as the students may have *learned* about social justice? Certainly the development of improved pedagogical approaches has the potential for making a more socially just system and, as Vicars notes, particular challenges existed in the light of the culturally complex classrooms. This highlights the importance of co-creating knowledge. In taking this approach, the students were able to develop cultural understandings from the Myanmar teachers, who in turn were able to develop new pedagogical understandings. Sharing those ideas – and contextualizing them in a rigorous theoretical framework – facilitated the construction of culturally appropriate child-centred approaches which 'recognised the autonomy of decision makers at different levels in the system' (Stenhouse, 1975: 211, citing MacDonald and Rudduck, 1971). While concern for a marginalized community (such as excluded children in Myanmar) can lead to ethnographic or practitioner research concerned with those groups, from a position of privileged outsider, belonging to a group may provide an even stronger motivation to promote social justice through education and research as a means of addressing societal inequalities.

Insider research and social justice

The researcher–participant relationship in studies within oppressed communities presents a critical opportunity for the emergence of marginalized and often silenced voices to be heard. As researchers we are often most inspired to explore the topics that have touched our own lives. This is evident in Lisa McKenzie's work. Lisa is a former mature access student whose research *Getting By* (2015) is based on St Ann's estate in an inner city area of Nottingham, England. It is the outcome of eight years' *insider* ethnographic study, based on both theory and practice. The 'insider' status enables us to hear the stories of its residents, often wary of outsiders, through the lens of Lisa's own journey. McKenzie illustrates how the working-class people and the communities in which they live have been devalued to such an extent that they are perceived simply as 'problematic' and thus in need of 'making better'. She repositions this deficit misrepresentation of a community which is the home to resourceful, ambitious people who are 'getting by' despite deep austerity. The narratives are recounted with humour, love and care, all grounded in social and cultural context. Similarly, Lyn Hanley (2007) was positioned as an insider in her research. She was raised just outside of Birmingham, England, on what was then the largest council estate in Europe and lived for years on an estate in London's East End. She argued in her personal memoir and social history of estates that children who live on estates and attend the local school receive a 'council estate education' where 'you can't ever hope to reach your potential; it's just that very idea of having lots of potential to fulfil that isn't presented'. In these studies we can see the historical thread and geographical landscape that link these insider researchers to their participants and their communities.

These are both examples of 'connections' with researched communities whose experiences have resonated with our own personal experiences and are consistent with our values. Such relationships with researched communities are common. From a practical perspective, most of the unfunded research in education (which is a majority of it) is conducted by students and practitioners. Insider membership of a community which is being researched offers particular opportunities for the researcher and can be a catalyst for participating in socially just research. This is often predicated on the need to offer reorientations that challenge inequality. As Marx argued, 'the philosophers have only interpreted the world in various ways: the point is to change it' (Marx, 1998: 49). Such connections can exist even where the researcher is not a member of the group being researched (e.g. a teacher researching student attainment): immersion in the community offers a critical positioning whereby the researcher has insider knowledge of the lives, motivations, pressures, hopes and dreams of those being researched (see Giroux, 1997; Macedo, 1994; Shor, 1992).

Such knowledge can often provide points of reference which can help the researcher and the participants to develop a relationship associated with shared experience, history or sense of place, for example. However, while this might help to develop an insider perspective to some extent, particularly where the researcher positions themselves as, for example, a privileged outside, it is still necessary to be acutely aware of the difference between the researcher and the researched and develop understanding of how that might impact on the research and all those involved, in terms of methodological, ethical and moral concerns. For example, as 'insiders' the impact of our positioning on data analysis is a major consideration (see Miles and Huberman, 1984). By ensuring transparency in changing role and positioning it is possible to develop greater rigour in research, particularly where this is a collaborative process with the research participants.

Privileged outsider

There has been extensive debate about the strengths of researchers being *outsiders* or *insiders* to the communities they study (e.g. see Banks, 1998; Merton, 1972; Rose, 1997). These debates are not straightforward, reflecting the complexities of some of the research relationships discussed in this chapter. Researchers often enter communities as outsiders, whether by virtue of their affiliation with a university, level of formal education, research expertise, ethnicity, socioeconomic status or other characteristics. As the boundaries between researchers and participants are ruptured, the issue of trust emerges as critical to creating and sustaining successful relationships. Building relationships of trust between researchers and participants often means reaching across class, gender, racial, ethnic and social divides, among others. The crossing of the divides and forging of meaningful and trusting relationships may be viewed as a *privileged outsider* position.

Case example

Shakespeare in prisons: Working as a privileged outsider
Laura Louise Nicklin

For over two decades Shakespeare-focused education programmes intended for criminal rehabilitation have emerged in the United States, becoming alternatives or supplements to incarceration. My multi-sited ethnographically informed research examines such initiatives as although incarceration is heavily used globally, outcomes rarely match intentions, with 45.2 per cent of UK adults and 68.5 per cent of UK juveniles released from prison in 2013 reoffending by 2015 (Ministry of Justice, 2015). There are Shakespeare-focused education programmes that continually produce far greater impact on recidivism, with some boasting exceptionally low rates at 6.1 per cent (Shakespeare Behind Bars, 2017). Where such programmes seem so successful, I researched their specific practices and perceived outcomes, exploring why specifically Shakespeare, and whether subject matter was most relevant to the impact. Most critically I wanted to know from the offender perspective what their perceived outcomes were from engaging in this work.

Social justice research is not only about engaging in related projects but also conducting research in a socially just way. My research philosophy places participant voice at the heart of authenticity, and I did not want to approach as a privileged outsider interpreting their world, but rather co-construct an accurate representation from voices within it. For this reason, I selected an ethnographic research approach as the best approach to this research, a method allowing me to position myself as researcher engaging within but not speaking for participant groups.

The research methodology was heavily informed by the style of ethnography which calls for a series of methods to be interwoven into a larger tapestry providing a full image of the situation under consideration, usually in non-mainstream participant societies (Hammersley and Atkinson, 2007; Richardson and St Pierre, 2008; Sobers, 2011). My research strategy necessitated a process of personal engagement within the programme groups, not only asking about the programmes but also engaging with them and witnessing them first-hand as a participant researcher situated within the investigated world. Where this practice is so specific, and therefore until recently so sparsely used in the prison context, I was very fortunate to be permitted access into pioneering programmes in this field. As there were so few of these phenomena in operation or accessible at the time, I utilized all opportunities to attend as much as possible, gathering data across multiple sites and states to build up a wider portrait and develop a rich dataset. I therefore undertook a multi-sited approach to this research study, collecting a range of relevant data from multiple field sites to construct an informed portrait of the research matter under investigation, reaching out for more data than traditionally single-sited investigations.

The structure of the data collection process was somewhat unstructured, where types of data collected vary and are often unpredictable in this type of study, and the approach is grounded in experience. What is available to the researcher varies greatly so I needed to be flexible in my approaches from accepting written pieces to making notes and recording stories through my own researcher diaries. The sample was taken by convenience through willing active participants with the groups at the time of data collection and included active participant testimony, group discussions, researcher diaries, written work, statements and observations that were recorded in research diaries and through written contributions from programme participants, ex-offenders and stakeholders such as practitioners and prison staff. Though there are many diverse practitioner justifications for this work, I selected the voice of participants as the most significant voice in this study as they are the ones most directly impacted by it.

Much ethnographic analysis does not necessarily use one traditional analytical style, but rather a combination of approaches to help source avenues into the subject matter. In this case, several styles were introduced including thematic, descriptive and free-form analytical approaches, to draw out broad themes and break them down to show a deep and detailed image of the phenomena. As is typical in ethnographically informed research, the analysis developed into more free-form exploration to draw out the findings, construct and draw meaning where description and reflection form a crucial part of establishing the research findings. Through this I was able to critically connect the constructed narratives with my research questions underpinned by appropriate literature and theory to offer a full image of the potential the programmes held. As several sites were investigated in a relatively short period, it was vital that as much relevant data could be gained as possible; therefore, this was an ideal way to ascertain high volumes of data, analyse each type of data appropriately and offer several layers in terms of results and findings. Denzin and Lincoln (2011) highlight the potential for interpretive approaches conducting 'bricolage', meaning that the portrait is created through the incorporation of multiple perspectives, sources and types of data to formulate the complete picture. This is not an uncommon approach for ethnographers, where the researcher becomes a builder using the available materials to construct an overall insight (Eglinton, 2008; Kincheloe, McLaren and Steinberg, 2011).

My research area, philosophy and approach brought with them significant responsibility as a social justice researcher, to ensure that what is being reported is not merely an outsider's rationalization or interpretation of situations, but rather an accurate representation drawn from within. I drew on a wide range of data types, identified by participants as the most appropriate for communicating their experience, and gained first-hand experience ensuring authentic findings. Investigating multiple sites provided an ideal way to ascertain high volumes of data, offering multiple routes into formulating the complete picture, through the incorporation of multiple perspectives and approaches.

My research draws on a broad range of theoretical perspectives as it is interdisciplinary. My theoretical considerations reflect this, with a critical focus on the theories underpinning applied theatre and arts-based therapeutic and educational practice (Boal, 1979; Jones, 1995; Landy and Montgomery, 2012; Nicholson, 2015; Prentki and Preston, 2013), coupled with related educational and prison-focused theory surrounding the impact of prison practices and purpose, power-dynamics, dehumanization and education (Fitch and Normore, 2012; Foucault, 1977; Freire, 1970). I connected the practices and outcomes of Shakespeare-focused educational interventions with such theories, including empathy and emotional development, interactive and reflective education, participant-led collaboration, empowerment and re-humanization, and life-drama connections. Shakespeare-focused initiatives intended to empower, educate and reconnect participants to real-world situations, developing personal, practical and emotional skills, while also empowering them to overcome personal and societal barriers and take authority over their own life trajectories. I discovered that the initiatives I considered are devices for rehabilitating and reintegrating offenders, through specific Shakespeare-grounded activities, facilitating reflection, re-humanization, and reintegration skills to be applied within and beyond incarceration, and in turn demonstrating both to society and to participants themselves prisoner capabilities beyond their criminal histories and stereotypical expectations.

The scope of social and ethical issues that emerged throughout my research highlights critical social justice issues. It is an unfortunate feature of society that offenders are assumed to be 'savages', 'animals' and other derogatory variations, rarely considered 'human' (Vasilyevic and Viki, 2013). Such attitudes towards offenders reflect a marginalizing dehumanization of them, revealing a vital need for social justice work, reaching marginalized communities. Not only does this perception exist but participants shared awareness of this, viewing themselves as separate from society. Society marginalizes offenders, making employment and progress limited. Meanwhile, offenders are unlikely to care about their impact on a society not caring about them. Long after physical barriers are removed upon prisoner release, constructed divisions remain, cementing discord. It is a vicious cycle that in part maintains the current cycle of recidivism. Where prisoners are a marginalized community, treated differently from and holding less power than the society at large, there is a great need for social justice. However, there are several barriers that make such research particularly difficult. There are significant physical barriers in terms of gaining permission and access to communities intentionally separated from society, coupled with more deeply embedded socially constructed divisions that stigmatize offenders beyond sentence completion. Initiatives for prisoners are notoriously controversial, with educational initiatives frequently labelled as treats rather than the treatments they are intended to be. In knowing this, several organizations shared that they would want their participants to be involved in my research; however, they could not, explaining a shared awareness that they were maintaining their survival in a turbulent environment.

I did gain access to several programmes willing to engage with the research; however, discrepancies in critical social justice issues including inequality and rights of prisoners quickly became evident within the prison context. This meant that although I could conduct my research, I had new challenges due to conflicting requirements from my research institution, supporting participant organizations, research sites and my own research philosophy. Informed consent, for example, is essential in just research practice; however, some research sites claimed that institutional blanket consent was enough for participants to be researched, particularly significant in theory surrounding prisons, power and enforcing control (Crewe, 2012; Foucault, 1977). Supported by participant organizations, I instead made the decision to still seek and value individual participant consent, but even where I made this choice participants were shocked or amused I was even asking. I was perceived as mistaken for asking permission, as though I did not understand they were not deemed worthy of choice. Prisoners have rights and freedoms removed from them, essentially told when to function with minimal scope for autonomy. My research approach and philosophy ensure that these people are treated justly, that participants want to engage in my research work and that they have the strongest voice in research outcomes that impact them.

Conclusion

Research for and about social justice is undertaken to challenge inequality, to give voice to and advance the well-being of particular populations. It can be an extremely rewarding activity. Both professionally and personally, it is extremely fulfilling to conduct research with the potential to empower individuals, their families and communities. The impetus of the research may be to generate knowledge that illuminates the constraints and challenges in people's lives and offer resistance; this might include subverting negative representations and presenting evidence that speaks back to politicians and policymakers to challenge the status quo and drive forward social and educational equality (Johnson and Duckworth, 2018). Disseminating research at professional conferences, in journals and on virtual platforms such as blogs and social media helps to generate critical discussions about how new knowledge and understandings can make a real practical difference in the lives of the participants.

Researchers can make their own decision on whether to position themselves as insiders or outsiders, as both insiders and outsiders, or as insiders first and then outsiders; in addition, they also have the dimensions of alongsider and inbetweener. However, as suggested by Wilkinson and Kitzinger (2013), we 'cannot escape being both insiders and outsiders', so it important for us to make good use of these positions (p. 254).

It is worth noting that Insider Research also brings with it challenges and tensions. For example, throughout this chapter, we have highlighted the notion of the insider/outsider and questioned the extent to which this is a false dichotomy or oversimplification given our multiple indices of difference in relation to the researcher's positioning in the research. We have concluded that while it is certainly an oversimplification, any discussion of the ethical and methodological implications of a research project must include consideration of the researcher's position in relation to the researched, particularly where that research is politically and/or socially motivated or is a form of social action. We also acknowledge that much educational research is critical inquiry conducted by practitioners, who are, by definition, insiders in their own classrooms. We examine the role of the researcher practitioner and the impact of this in developing as a critical educator who can contribute to the development of a more socially just and equitable education system, considering how this is located not only in the research questions but also in the methods and methodology and the way the research is carried out and how it is written. We have positioned research as a political activity in the process and how it is written: it is an activity which challenges practitioner-researchers to question and re-examine the nature of their practice. It also focuses upon the assumptions, the implicit value-judgements that often affect and direct the ways in which practice operates. For all these reasons this kind of research is of great value to those who participate in it, at whatever level. Whatever approach a researcher takes, it is important that *outsiders* – many of them privileged outsiders as illustrated in Laura Nicklin's case example – feel just as competent as insiders and vice versa, in critically engaging with research, theory and pedagogy in ways which facilitate the construction and co-construction of knowledge. In this way, Insider researchers can promote social justice by seeking to produce 'practical, pragmatic knowledge . . . a bricolage . . . judged by its . . . ability to produce praxis or action' (Denzin and Lincoln, 2013: 193).

Further reading

Atkins, L., and Wallace, S. (2012), 'Insider research', Chapter 3 in *Qualitative Research in Education*, London: BERA/SAGE.

Carr, W., and Kemmis, S. (1986), *Becoming Critical: Education, Knowledge and Action Research*, London: RoutledgeFalmer.

Iredale, A. (2018), 'The journey into praxis: Confidence, excellence and routinised practice', Chapter 5 in *Teacher Education in Lifelong Learning: Developing Professionalism as a Democratic Endeavour*, London: Palgrave Macmillan.

Johnson, C., and Duckworth, V. (2018), 'A tale of two adult learners', in A. Benoit, Joann S. Olson. and C. Johnson (eds), *Leaps of Faith: Stories from Working-Class Scholars*, Charlotte, NC: Information Age Publishing.

Sikes, P., and Potts, A. (2008), *Researching Education from the Inside: Investigations from Within*, Abingdon: Routledge.

PART TWO

Researching for social justice and equity in context

CHAPTER FIVE

Education, marginalization, voice and socially just methods

Introduction

This chapter focuses on one study which, underpinned by theoretical and philosophical frameworks associated with social justice, sought to 'walk the walk' as well as 'talk the talk'. In particular, this involved giving consideration to the different ways in which participants in the study could collaborate, as well as to how the methods utilized could be applied in ways which were socially just. Social justice–driven researchers are transparent about the values that researchers should adhere to, most notably, democratic values: concern for marginalized and minority rights and dignity, commitment to the common good, conviction in the power of individuals to have agency, belief in the importance of dialogic engagement and the transparent stream of ideas, reflexivity and the central premise of individual and collective responsibility for others. This forms part of their acknowledgement of the assumptions about power, oppression and socially and historically constituted inequalities which underpin critical theory, research and pedagogy (Kincheloe et al., 2013: 341) and means that they work within a critical framework which positions the researcher as a 'transformative intellectual' who is both advocate and activist (Lincoln et al., 2013: 203). However, this in itself raises another controversy explored by Lincoln et al. (Lincoln et al., 2013: 241), and this centres on who has control of the study, in terms of determining who initiates it, who determines the key questions, what and how data will be collected, interpreted and disseminated. These are critical questions which are bound up in conceptions and questions of voice and reflexivity and therefore significant in any research claiming social justice as part of its framework or purpose.

Lincoln et al.'s argument that the 'transformative intellectual' is 'both advocate and activist' is also significant, relating as it does to conceptions of social justice as a political ideology which implies action (e.g. see Atkins, 2009; Griffiths, 2003; Walker, 2003, quoted Griffiths, 2003). Calls for action addressing the structural issues leading to increasing inequality and marginalization of certain communities have become louder across the Western world since the banking crash of 2008 and subsequent economic crisis (e.g. see Davis, 2017, Dorling, 2015; House of Lords Social Mobility Committee, 2016; Gibb, 2017; NUT, 2017). These have been given greater imperative in the UK following the Grenfell fire which drew into sharp focus the ways in which less affluent working communities – as well as those characterized as marginalized – can be denied access to safe, decent housing and led to wider debates about differentiated access to health, welfare and education (e.g. Duckworth and Smith, 2017a and b; Hanley, 2017; OxfamBlogs, 2017).

Recognizing issues of differentiated access to education (e.g. see Tomlinson, 1997, 2001, 2013), Liz adopted a social justice perspective for a study which aimed to enable marginalized level 1 learners to have their voices heard. In doing so she utilized a participatory and inclusive approach. The practice of inclusive research is limited but has its roots in disabled people's movements (Björnsdóttir and Svensdóttir, 2008). Nind (2014b: 526, citing Walmsley, 2001, and Walmsley and Johnson, 2003) notes that it was originally proposed as a means of involving people *with* learning disabilities in research *about* people with learning disabilities. It has much in common with the participatory approach that Kellett (2010: 49) advocates in research with children; indeed, in other work Nind (2014a) has extended Walmsley and Johnson's notion of inclusive research to include the participatory approaches advocated by Kellett, as well as a range of others including, for example, decolonizing research, user- and child-led research, and community research as well as activist scholarship and democratic dialogue. Inclusive approaches can present particular challenges in terms of facilitating a conceptually challenging process. However, they are consistent with the social justice philosophies of empowerment, inclusion and participation. Further, critical social justice approaches to research have become increasingly common over the past two decades as scholars have sought to utilize social science as a means of 'redressing a variety of historically reified oppressions in modern life' (Denzin and Lincoln, 2013: 580). In relation to this, young people such as those involved in Liz's research (below) might be regarded as subject to significant structural inequality and oppression as a consequence of a range of exclusionary characteristics including, but not limited to, class, race, gender and disability.

Research context

Liz's study explored the aspirations and learning identities of three groups of level 1 students in two English General Further Education (FE) colleges. Data were collected over a single academic year, but varied between colleges due to constraints such as external OfSTED[1] inspection and external examination periods. Level 1 is the lowest point in mainstream education post-16 but is somewhat ambivalently positioned. Bathmaker (2001) noted that some colleges located it as mainstream and others as part of their Special Educational Needs provision, despite the fact that a majority of young people engaging with level 1 programmes will have progressed from mainstream schools and been entered for GCSE's at 16+. This position has remained unchanged in almost two decades since Bathmaker's study. Located at the bottom of the mainstream hierarchy, these young people are characterized by multiple forms of oppression and inequality, related to, for example, social class, gender, race and disability as well as their low educational attainment at 16+ which effectively debars them from

---

[1]OfSTED – The Office for Standards in Education, Children's Services and Skills is an organization responsible for the formal inspection and regulation of services that care for children and young people and services providing education and skills for learners of all ages on behalf of the government in England and Wales.

more prestigious forms of FE such as A levels or apprenticeships, thus having significant implications for their future transitions to the labour market.

Warin (2010: 46) has suggested that school-to-work transitions are a significant phase in identity formation. Since the collapse of heavy industry in the late twentieth century, however, these transitions have, particularly for low-attaining youth, become increasingly 'extended, fractured, difficult, troubled and/or precarious' (Atkins, 2016: 1) experiences characterized by a relentless 'churn' between low-level education programmes, low pay, low skill work and being Not in Employment, Education or Training (NEET). Within this context, these young people are characterized as 'disaffected' and 'disengaged' and seen as failing to meet their perceived civic responsibility of engaging with lifelong learning, placing them firmly within a government deficit model of failure to engage with vocational 'opportunities' and resulting in blame being attributed by the state to the individual (Ainley and Corney, 1990: 94–5; Atkins, 2010a: 262). This occurs even where the 'opportunities' on offer are lacking in any meaningful exchange value and is now sanctionable via loss of benefits.

Consequently, learners at this level are perceived within and beyond educational institutions to be less valuable learners, perhaps reflecting the 'sharp divide between valuable and non-valuable people and locales' described by Castells (2000: 165). In recognition of this low value, the project was structured within a social justice framework which sought to demonstrate respect and value for the young participants during its process, as well as to understand the young peoples' lived experience of engaging with level 1 study, their hopes and aspirations, and how these were variously constrained and enabled by their social and educational positioning.

Developing the research

Planning the study raised issues concerning my positioning vis-à-vis that of the young people I hoped would participate in the study. Similarly to Back (1993, cited Warren and Hackney, 2000) my choice of study related to an area closely related to my own personal experience – not only had I spent many years teaching in FE but I had been a vocational student in FE myself after failing my post-16 exams. In the (long) intervening period, however, supported by my FE experience, I had made a significant transition in terms of education, occupation and class positioning. I was now much older than the young people, something which engendered a different kind of distance from their experience. I recognized that this meant that I no longer had any meaningful insight into the lives and experiences of young people undertaking contemporary vocational programmes, although I recognized the inequalities they experienced and was committed to trying to address these. This informed my decision to involve young people from the outset, not only in the actual investigation process but also in terms of developing the research instruments.

As well as being moral issues, concerned with respecting the participants and valuing their contribution, there are good methodological reasons for this inclusive type of approach. It ensures that the investigation is grounded in the actual reality of participants, rather than that perceived by the researcher, and as such avoids the risk of asking 'Catholic questions of a Methodist audience' (Lincoln and Guba, 2000: 175), meaning to pose questions which are meaningless to an audience who have no frame of reference for them. This is a significant risk in any exploration of identity, a concept which has been argued to be 'partial, contested, and, at times, contradictory' (Tierney, 2000: 547) and sometimes situationally specific (Angrosino and Mays de Perez, 2000: 689). It is also individual, influenced by life experiences and intersectional characteristics such as class, race, gender and dis/ability. This was illustrated in the activity undertaken with group A, sixteen level 1 students to whom I had negotiated the earliest access. My starting point was to establish what aspects of their lives were most significant and worthy of investigation to the young people in a study which sought to include young people in research about aspects of their own lives and to facilitate them to 'have some impact on aspects of the research process' (Holland et al., 2008: 4). This involved choosing methods that the participants could 'do' rather those 'beyond their immediate capacity' such as more traditional methods that could be potentially unfamiliar or uncomfortable (Nind and Vinha, 2013: 21; 2012). Thus, I began by asking questions such as, *what do I need to ask you to find out about your lives and what is important to you? What sort of things could we do together that would help me to understand your lives?* To ensure they felt comfortable, the conditions for their responses involved a classroom-based activity, designed using media with which the young people were familiar (flip charts and pens to use in small group work) undertaken in small, self-selected groups. Such an approach is consistent with practices in inclusive research where individual methods of data generation can be repurposed as group processes (Bigby et al., 2014, see also Nind, 2011).

I explored the questions I wanted to discuss with group A by utilising Ball et al's (2000:148) model of 'arenas of action and centres of choice', originally developed to provide a framework for understanding the ways in which young people experience their school to work transitions. The original is diagrammatic and utilises complex language. To facilitate accessibility I developed a simplified version in pictorial form which used three key headings (family, work and education, and leisure) and explained its meaning to the participant group. They were then divided into 4 small (self-selected) sub-groups, and asked to use the model to generate ideas about the things that were important to them, recording their ideas on flip chart with marker pens, similarly to the group activities they were familiar with from their course work. There was some slight difference in emphasis in terms of the themes which arose from this activity, but despite this all ascribed importance to broadly similar areas. Two sub groups placed significant emphasis on money as well as their college course.

A third sub-group, consisted of three students, all young British Asian men, had particular concerns with their work futures and ambitions, which they envisaged in terms of working in or establishing 'a good business' and how the course they were enrolled on might facilitate that. Finally, a rather larger group consisting of 3 young women and 2 young men engaged in considerable debate and was most productive in terms of ideas and outcomes. These young people had a wider range of important issues to share all of which suggested a greater concern with the family and leisure activities than their course, and may have reflected the gender split within the group: all came from traditional working class backgrounds with fixed gender roles.

The ideas arising from this activity was fundamental to the way in which the methods used in the study were designed and applied. The ideas successfully generated the questions for the student interview schedule and the interview schedule used with tutors as well as providing themes for the initial data analysis. At this early stage comparison of the questions and ideas reflected common themes consistent with Cote's (2005: 223) suggestion that career choice and lifestyle preferences are fundamental to adult identity formation. However, there were also significant gender and racial differences in the identification of 'important' which would need further exploration at the data analysis stage.

(Atkins, 2013a: 148)

Ethics

Given the limited literacy skills of the young participants, standard documents outlining the aims, purpose and methodological approach of the study were inappropriate: such documents could have been signed, but I did not feel that this would necessarily imply 'informed' consent or, indeed, any meaningful understanding of what they were to participate in. Therefore, I gave a verbal presentation about the study during a meeting with each group, which was supplemented with a single-sided A4 handout. This made use of illustrations and white space, was checked for readability and outlined the ethical framework for the study, consisting of statements such as:

- I will keep your information confidential (as secret as possible).

- I will not talk to other people (such as your tutors, friends, or family) about what you have said. I will just write about it in my book.

This approach meant that the document was accessible to all members of the participant group, bearing in mind that most had very low levels of functional literacy and some had English as a second language. It also included contact details in case any participant had questions or concerns they wished to raise at any time.

Methods

The design of the methods was informed by activities undertaken with the young people prior to the fieldwork in which they identified areas of importance in their lives (see Chapter 4). A multi-method approach using five different techniques was utilized. Methods included semi-structured interviews, conducted with both students and professionals, classroom observation, written data provided by the young people and some limited documentary evidence. Serendipitous data arising from the collaborative nature of the research process was volunteered by students and also contributed to the final analysis.

The choice of research methods was determined by the imperative to evolve an inclusive research process which demonstrated respect for the participant group and their needs and preferences consistent with the social justice framework for the study. This imperative determined all my decision making during the project, but most significantly my decision to use what I termed serendipitous data, something which I recognize that others might challenge. At the beginning of the study I did not know what this might be, but having taught level 1 students I was aware that I was likely to be offered material which might contribute to the data by the participants. It seemed self-evident that an inclusive research process must demonstrate a value for any contribution and that that must be an honest and moral value: I could have chosen to thank the students but not use their data. This would have been unacceptable from a social justice perspective, reflecting a misuse of power and lack of morality and was thus incompatible with the aims of the study. As anticipated, much serendipitous material was offered. These data included material such as work which the students wished to share (e.g. Figure 5.1), particularly where this was electronic and could be emailed to me. On one occasion, this included the draft pages for a website asking for my comments, but most contributions were PowerPoint presentations undertaken as part of their coursework. Visual data of this nature was not only generated independently by the young people but, as in Holland et al.'s (2008) study, provided 'rich insights' into their lives and identities. Ultimately, this not only enriched the process in terms of human relationship and experience but also enhanced the research in terms of the wealth of data which was ultimately generated.

Al's My Favourite Food

- 8oz rump steak with chips
- You can eat this with chip and you can have steak well done, medium or rare

FIGURE 5.1 *Serendipitous data: Sample slide from Al's PowerPoint presentation.*

Interviews

Interviews were indicated as a key data source due to their flexibility, adaptability and potential to elicit rich data from diverse participants. I elected to use informal, semi-structured interviews as these seemed most likely to elicit most data, being focused but allowing for prompting. I anticipated that the students might not articulate well and that individuals may need different degrees of prompting. However, these fears proved to be mainly unfounded, and most students made a voluble and articulate contribution, illustrating that I, too, had taken a diminished and deficit view of this group of young people. This was a particularly challenging moment in the research, as I had to confront and acknowledge the difficult truth that my perceptions of this group of young people othered them in potentially negative ways, however benevolent my intentions.

The choice of interview raised a number of questions: would a group or individual approach to the interviews be better? How could this process be adapted to maximize the involvement of the participants and to give them some control over how it evolved and was designed and managed? Precisely how should the questions be framed, and what should they include or exclude to facilitate a clearer response to the research questions? I also had to consider the relative advantages and disadvantages of different approaches to interviewing (e.g. Punch and Oancea, 2014: 184/186; Atkins and Wallace, 2012; Wellington, 2015: 148; and Fontana and Frey, 2000: 652), placing these in a context which demanded an approach that could be argued to be socially just. Power dynamics were a significant issue in this context. Madriz (2000: 838) has argued that individual interviews can create the potential to reproduce the power relationships between the researcher and the researched, and these were significant in this study, given the differentials between me and a group of teenage level 1 learners. Madriz's argument is well supported by her earlier reference to the words of a young Dominican woman who participated in a focus group with Madriz in 1995: 'I'd rather talk this way, with a group of women . . . when I am alone with an interviewer I feel intimidated, scared' (Madriz, 2000: 835). Focus groups are also highlighted as a potentially empowering method in the literature on inclusive research (e.g. see Nind and Vinha, 2012). Madrid's work, and that of Nind and Vinha, is concerned with social in/justice, and therefore these arguments make a strong case for group interviews. However, such approaches can be problematic, particularly in terms of interference with individual expression or domination of the group by one individual, and it is clearly important whatever interviewing technique is chosen to be aware of the implications, pitfalls and problems associated with its use (Fontana and Frey, 2000: 652). Taking this into consideration, I opted to offer students a choice between participating in a group or individual interview while bearing in mind the potential risks and advantages of both in order to ensure that they were empowered to take some control of the process and that any potential inhibition related to power dynamics or an unfamiliar social situation could be minimized. This approach also demonstrated respect for individuals and placed a clear and explicit value on their preference and promoted the collaborative approach I was attempting to develop. The interviews were audio-recorded and transcribed. The young people were interviewed twice each – towards the beginning and end of the academic year – in acknowledgement of the fact that identities and aspirations might change and develop over time. This approach also provided a further opportunity to confirm the emerging themes of the study.

Observations

Semi-structured observational strategies (Punch and Oancea, 2014) were utilized to establish whether behaviour, thoughts and ideas expressed in a less formal setting reflected those expressed by the students during the interview process (Wellington, 2015). Despite the time investment associated with undertaking observation (Yin, 2003: 86), it offered the potential to gain rich and illuminating data with minimal interference to the college day. The observations took place in the classroom and were recorded using a stream of consciousness or 'open-ended narrative' method (Angrosino and Mays de Perez, 2000: 674). They were conducted using a participant approach within the spectrum of observation proposed by Wellington (2015: 169), an approach informed by both the research questions and the participants' work identifying areas of importance in their lives.

The level of my participation between groups varied as it was dictated largely by the individual tutor on each occasion. For example, during one session the tutor was only prepared to allow me to sit and take notes and on another occasion there was some interaction with both students and tutor. The greatest degree of interaction took place with a participant group which was studying Health and Social Care, my own area of expertise when I was an FE teacher. The tutor and students were aware of this and asked me to contribute to the lesson. Conscious that I had predicated my research on respect and collaboration, I recorded my observation notes with the participants while simultaneously supporting them with their assignment work. Ethically, this worked, but methodologically it illustrates the impossibility of replicating specific sets of circumstances in ethnographic research and highlights the necessity to be conscious of the way in which different relationships and perceptions of the process might influence the outcomes.

I had considered more structured approaches to the recording of data such as the formal observations and protocols discussed by Yin (2003: 92) and by Punch and Oancea (2014: 194/196), but I felt that a very structured approach may lead me to pre-judge what was important. In order to avoid this and to ensure that the opportunities for gathering useful data were maximized, a more informal, largely unstructured approach was used. Within this, the observation was focused by noting specifically two aspects of behaviour which related broadly to the research questions. These were evidence of engagement with study and anything relating to the students' lives outside their college course. This broad coverage ensured that I did not 'miss' any potentially useful data (Wellington, 2015: 248) and also addressed the issue of selectivity, identified by Yin (2003: 86) as a weakness of observation.

In order to address Vidich and Lyman's (2000: 39) argument that observations are mediated by a framework of cultural meanings and symbols arising from the observer's own life history, the participants were given the opportunity to read and comment on the notes that were taken, as well as contributing their own opinions about what was happening in the class. As with the interviews however, no changes were made to my notes or interpretations, and this was the same for all groups even where, as with the Health and Social Care group, most of my notes recorded leisure-related activity while the students separately identified that they had been 'working hard'. This may have been for similar reasons as those hypothesized in respect of the interview transcripts. However, a second consideration is the use of language in my observation notes, essentially written for myself, as 'fairly accurate renditions of what I see, hear, feel . . . and so on' (Richardson, 2000: 941); thus, the language used was more sophisticated than that in the documents I prepared for the students and some at least may have had some difficulty understanding them. Therefore, from a social justice as well as a methodological perspective, this leaves this aspect of the study open to criticism in that I could have considered more creative ways of enabling the young people to participate more fully with this aspect of the research process.

Despite this, reproducing my notes in a less sophisticated form could have been argued to mediate them further. I might have asked a student to make contemporaneous notes but this was not feasible in the context of levels of literacy. A more realistic option might have been to hold a discussion around what they thought happened and what I might have observed at the end of the session or at a later date to use as a comparison to my own notes. Despite this difficulty, the observation data ultimately formed part of a broader collection of data. The young people did engage with a review of the initial analysis of that data and confirmed my early interpretation of it, suggesting some extent of agreement in terms of the observation records and their interpretation.

Additional data

A range of additional data sources were used to support that derived from the interviews and observations. These included some written data provided by the young people as 'personal profiles' – self-descriptors in the form of interactive handouts to help determine what aspects of their identity were most important to them, and completed early in the academic year. Some limited documentary evidence was requested from the colleges relating to attendance, achievement and intended destination. Hodder (2000: 703) argues that material evidence is of particular importance in 'providing insight into components of lived experience'. In terms of this study, the documentary evidence was limited and provided only a partial and patchy picture of the participant groups. However, it did provide some additional evidence to support and amplify the voices of the participants, particularly in terms of whether, at the end of their programmes, their destination suggested that they were continuing to pursue their original career aim. Further documentary evidence was provided by some tutors including disciplinary records and other information about individual students but was disregarded as not being relevant to the research questions, although some of it did demonstrate the problematic and deficit lens through which some tutors perceived this group of learners. A final data-gathering activity took place at the end of the academic year. This took the form of a paper-based activity exploring their future expectations. This also provided an opportunity to triangulate other data and asked the following questions:

- *What will you be doing in September?*
- *What will you be doing in 10 years' time?*
- *Do you know anyone who is already doing this?*

This activity had the advantage of being undertaken when more concrete decisions had been taken about the following academic year and was successful in generating considerable data. This final meeting also provided an opportunity to wish the young people well and thank them for their contribution to the study.

Shared interpretation?

Consistent with the aims of demonstrating respect and developing an inclusive and collaborative research process, the young participants were – to an extent – involved in the data analysis. From both methodological and social justice perspectives, this was possibly the most challenging and problematic aspect of the research process. The importance of analysis or 'the separation of something into its component parts' (Denscombe, 1998: 239) is a critical activity which should provide a credible response to the questions posed within the study. That demands that any analysis is conducted in a systematic and structured way which recognized issues such as bias or threats to the validity of the study, in order to develop and sustain a rigorous and credible argument. Reflexively, I had to acknowledge that I would influence both the methodology and the results of the research. The researcher and research are integral parts of the world they are investigating and, as such, cannot offer an impartial view of a world of which they are a part (Denscombe, 1998: 240; Hammersley and Atkinson, 1983: 234; Wellington, 2000: 42). In collaborative research situations where control is dispersed among group members, it remains the case, as in this doctoral study, that leadership of the research process often rests with a senior researcher (Bigby et al., 2014: 8). It is also important to note that the process of analysis and interpretation is conceptually demanding (Bigby et al., 2014: 8) and that (citing Stalker, 1998: 15) 'very little is known about the potential implications of intellectual impairment on the research process'. It is important to note here that these students did not have learning disabilities. However, they did have very low levels of attainment and were positioned at the bottom of the mainstream hierarchy. Thus, the complexities of the data analysis were possibly beyond the immediate capacity of many of the level 1 learners. Therefore, I made the difficult decision to conduct an initial analysis myself and to ask the young people to independently evaluate my interpretation.

In terms of the practicalities of the analysis, all interview and observation notes and audio records made in the course of the study were transcribed and reduced to a paper form where they were thematically analysed using a manual approach by category (e.g. male, female, college, group) and by themes emerging from the data and the literature during the research process. This was time-consuming and required total immersion in the data for several weeks. Once the analysis was complete, the key themes were summarized onto a handout for the participants, structured similarly to the ethical framework. Making use of image, white space and clear, unambiguous language, it consisted of a series of statements which corresponded to the key themes emerging from the data, together with notes to encourage clarification if I was uncertain of my interpretation. Examples included the following:

- *A lot of level 1 students have a job as well as doing their course*

- *Some students also have caring responsibilities*

As with the transcripts, the young people were each given two copies – one for annotation and one to keep – of the emerging themes' (or *what we have found out*) handout. To facilitate a level of evaluation, they were asked to note whether each statement was 'true' or 'false' and to explain their reasoning. Levels of participation varied. Some students simply identified true or false. However, this was a minimal contribution. Others wrote copious notes such as:

- *Agree because everyone nearly wants to have a good job* (in response to the statement: *Most level 1 students have high aspirations (dreams and ambitions). They want to do a lot with their lives*).

And

- *Agree. Most people don't but they could always ask at Contections* [sic – *Connexions*[2]] *or teachers/tutors to help them decide* (in response to the statement: *Many Level 1 students do not know how to achieve their ambitions. They do not know which courses to do or how long it will take.*)

Such contributions considerably aided the final analysis. Others gave verbal feedback which I recorded as field notes. Yin (2003: 99) has suggested that this approach, in which the participants effectively checked that my interpretation accurately reflected their views and attitudes, is a form of methodological triangulation. However, I would argue that the instrumental value of this checking process as a form of triangulation was much less than its moral and ethical

---

[2]At the time this study was conducted, Connexions was a national careers advisory service for young people aged 13–19. It was established in 2000 and emphasized the needs of marginalized youth. It was replaced by the National Careers Service in 2012.

value, in that although the young people were able to make only a limited contribution in terms of analysis, the process provided a further mechanism for demonstrating respect and value for them. Further, as Schwandt argues, such an approach also provides a basis for greater insight into the feelings and views of the participants, something which aided my own interpretation of the data:

> Conceiving of the activity of interpretation in terms of an ontological condition (i.e. as a fundamental grounds of our being-in –the-world) rather than as a methodological device is what puts the inquirer on the same plane of understanding, so to speak, as those he or she inquires into.
>
> (Schwandt, 1998: 229)

Ethical and methodological challenges

Verbal and written communication with the participant group presented what was possibly the most challenging methodological issue of the research. Explanations had to be made using language which was unambiguous and expressed with clarity in terms the participants understood, but which avoided any loss of meaning. Ultimately, for example, this meant describing research as 'finding out'. The lay language used in the explanation was necessary to engage these young people and facilitate them to have sufficient understanding of an abstract process to contribute to it in a meaningful way. Despite the lack of sophistication in the participants' own language, they were able to communicate clearly and without ambiguity, as they described their lives, hopes and dreams in the context of their transitions from school to work. Fine (1994: 20) has previously reported American low-income adolescents as giving 'vivid' accounts of their lives, something which suggests they too had relatively high levels of verbal ability and social awareness, similarly to the participants in this study. For example, Samir, a young man with a physical disability who had been educated in a Special School, mentioned university, in a rather wistful acknowledgement that this would not be part of his own transition: '*I know I can't go to university [because] they have exams, very long exams. After their exams they can do anything they want to*'. In contrast, his future consisted of being cared for:

> We tried to get me married off but it hasn't worked yet. [I will probably have] a job – I would like to work in an office answering phones, messages for anybody, working on computer . . . bringing up a good family that can look after me, go to Pakistan.

His comments also reflected his engagement with leisure activities:

> For me, me and my mates meet up. We sometimes go [to the pub] for a drink, we all like the same. We sometimes go to McDonalds; we have a really good time. At home I play on play station or watch telly. A lot of time is spent playing on the play station or watching telly but on Saturday I meet up with my mates and have a good time. I do whatever they do. I really do whatever they do.

Despite this eloquence, some participants did occasionally find themselves 'lost for words' as they struggled to express a feeling or opinion in written form. It seems likely, however, given their verbal skills that this reflected a low level of functional literacy, something which was evident across each of the groups who participated. Wellington and Cole (2004: 103) noted similar difficulties in their research, reporting that they had to support articulate young people to complete questionnaires when it became apparent that they had difficulty with the written word. This suggests that even where every attempt has been made to ensure accessibility, data-gathering instruments which require the use of the written word may, for some participants, elicit more limited data, thus diminishing those participants' voices. It also raises questions about the degree of inclusivity where the assumption is made that all participants have some – albeit limited – literacy skills and implies that greater utilization of verbal methods (such as evaluating the emerging themes in small groups, akin to the interview groups, and recording comments) could have generated richer responses.

The second, related, issue was the representation of voice, apart from my personal ethical concerns about mediation, and the impact of power dynamics during the interview process; the most significant practical issue that arose was actually related to anonymization of the participants. The young people had participated enthusiastically (including often critical opinions on my initial data interpretation!) and were undiscriminating in their disclosure of information. Reflecting their often troubled and chaotic backgrounds, I became the recipient of confidences relating to histories of being looked after children, contact with the youth justice system, abortion, caring responsibilities, heavy drinking and drug misuse. With one exception, the college staff were aware of these problems, which were made almost ordinary in the context of the language and lack of emotion used during each disclosure, perhaps reflecting the significant complexities of life faced by these young people on a daily basis. However, these issues did create an ethical imperative for absolute discretion, which came into conflict with the participants' universal wish for recognition for their contribution. Thus, a dialogue developed around not what data I could use, but around the necessity for anonymizing the young people who could not comprehend the potential implications later in life of some of this information being in the public domain.

Ultimately, I felt that I had to deny the young people the voice that they might have chosen, and which seemed to be related to notions of fame and celebrity, in order to give them a more public voice which could (and did) contribute to the debate on level 1 provision and the lives of students who access it. This choice, however, was mine and was made in the context of the demands of a research project and from a different value base and illustrates the way in which, despite my intention to collaborate with the participants, the ultimate control over the study was mine alone, highlighting questions of empowerment and the 'extent to which power can be "bestowed" upon people through the medium of education or research' (Johnston, 2000: 78/79). The debate did, however, lead to a compromise in which the young people chose their own pseudonyms. Clear gender differences emerged from this decision: amusement and the opportunity for a 'joke' among the male students, most of whom identified pseudonyms which were related to aspects of perceived masculinity, such as sexual prowess, possibly in an attempt to shock, but also corresponding to the working-class notions of masculinity (e.g. supporting a wife and family) they had described in their interviews. Others, including all except one of the female students, identified 'celebrities' as their pseudonyms. Some were, indeed, well known, others were established to be characters from soap operas and other television shows. Irrespective of this, there was a relationship between these choices, which appeared rooted in notions of wealth, fame and celebrity and the aspirations expressed by the students during interview.

Power and voice

The use and interpretation of voice presents many challenges, some of which are clearly illustrated in the data from Liz's study. For example, from a theoretical perspective how do they reflect power differentials and how can those be addressed? At a more practical level, where the participant articulates ideas which are at variance with one another, what is the socially just and ethical response? In the study, a participant known as Pete explained how he valued the support he received from the tutors:

> *I love it me, I think it's brilliant. I like how the lessons are handled because they explain better, they actually run over it different ways what you actually have to do on the course so it's more easier to understand'.*

This perspective was supported by a PowerPoint presentation he contributed (*All about college*) which included a slide reading: *The teachers teach the students about the course and help out the students if they need help with their work.* Similarly, during his interview he identified a range of typically teenage, though often solitary leisure activities:

> *Play on the play – station, go on computer. Sometimes I go swimming or go out with my mates – half the time I am with my mates. I enjoy rock music and sci-fi space programmes. I collect Warhammer*[3]

However, these data were significantly at variance with the perception of himself as an adult (in fact, he was 19), which

---

[3]Warhammer is a strategy game involving the collection and decoration of small figures which are then used to act out battles in a similar way to old-fashioned toy soldiers.

was reflected in his occupational ambition to progress through college and join the RAF, his well-articulated understanding of the relationship between college and work (*'you will go far with good qualifications behind you'*) and his participation in activities such as 'going to the pub' which he regarded as adult. Indeed, he discussed his heavy drinking at length in class and produced a presentation on 'My favourite food' which comprised a series of slides listing a vast range of alcoholic drinks. So, from a socially just perspective, how should Pete's voice and person be represented? He would expect to be represented as an adult, but the data implies that he is a young man in need of support; data about his heavy drinking was drawn from observational and serendipitous data. Would Pete recognise that, particularly if he did have a drink problem? And is any representation of his drinking permissible (for example, in terms of understanding cultural and leisure practices) or should it be accompanied with an outline of his traumatic and chaotic life experiences? How does any of this sit with the dichotomous policy models of 'vulnerable' and 'problematic'? Other issues arise from the use of Kate's voice, as she discusses her career aspirations:

> L *What sort of job with children would you like?*
> Kate *Class Assistant, a nanny something like that.*
> L *OK. Do you know what sort of qualifications you need for that?*
> Kate *Yes.*
> L *What do you need?*
> Kate *I can't remember.*

This extract was used to illustrate the lack of knowledge about career pathways common to level 1 students. However, it has the potential to generate deficit perceptions of Kate. Does the need to communicate the problematic positioning of all level 1 students (or, indeed, any other marginalized group) outweigh the representation of individuals as 'not knowing'? These are challenging questions to which there are no easy answers, but which reflect the ongoing need for critical engagement with theory and methodology as well as highly developed reflexive practice throughout the research process. The decisions made – be they ever so ethical and moral – still reflect the fact that for most research, control lies with a particular individual or small group, and in the case of much socially just research (such as the examples given in this book) those groups or individuals do not form part of the marginalized community they are researching. That control – and sitting outside the researched group, even with privileged insights – can lead to concerns about power relations and their impact on individual participants, the data and its interpretation, and, by extension, the extent to which a project has achieved its aim of being socially just.

Conclusion

The issues concerning power, voice, collaboration and social justice arising from Liz's project raise the question of whether social justice is done, and if so how, to whom and to what extent? In terms of the process, this chapter reveals the extent to which her aim of 'walking the walk' as well as 'talking the talk' was problematic. Collaboration and inclusion were intended and attempted at each stage of the process. However, at each stage she could only claim partial success in achieving this, although some of the challenges were associated with the participants' levels of education and life experience. However, the strategies employed facilitated a far greater degree of involvement than would have been possible in the absence of engagement with the theoretical and philosophical social justice framework. In terms of the outcomes of the work, which was originally published in 2009, some things have changed, but slowly. Level 1 students remain Othered as having 'failed' at school, as vocational students, as low-level students and as disaffected and disadvantaged, still regarded as the 'embodiment of deficit' (Colley, 2003: 158). They continue to have limited access to valorized capitals and limited opportunities for developing the agency (and capital) to enable them to negotiate the structural forces which appear to be irresistible barriers to movement beyond their immediate field/habitus.

The lack of access to dominant capital may be compared to the adult learners in Vicky's study (2013: 186) where the learners' accounts of their experiences 'showed that access to capitals and positioning in the field they inhabit can influence symbolic capital and power and also influence the possibilities open for their future trajectories. . . . Illustrating the learners' capacity for agency and flexibility, showing the habitus is involved in resistance and reflexivity as well as compliance.' Developing their agency would require young people to receive a more socially just education (see Reay, 2012) and to be exposed to a different, more political pedagogy, which encouraged them to develop awareness of and to question societal structures. This is not a new concept: Avis (1996) and Bloomer (1996) are among those who have highlighted the need for a more political education for citizenship, and Liz and Vicky have both repeated these calls more recently: indeed, this was a main driver for this book. However, dissemination of the work led to it contributing as evidence to the Wolf Review (2011) and the House of Lords Select Committee on Social Mobility (2016) report *Overlooked and left behind: improving the transition from school to work for the majority of young people*. The Wolf Review in particular led to policy change (DfE, 2011), although the curriculum impact on level 1 programmes was minimal, effectively being a 'rejigging' of the existing offer which had been criticized as 'busy work' (Atkins, 2009) and which fails to articulate with entry to the labour market (Keep, 2014). At the current time, more young people are accessing vocational education – not only partly due to the raising of the participation age in 2013 but also partly due to structural changes in the youth labour market (MacDonald and Marsh, 2005) which have contributed to persistently high levels of young people being NEET (Thurlby-Campbell and Bell, 2017). Liz's project has informed her other research which has continued to contribute to debate (e.g. Atkins et al., 2011) and which is slowly developing an empirical basis to support more critical pedagogies at level 1 (e.g. Defeyter et al., 2017) and includes an ongoing Participatory Action Research project (see Atkins and Misselke, 2018) which seeks to develop more critical forms of pedagogy at level 1, conferring valorized capitals as well as knowledge and skills. Social justice is often described as a journey. It is, it seems, a slow one.

Further reading

Ball, S. J., Maguire, M., and Macrae, S. (2000), *Choice, Pathways and Transitions Post-16 New Youth, New Economies in the Global City*, London: RoutledgeFalmer.
Dorling, D. (2015), *Inequality and the 1%*, 2nd edn, London: Verso.

Griffiths, M. (2003), *Action Research for Social Justice in Education Fairly Different*, Buckingham: Open University Press.

Holland, S., Renold, E., Ross, N., and Hillman, A. (2008), *Rights, 'Right On' Or The Right Thing to Do?*. ESRC National Centre for Research Methods NCRM Working Paper Series 07/08.

Johnston, R. (2000), 'Whose side, whose research, whose learning, whose outcomes? Ethics, emancipatory research and unemployment', in H. Simons and P. Usher (eds), *Situated Ethics in Educational Research*, London: RoutledgeFalmer.

Wellington, J., and Cole, P. (2004), 'Conducting evaluation and research with and for 'disaffected' students: Practical and methodological issues', *British Journal of Special Education* 31(2), 100–104.

CHAPTER SIX

Education, literacy, and socially just methodology

Introduction

This chapter will explore education, literacy, inequality and different approaches to applying socially just methods and methodologies. In order to frame the exploration it is important to note that literacy is not neutral. Literacy is political. The positioning of literacy and the lens employed determine what counts as literacy in educational and social policy contexts and in terms of whose interest it serves (Duckworth and Smith, 2019b). In the last two decades we have seen a greater focus on literacy, primarily among countries participating in the Organization for Economic Cooperation and Development (OECD) (Duckworth and Smith, 2018c, 2010; Hamilton, 2014). The OECD's (2013) report makes clear that the implement for measuring literacy levels across countries is the specifically designed OECD Programme for the International Assessment of Adult Competencies (PIAAC). The policy discourses that draw on OECD and PIAAC data tend to value literacy almost exclusively in economistic terms, seeing a minimum level of attainment in literacy as the basis for employability and from there linking it to the economic competitiveness of industry and nations.

This economized version of literacy has a specific alignment with neo-liberal notions of human capital and is expressed, for example, through the concept of 'functional' skills that enable individuals, as well as countries, to become more productive and competitive in the labour market based on the premise of a 'knowledge economy' (Ade-Ojo and Duckworth, 2015; and see Atkins, 2016a; Billet et al., 2010). This instrumental and reductive stance sees one of the most significant responsibilities given to education as being to provide a flexible, adaptable and skilled workforce to make countries competitive in the globalized economy.

In the UK and internationally, democracy and notions of community are being (re)conceptualized through the lens of neo-liberal ideology. Neo-liberalization is the dominant political force of our time, bringing with it a focus on de- and re-regulation, economic competitiveness (both national and institutional), all framed by discourses of globalization (Davies, 2014). We have seen as a result the notion of 'free market' competition displacing social democratic policy as a structuring force in many areas of public life, including compulsory and post-compulsory education. This has, in turn, impacted on the way literacy is represented and conceptualized by policymakers.

As identified by Duckworth and Smith (2019b) in the neo-liberal imaginary of which the so-called knowledge economy forms a part, for adults there are new ground rules. These rules exert influence on people, their lives and communities. Notions of *success* in the knowledge economy require the acquisition of particular skills and competencies and the ability to adapt to a wide variety of knowledge domains. This mythology insists that people must be able to apply these skills effectively to be included in the ever-changing knowledge economy. Lifelong learning is positioned as a mechanism for ongoing 'upskilling', whereby a person must expect and make ready for transitions throughout her/his life (Duckworth and Smith, 2017a, 2018b; Field, 2000, 2008; Field et al., 2009). Where circumstances mean that an individual is unable to engage with lifelong learning 'opportunities', blame is attributed by the state to the individual (Ainley and Corney, 1990; Atkins, 2009, 2010a) for failing to meet their perceived civic responsibility of engaging with lifelong learning.

This upskilling includes developing appropriate and adequate literacy/language/numeracy skills as well as those associated with new and emerging technologies. In the UK the current funding landscape in Further Education requires adults to be prepared to invest in their future. Their choices are tied tightly to financial considerations. Further education is seen as offering upskilling opportunities related to work, in ways that view education as a commodity. This commodification often blurs key issues (which will be addressed in this chapter) that include economic, political and social equality considerations. Both in the UK and internationally, the current discourse around literacy is driven by international surveys that have become increasingly important over the last twenty-five years (e.g. those produced for the PIAAC). Produced and promoted by a range of agencies including the OECD, United Nations Educational, Scientific and Cultural Organization (UNESCO) and the European Union, national governments commit considerable funding to these surveys and countries and then compare themselves against one another using the results. Hamilton (2017) argues that international, large-scale skills assessments (ILSAs) shape our uneasiness of educational achievement at a profound and ubiquitous level and yet she argues there is minimal evidence of any successful attempts to challenge and shift this discourse of metrics value basis and terms of the debates about the measures themselves.

The discourses that prevail are reductive; they are not neutral but are imbued with a system of norms, values, symbols, beliefs and behaviours that form our world. They are cultural practices that shape engagement, beliefs and assumptions which feed into identity, how we view ourselves and the choices or lack of choices we have. Framed by these human capital discourses, at the level of the individual, literacy becomes a technology for stratifying human beings as embodied labour power (Duckworth and Smith, 2019a). In many ways this 'economization' of literacy serves to depoliticize it. This is consistent with a neo-liberal hegemonic view that typically attempts to neutralize politics through a common-sense assumption that economic considerations are sovereign (Davies, 2014).

The relationship between struggling to read and/or write and the ability to articulate one's rights can result in adult literacy learners being marginalized, silenced and losing a sense of agency. Struggling with literacy (and numeracy) is not just related to employability. Such struggles hold people back at every stage and in every area of life, having an impact on health and well-being, democratic engagement and political participation. The impact is also felt in relationships with others and has intergenerational consequences, ultimately influencing children's life chances (Duckworth and Smith, 2018b, 2019a,b). For example, the University College Union (UCU) research project led by Dr Vicky Duckworth and Dr Rob Smith, *FE in England – Transforming Lives and Communities*, includes a strand which explores the intersection between women, literacy and adult education. The research data illustrates that further education is disruptive of the rigid linearity of the model of 'learning progression' at the heart of neo-liberal models of education that assesses and sorts individuals according to a qualification/age matrix.

Literacy is crucial for promoting people's rights and for their empowerment. It plays a vital role for Lifelong Learning through the different ways that it fosters capacities, reduces vulnerabilities and improves the quality of life for women, their families and the wider community. Indeed, women are marginalized and often silenced if they are unable to access the powerful tools that literacy offers and which can enable them to transform their lives (Duckworth, 2013; Duckworth and Smith, 2019b; Robinson-Pant, 2016). A broad-based notion of literacy is one of the crucial grounds of other life skills; it has distinct importance for the empowerment of women and has a strong intergenerational effect.

Models of literacy

Adult literacy has elaborated two models of literacy: the autonomous and the ideological (Street, 1984). The former treats illiteracy as an independent variable, a deficit position that needs to be cured by a medicine of skills; the latter views literacy in terms of social and cultural practices and thus, in recognition of the range and variety of such practices, speaks of *literacies* rather than of a unitary skill. The view of literacy as ideologically and socially embedded is supported by an increasing awareness of the importance of context and how the circumstances in which learners find themselves influence their perceptions, understandings and their uses of literacy (Ade-Ojo and Duckworth, 2016).

Literacy research has explored the role of access to resources in the negotiation of lived experience and the agency and voice of individuals and their families and communities (Duckworth, 2013;

Duckworth and Smith, 2018c). The case studies below argue for the ways in which the field of literacy is positioned to take up the challenge of transformative social justice. In order to address issues related to class, gender, ethnicity, literacy and empowerment it is helpful to consider how 'literacy' is defined and positioned as an ideological discourse. Literacy practices shape the way we relate to and interact with literacy and are interwoven with our identity and practices. As identified in the opening lines of this chapter literacy is not value-free; it is not neutral but deeply political.

The politics of literacy and its link to learner identity and empowerment are explored in Duckworth's (2013) study and that of Duckworth and Smith (2018b and d) from the standpoint of how the learners' everyday lives have been shaped by the lack of, and development of, literacies. Part of the praxis of the research draws on participatory and democratic pedagogical practices as a way of countering dominant models and questioning how power and knowledge are valued, what counts as literacy and what does not, who benefits from this and who is marginalized. The impact of dominant literacies on the learners' trajectories and the use of socially situated models in my practice are unpicked to explore how a critical curriculum can empower the learners and lead to emancipation and transformation in their personal and public trajectories.

Context

The 2013 research explored how sixteen former literacy learners have been shaped by the public domain of schooling, college and work and the private domain of family, friends and home. The learners were all enrolled on basic skills courses at a further education college in the north of England. The research was based on a feminist, qualitative, longitudinal, ethnographic and participatory approach. While the interpretation uses a critical perspective, drawing on Bourdieu's work as the theoretical framework, it also uses a range of feminist sociologists of education and literature on the ethics of care and critical literacy pedagogy work, including New Literacy Studies (NLS).

The study draws on a combination of research principles including a feminist worldview, a qualitative approach to research, a quasi-longitudinal process of data gathering, as well as ethnographic and participatory approaches. It takes life history as a starting point for the action research reported in this study (see Plummer, 1995). Within this context, it places the individual at the centre of the narrative and as the driver for the action. It is a manifestation of a shift from viewing society as a disembodied structure to setting the narratives of the respondents against the backdrop of a cultural, historical and political landscape, providing a life history methodology where the groups could make sense of their lives through reflection on their experiences and the choices or lack of choices they have experienced in their public and private trajectories.

The research was based on Vicky's personal position as an 'insider' with 'insider knowledge' of marginalized communities. This was the catalyst to her becoming a basic skills tutor and becoming involved in the study (Duckworth and Hamilton, 2016). For example, her own life history has greatly influenced the commitment she had for finding opportunities to enable others to take agency and aspire to reach their potential (Johnson and Duckworth, 2018). She was born and brought up in the same community as the learners, attended the local state school and was the first generation of her family to enter college and university; her subsequent trajectory has also contributed to this commitment. Below Vicky describes the research and the drive towards challenging notions of the educational system being meritocratic. The study recognizes that childhoods are experienced differently depending on the different capitals (including social capital) the family has. As Franklin (1995) states, childhoods are varied and are 'social constructs formed by a range of social, historical and cultural factors'. These factors include the type of family (field) they live in and how this is shaped by and shapes their experiences, choices and identity. For example, homes and family may appear to be neutral, but through symbolic representation, the cultural capital a middle-class child brings from home (knowledge of books, experience of going to the theatre) to achieve success in the accruing of qualifications can be seen as 'natural' rather than the result of them transferring this 'inherited' cultural capital into academic success, 'qualifications' and cultural capital, while the street capital a child brings to school (being able to take care of themselves, strength, street savvy, cook, clean, look after siblings and so on) is deemed redundant and not of equal parity at school, although it nevertheless provides them with survival tools on the streets.

> ## Case example
>
> In Vicky's (2013) study, on arrival at college the literacy learners' perception included a strong feeling that, mirroring their experiences at school, they would be judged and pathologized by others. This learner marginality related to the dynamics of symbolic violence (Bourdieu, 1991). In the discussion with the learners there was a link between what they considered their 'poor' literacy skills and viewing themselves as child-like because of that. This is hardly surprising when in all aspects of society including entering learning, basic skills learners are labelled as lacking and in many case put to the bottom of the list when it comes to the hierarchy of employment and courses offered in college. Further, the dominant discourse that runs through Adult Education (like that of compulsory education) is often constructed on a deficit model which positions the learners as lacking in relation to what are widely deemed as the norms of literacy. Stella described how:
>
> > *You just feel thick. The worst is when you've got to read something in front of someone. I hate that.*
>
> while Craig noted,
>
> > *I'm ashamed really of not being able to spell properly. It's okay as a kid, but at my age it's not right, it's not. I'd be mortified if me mates down the pub knew.*

A key drive for all the learners attending the basic skills classes, whether attending voluntarily or compulsory attendees on New Deal Programmes, was to become literate. The New Deal (renamed Flexible New Deal from October 2009) was a workfare programme introduced in the UK by the first New Labour government in 1998. They purported that the initiative was intended to reduce unemployment by providing training, subsidized employment and voluntary work to the unemployed.

New Deal attendance was mandatory and, indeed, may be argued to have been punitive; it had the power to withdraw benefits from those who 'refused reasonable employment' and indeed who did not attend college courses.

Approaches

Participatory Action Research (PAR), critical pedagogy and the curriculum were a central focus of the research. There is a rich educational tradition of literacy and empowerment. Paulo Freire's (1996) seminal text *The Pedagogy of the Oppressed* addresses who and what education is for and whose group interests are promoted. Linking literacy with critical pedagogy, he examines the ideologies of classroom practice and the 'banking' theory of knowledge. Within this theory, he argues, traditional pedagogical practice is a means to fill the learners with information/knowledge that serves to maintain the status quo of structural inequalities and unjust hierarchies of power. The learners come to be passive receivers of information and accepting of the dominant hegemony. (Vicky employs Antonio Gramsci (1891–1937), a leading Marxist thinker, who used the term hegemony to signify the power of one social class over others, e.g. the bourgeois hegemony.) Hegemony embodies not only political and economic control but also the ability of the dominant class to assign its own way of viewing the world so that those who are subordinated by it accept it as 'natural'. Gramsci's ideas have influenced popular education practices which are drawn on in this study, which include the adult literacy and consciousness-raising methods of Paulo Freire in his *Pedagogy of the Oppressed* (1996) and methods of PAR.

PAR, as used in this study, therefore builds on Freire's critical pedagogy (2004) and offers learners the means to 're-appropriate the structures of their own thinking' (Grenfell and James, 2004: 5). The design and implementation of curriculum and pedagogy thus shift away from formal models of education, where the teacher takes control of power and imparts information to the students, who are perceived as passive empty vessels waiting to be filled. The pre-existing model ultimately fails to recognize the powerful knowledge learners bring into the classroom with them, such as socially situated knowledge (Barton and Hamilton, 1998). In this vein, the main goal of PAR was for both researcher/practitioner and participants to work within an egalitarian framework which facilitates an effective dialogue and critical consciousness and, in the case of this study, through a critical curriculum over a sustained period of time (Tummons and Duckworth, 2012). To reflect the democratic and participatory nature of PAR, therefore, it was very important that the participants (learners) were involved in the research (and curriculum design) process. This included what West (2016) describes as developing 'democratic sensibilities' which included 'cultivating qualities of space that might nurture people's capacities, in multicultural communities, to remain open to difference' (p. 4). Within this space there was a shift where the learners took the lead in the classroom and were able to decide how they wanted to shape the curriculum in relation to drawing on their own socially situated practices as a hook to develop their confidence, knowledge and skills. A plan was also put into place on how they wanted to move forward in the public domains of their life, which included employment and formal learning, as well as private domains such as home life. Their personal and shared analysis highlighted the connectivity between learning, critical reflection and praxis. The PAR also included counternarratives that expose how the communities are resourceful, resistant and agentic and what hooks (2000) describes as awareness, not isolation or victimization.

In this shift whereby there was a deep awareness of the agency and resourcefulness learners had, there was also a recognition of the vernacular literacies and other embodied knowledge that they (and the teacher) brought into the classroom. In engaging with collaborative research the expectation was that it would create a rupture which would facilitate participants' acquisition of the necessary critical tools in order to transform their own lives in line with the principles embedded in praxis (Freire, 1996).

Findings

The development of literacy skills, confidence and self-esteem was linked to the learners seeing other possible choices in their lives. For many of the learners the adult literacy classes were their last hope of education. At the beginning of the course Stella, a married mother of three, had struggled to read and write. She was working as a cleaner and wanted to change jobs and become a care assistant in a care home for the elderly. However, she did not have the confidence to apply, as she noted:

There will be things I have to write, yer know and carers now need to do their NVQ in care. I can't even spell so that's way beyond me . . . I just want to be able to write and spell yer know so that I can do a job I know I'll love. I'm really sick of cleaning, done it for years and it's mind numbing, pointless like and makes me feel what's the point. Caring, well there's a job where you can make a real difference, yer know like make someone feel better about themselves, give them some dignity at the end of their life. But it's maybe a dream or summat, daft to even think about leaving cleaning.

As the course progressed, there was a transformation in Stella's self-belief, a transformation built on the recognition and reality that she (and others in the group) could 'learn to read and write properly' and indeed aspire for and realize her dreams. Working in a collective was a way for the learners to begin to see themselves differently as individuals and question their positioning in unbalanced power relationships that have marginalized them and their practices of literacy, and act to change them. Stella progressed onto the level 2 programme (broadly equivalent to GCSE, or the level expected at 16+) and subsequently completed the level 3 in Health and Social Care. The cultural capital Stella developed led to resistance and empowerment for her family and self.

Joanne, a single mum with three children arrived at college struggling to read and write and sat at the back of the class; she avoided eye contact and neither spoke to myself nor the other learners. After Joanne joined the research group, we began to spend more time together. This allowed me the opportunity to speak to Joanne in detail about the barriers she had faced and her hopes and aspirations for the future. Joanne spoke of how her stepdad put all the family down with his verbal attacks:

Resp: *He was always on at us. What he said we did otherwise he'd have a screamin' match. It was easier to keep the peace'*
Int: *How did it make you feel listening to his screaming?*
Resp: *I hated it. When I was younger I'd stay in me bedroom and put me radio on just so I couldn't hear him bangin' on at me mam. It made me feel sick. I'd pinch meself 'til I bled cos the pain felt better than what I was hearing. He'd pick on owt to get an argument. He had to let us all*

> *know he was the big man. As if. It was a joke he wasn't even our dad.*
> Int: *Did you tell anyone?*
> Resp: *No chance, you kept it to yourself.*

The violence that was going on in the house stayed behind the walls. These unrecorded silences hide the pain and distress inflicted on families by domineering men (Duckworth, 2013). The symbolic violence inflicted on Joanne led to her hurting herself. As identified by Barton et al. (2007: 43) violence is 'part of everyday experience'. For the learners in the study it shaped the way they viewed themselves and their identity. Their identity was linked to silences they could not share, secrets of shame. This shame was manifested in the act of self-harm carried out by two of the learners in the group.

Drawing on the barriers faced by the learners, which included the emotional scarring of the violence of child and adulthood, the learners' lives and experiences were embedded into the curriculum using their narratives, poetry and so on. This offered a safe space to express their emotions, validate their experience and deconstructed the old knowledge, where they blamed themselves for being 'thick', 'stupid' and 'no-hopers' because they struggled in literacies and were poor and substituted it with the construction of new, shared knowledge where they were able to see the inequalities and violence in their lives this had stemmed from.

The development of literacy and confidence also ruptured the cycle of deprivation. One participant, Joanne, voiced how she hadn't been able to help her eldest son when he was at school 'cos I didn't know how to do the things like spelling meself' and 'couldn't see a future out of the estate like I can now, I thought it was the right way to wag it an' that'. The estate she lived with its own rules, its own field, fed into a habitus in which 'respect was given to those who put their two fingers up at education'. Together with her eldest child, Joanne did not feel that it was important to help her son with his homework:

> I feel a bit guilty now, but with our L it was different than my two youngest. I never bothered helping him. It's not that I didn't think it was important, I didn't even think about it. I just wanted him to leave school and get a job like I did.

However, as Joanne accrued cultural capital at college (qualifications), her position in the field changed her view of what motherhood entails and the cultural support a child needs:

> Resp: *It's my job to make sure our B and L do their homework. I sit with them and go through it. I'm really strict.*
>
> Int: *Why do you think it's important to help them with their homework?*
>
> Resp: *So they don't end up at my age with a load of wasted years behind them. No, I'd like them to get a decent job and do something with their life.*

Joanne's behaviour and notion of motherhood has changed as her habitus (way of being) has been shaped by the field of education (literacy course, access course and then nursing course at university) and job (nursing). This has resulted in higher expectations of the jobs her youngest children progress to.

David from the Further Education UCU *Transforming lives* study, a participant from a traveller background, also spoke about his motivations for learning as being able to read to his four-year-old daughter. For David, literacy was also a catalyst to take part in our democratic processes:

> Now I can actually read and write and sign my own name. When I go to the doctor, I can sign a note . . . You need education to know what's going on outside: the politics and all that. I'd never voted in my life, ever. I read the thing that came through the letterbox and I voted for the first time.

The research has shown the ways in which the learners' experiences are shaped through classed and gendered processes which result in different dispositions in the public and private domains and impact on their trajectories. Histories, while always social, are also distinct enough to merit closer attention to the details that contribute to significant differences in learners' habitus (ways of being) and choices or lack of choices across the fields they inhabit, especially in such cases where the product being examined (capitals) is defined by the dominant lens of distinction from the start. Learners are tied to their physical space which, in turn, is reflected in their positioning in social space (Bourdieu, 1985). The learners have described the difficulties they encounter when trying to move outside their space, for example, returning to college. The learners' stories challenge fields they enter, where, specifically, education is problematic. The depth of misrecognition within the dominated space means that unmasking domination cannot be conducted at a distance and, as a practitioner-researcher adopting PAR, it allowed me a close engagement with the learners and their communities.

The research conversations from both the research projects provided participants with an opportunity to share their narratives, allowing for the sharing of obstacles and the solutions to overcome them. In the UCU *Further Education: Transforming Lives and communities* project, Vicky and Rob's research illuminates how through the medium of video, these narratives themselves then constitute capital which can be shared with and drawn on by others to inspire and offer strategies to move forward. The research conversations were dialogical because stories were exchanged and views, opinions and feelings shared. The collective and interactive experience of the website enabled the sharing of challenges to the neo-liberal educational discourses which privilege individual over collective learning.

A key element of our methodology was to provide the environment and tools to facilitate learners to celebrate their ways of knowing and doing. In order to facilitate this we drew on a praxis-orientated philosophical stance that involved the participants and the local and wider community in the research process (Habermas, 1987: 89). That informed the care that we took to frame research conversations (we use this phrase in preference to the term 'interviews') to foster a sense and drive for equality between the participants and the researchers. These research conversations usually took place in the further education setting where participants were studying; however, if family members took part in the conversations, we were invited into the learners' homes. Reciprocity was also important: we shared our own stories to establish openness and informality, acknowledging that the research aspect of what we were doing was one part of a broader social encounter. The research conversations provided participants with an opportunity to share their narratives through the format of video. These video narratives were shared publicly through a project website. This resulted in stories that had been hid in shame being reclaimed then as stories of success while recognizing the structural inequalities that they challenged and resisted to take agency in their lives and communities (Duckworth, 2013; Duckworth and Smith, 2018b), the drive being to invest in research that 'fosters belief in learning and knowing together – in co-production' (Nind, 2004a: 537).

Drawing on their narratives, the significance of symbolic capital or the lack of it across the different domains of their lives and the impact of these factors were identified. Uncovering and understanding what are often invisible forms of symbolic capital and trying to understand how these impact on the lives and the communities of the learners offer valuable knowledge. Indeed, drawing on the learners' narratives, we are able to identify features of symbolic violence embedded in everyday life. This allows us to explore the different forms of violence that can co-exist and support one another, each impacting on the other in a seemingly unending cycle of violence. In unfolding the learners' narratives, there was recognition and understanding of the narratives against the backdrop of wider socio/economic/political and historical contexts (Duckworth, 2013; Goodson and Sikes, 2001; Goodson, 1992). The element of critical education that is recognized in this study offers the opportunity to extend on Bourdieu's concept by including this as a lever for change and the potential for learner empowerment (Duckworth, 2013: 14; Duckworth and Smith, 2018c).

Importantly, it is vital to recognize that in an age of neo-liberalism and globalization, the Freirian concept of empowerment, based on the premise that by overcoming oppression people will move towards true humanity, can be problematic. Indeed, transformation and empowerment of the learners/teacher, if individually focused rather than collective and connected to critical consciousness, could simply lead to the oppressed becoming the oppressors and a failure to engage in social justice and liberation. But in Duckworth and Smith's work (2017a, 2018a) transformative teaching and learning is viewed as a continuum and as having a spectrum of features that, most fully expressed, radiate beyond the individual to their family and community in ways that challenge existing inequalities more broadly. Literacy education creating a discourse community offers 'differential space' (Lefebvre, 1991) that is emancipatory for many learners at the local level of family and community. Adult literacy education becomes disruptive of the rigid linearity of a model of 'learning progression' that sorts individuals according to a qualification/age matrix. Instead, it can offer organic tools for resistance, through consciousness-raising and transformation by acting as what Duckworth and Smith (2019b) describe as a 'hope catalyst' for changes in both learners' lives and teachers' practice that ruptures the negative impact of a classificatory education system and instead allows learners to rearticulate the relationship between their education and their futures.

Case example

Developing a 'Reading Habitus'
Chelsea Swift

Overview

Chelsea's research moves the focus from Duckworth's (2013) research with adults to exploring young people's development of a 'reading habitus', their ways of reading, being a reader and the extent to which they view themselves as 'someone who reads.' She explored how young people negotiate the various ways of reading and reading they are exposed to, as they move between and within fields, in order to develop a sense for themselves of what it means to be a reader. This research topic was, to an extent, a product of her own personal reading journey and educational trajectory, in addition to her academic studies in English and Education. Reading, libraries and education more broadly have played an important role in both Chelsea's personal and professional trajectory. They were central to shaping her aspirations, her sense of who she was and who she could be, instilling in her a strong sense of the importance of reading, literacy and access to books for social justice.

Approach and methods

This research was conducted in two state secondary schools in relatively deprived coastal areas of Yorkshire, England. Two classes of year 9 students (aged 13–14) in each school took part: two mixed attainment in the first school and one high and one low attainment in the second. A total of ninety-six young people took part in the first stage of the research, and twenty-eight of these also took part in the second stage.

The generation of data took part in two stages. First, I employed a whole-class critical incident charting (CIC) activity. This is a visual-based construct elicitation tool, which involves the visual mapping of the individual's 'assumptions, values, ideas and histories' (Burnard, 2012: 168). I intended to capture how both past and present experiences of reading, and the individual's movement between fields, shaped their reading journey and subsequent reading habitus. The task required the young people who took part to map, along a 'river' or a 'road', the events and experiences which they felt had been critical in directing their reading journey. They were also asked to rate themselves according to how much they enjoyed reading, how much they read in their spare time and how good they felt they were at reading. My use of CIC was shaped by my theoretical understanding of the concept of identity, detailed below. It acknowledges the social, situated nature of identity and recognizes and facilitates the individual's capacity for personal reflexivity, offering 'insight into the richly multifaceted and highly complex relationships by which identities are built' (Burnard, 2004: 7). Pupils were actively encouraged to reflect on what these experiences and events mean to them and to decide for themselves what has been important or significant in their reading lives, rather than relying on pre-specified criteria. The CICs shift the lens on the individual's interpretation of events and leaves room for a variety of responses, encouraging 'active involvement from participants in an emancipatory and democratic way' (8) and 'promoting reflection on and change in the self' (7).

I then selected a number of those who completed this first stage, to take part in a series of two semi-structured interviews. In the first interview, the young people were asked to expand on their CIC. I began by asking them to talk me through what they had written, providing further elaboration and explanation. This then formed the basis of subsequent discussion, with questions being shaped by participant's explanations of their CIC, attempting to generate further insight into why certain events held meaning for the individual. This gave participants some control over the content of the interview, as the experiences they had decided were critical and formed the basis of the conversation. I also repeatedly asked for clarification and further elaboration throughout the interviews, in addition to briefly summarizing participants' responses at the end of each, in order to confirm my understanding and provide opportunity for participants to correct me.

In the second interview, participation involved the sorting and discussion of a variety of reading materials, including newspapers, magazines, novels, online material, children's and young adult fiction and non-fiction text, which I had selected for discussion. I started by asking several open-ended questions which required participants to make judgements of the texts such as, which they found the most and least appealing and who they thought the intended audience for each of them might be. This was then followed by asking them to organize the texts according to a criteria of their choice and then to explain their thinking behind their choices. Again, this places control of the discussion in the hands of the participants, levelling the playing field between researcher and researched. This activity allowed me to explore the ways in which pupils view certain types of text and what they consider to be relevant reading material for them. It provided insight into the process of reading-related decision-making, highlighting the factors that attract or deter individuals from approaching particular texts. This is in line with the approach to identity which informs this research, which views choices and behaviours as the embodiment of an individual's identity, which form a guide to such action (Bourdieu, 2010; Hitlin, 2003; Reay et al., 2005).

Each stage of this research was designed to enable me to approach issues in a way that was accessible to participants, in light of their age and, in certain cases, their ability. The methods functioned as prompts for thinking about the issues in question, facilitating the participant's guidance of the discussion and foregrounding the meaning that reading experiences hold for the individual in the context of their daily lives. They are also consistent with the critical theory interpretive paradigm which forms the foundations of this research, which maintains that it is only possible to effect change through a critical awareness of one's situation.

Much current education and cultural policy positions certain groups of young people as lacking access to an elite culture, rather than valuing their culture and experiences within these contexts. With regard to reading in particular, this deficit discourse is evident in persistent attempts to redistribute cultural capital through education, informed by an understanding of reading as existing solely 'in heads'. This view of reading neglects the social and the processes by which literacies are positioned in relation to each other and differently valued in different social contexts. It places value in the text itself rather than in the valuing process, leading to what Milner (2005) describes as the 'fetishization of the object (6)', where certain texts are revered as intrinsically and universally valuable and, consequently, more worthy of serious consideration. This serves to mask the arbitrary nature of the value ascribed to particular texts and authors, and does not account for the contexts in which texts are used and produced, or the variety of social and cultural experiences an individual brings with them to the text. Consequently, blame is placed on the individual for failing to understand and appreciate particular texts and authors in particular ways.

In order to problematize this dominant discourse surrounding young people's reading, I needed a theoretical framework which would connect these micro practices of reading, which occur at the level of the individual or between individuals, to the macro structures of society. In order to achieve this, I drew on the Bourdieusian concepts of habitus, symbolic capital and field (Bourdieu, 1977), in addition to working with an understanding of literacy as a social practice. This enabled me to explore the gendered, classed and intergenerational nature of young people's reading lives, expanding social understandings of literacy by 'focusing on the production of literacy identities in relation to social structures and cultural worlds' (Bartlett and Holland, 2002: 12). The theoretical framework and methods used to generate data in this research allowed me to explore the implications of individual literacy practices for broader issues of social justice and equality, problematizing promises of social mobility through access to an elite culture of which certain young people have been 'deprived'. My findings demonstrate both the rich reading lives that many of the young people lead outside of school and the ways in which the current deficit model serves to make these lives invisible, not only in education policy and in the classroom, but often to the young people themselves. Placing emphasis on readers and reading rather than on specific texts, acknowledging the role of the social in acts of reading and learning, challenges the dominant model of reading and the inequalities it maintains.

Chelsea's research, like Vicky and Rob's, recognizes literacy as a plural concept which is important in challenging the dominance of the idea that there is just one way of reading and writing. The dominant instrumental models of literacies fail to value or recognize the everyday skills and practices that learners have and bring into the classroom. They draw on Bourdieu's work on education and its impact in the reproduction of social inequality (Bourdieu and Passeron, 1990) to provide a framework. Vicky and Chelsea both probe literacy in the realm of inequity, of what is valued and what is not, with literacy education positioned as a site of production and reproduction of power positions, and where certain literacy practices are considered more legitimate than others.

Clearly, educational institutions are not neutral in the value placed on the accumulation of capital, including linguistic capital, and its transmission. This is often reflected in the way that they ensure the profitability of the dominant classes' cultural capital where 'abilities measured by scholastic criteria often stem not from natural "gifts" but from the greater or lesser affinity between class cultural habits and the demands of the educational system' (Mills, 2008: 83).

The relationship between struggling to read and/or write can impact on the ability to articulate one's rights. A critical literacy approach which derives from Freirean notions of 'conscientisation' (Freire, 1972) encourages critical reflection on the relationship between literacy practices and the (mis)use of power, thereby providing the scope to challenge hegemony. Pedagogy of social empathy, care and solidarity can be driven by dialogue with students about their needs and interests; educators can also invite students to take part in a larger community discourse that attempts to solve problems and create alternatives to oppressive situations (Duckworth and Maxwell, 2015). Transformative and emancipatory approaches to education and research demonstrate how critical education can open up spaces for a more equitable approach based on the co-production of knowledge (Duckworth and Smith, 2019a). Evidence from the research presented demonstrated this critical pedagogical approach generating a curriculum which is culturally relevant, learner driven and socially empowering (Barton et al., 2000, 2007; Duckworth and Ade-Ojo, 2016; Duckworth and Smith, 2018c, 2019b; Freire, 1985; Jones, 2018). It facilitated the learners to generate a personal connection with the historical, social, economic and political structures privileged by the dominant ideologies. It empowered the learners and their families and communities, empowerment being the strength and will to challenge oppression and inequality, to have control over one's own life and the motivation and self-belief to contribute to the needs of oneself and the community. This emancipation originates in an awareness of the structural inequalities oppressing people and, where possible, challenging and changing these conditions, and this includes embracing methodologies which Nind (2014a) describes 'doing research inclusively (and consciously and reflexively), to study and further inclusive education' (Nind, 2014a: 536). However, as argued by Bearne and Marsh (2007) there is still a distance to travel to resist and challenge narrow and traditional conceptions of literacy. We would argue that these traditional conceptions are exclusive, marginalizing many learners and the powerful socially situated literacies they bring into the classroom, and that a drive and determination is needed to embrace wider and richer perspectives which encompass the real and tangible ways in which literacy practices are already embedded in everyday lives.

Case example

Virginie Thériault

Literacy Practices: Understanding the relations between the literacy practices used in the two community-based organizations and those of the young people in a situation of precarity who attended their activities.

Context

For Virginie's study we move across the waters to Canada. Her research was conducted between 2012 and 2015 in two community-based organizations for young people in the Province of Québec (Canada) (see Papen and Thériault, 2016; Thériault, 2016). The community-based organizations – the names Le Bercail and L'Envol are used as pseudonyms – were offering support to young people aged 16 to 30 who were experiencing precarity. Le Bercail and L'Envol were helping them to find work, return to education, stabilize their housing situation, improve their social relationships and so on. The study adopted a social justice and critical stance (Madison, 2005) as it challenged widespread deficit views about young people in a situation of precarity. For instance, previous work (Bélisle, 2006) indicated that some youth workers, and to some extent society in general, believe that young people in a situation of precarity do not like to read and write and simply do not engage in these kinds of activities. The selected theoretical framework is the NLS, as it considers literacies as social practices rather than technical skills (Barton and Hamilton, 1998). Looking at everyday life, literacy practices can foreground certain usages and strategies developed by so-called marginalized groups; their literacy practices are not necessarily valued by society and would otherwise remain invisible.

Objectives and outcomes

The main research objective of the study was to understand the relations between the literacy practices used in the two community-based organizations and those of the young people in a situation of precarity who attended their activities. One of the specific questions that the study pursued was: In what ways can the literacy practices used in these organizations potentially empower young people in a situation of precarity?

The results show that the young people at Le Bercail and L'Envol had rich and varied literacy practices including, for example, the use of new technologies (Facebook and text messages), reading novels and spiritual books, and writing poems and letters. Their literacy practices were often multimodal (including images, texts, spoken language, video and so on) and multilingual (e.g. Cantonese, Dari, English, French and Mandarin).

The vast majority of the young people participating in the study had had difficult experiences at school. The results indicate that the young people might have reconciled themselves with certain types of literacy (e.g. more formal or school-related types) through their participation at Le Bercail and L'Envol. Through the activities organized at Le Bercail and L'Envol, the young people were brought into contact with a variety of genres (e.g. leaflets, websites, recipes, CVs, bureaucratic documents and so on). The youth workers supported young people's learning with regard to all these different texts.

Also, because the young people were experiencing precarity, they needed access to the services of various institutions (health services, financial support, housing support and so on). The access to these services was mediated by bureaucratic literacies (e.g. form, online information, official letter and so on). The youth workers often acted as 'literacy mediators', helping the young people to cope with these literacy demands. They were undertaking this role with a focus on social justice and young people's autonomy and learning.

Methods

The methodology adopted was ethnographic, critical and participatory. The study had three main phases: (1) intensive participant observation sessions and research interviews, (2) participatory analysis workshops and (3) dissemination and knowledge exchange activities. In addition to traditional ethnographic methods (participant observation and research interviews) I also wanted to give a voice to young people and youth workers. This is why a range of participatory research methods were included throughout the study.

After two intensive months of participant observation at Le Bercail and L'Envol, I conducted individual interviews with fourteen young people and seven youth workers. Before the interviews with the young people, they were invited to bring a 'literacy artefact' (Pahl and Rowsell, 2010) that they considered important in their lives (e.g. mobile phone, personal diary, novels, tattoo, poems and so on). The artefacts selected by the young people were generally related to significant and transformative events in their lives (e.g. immigration, death of a parent, travel, change of school and so on). By talking around a literacy artefact, I had the opportunity to understand better how young people's literacy practices evolved through different spaces, time periods and interactions with members of their social network.

In the second phase, I developed workshops around seven important concepts identified in the first phase of data collected: (1) literacy practices, (2) digital literacies, (3) multilingual literacies,

(4) literacy mediators, (5) sponsors of literacy, (6) literacy learning, (7) empowerment and (8) literacy in the physical space. The design of the workshops was in line with the philosophy and kinds of activities that the community-based organizations would organize for young people. The methods used were visual, collaborative, creative and included activities such as mind mapping and card sorting. For one of the activities, I asked the young people to think about a letter they had received recently and that had an important effect on their lives (see Thériault, 2016). I provided them with a sheet of paper as a blank storyboard including the following sections: who had sent the letter, what it was about and what they did afterwards in relation to it. This activity allowed me to discuss the concepts of literacy mediation and literacy sponsorship in a more hands-on manner with the young people. They were able to have a say during the data analysis stage and influenced the study's focus and findings.

Areas for consideration

Literacy can be a very sensitive topic for young people who had had negative experiences with reading and writing at school. The young people who took part in my study had very rich literacy practices but still associated reading and writing with formal schooling. I used participatory research methods, as discussed in Calderón López and Thériault (2017), to present an alternative perspective on literacy (NLS) while respectfully listening and considering the research participants' own beliefs about literacy. It is only after having spent time and built trusting relationships with the young people and the youth workers that I was able to discuss their everyday literacy practices. Authenticity, transparency and a genuine interest in the participants' lives were at the core of my methodological and epistemological approach. The young people and the youth workers gave me access to some aspects of their private lives. In some cases I visited their home, talked about their family and friends, and discussed their personal difficulties. Some of the details shared with me were intentionally left out of my publications for ethical reasons and by respect to the participants.

Virginie's research illustrates how everyday literacies, which include the use of new and emerging technology, are often marginalized and inviable in favour of privileged institutional literacies. Like Vicky's work with adult learners Virginie's research highlights that literacy can be a very sensitive topic for young people who had had negative experiences with reading and writing at school. For example, at a critical time when our participants, as illustrated by Joanne and Stella, were becoming aware of themselves and how they fitted into the classroom, self-conscious emotions such as shame and guilt began to emerge. Whereas school should be a place where the learners feel comfortable and respected, our participants were anxious, confused and worried for their own well-being. The studies shed light on literacy as being historically located and socially embedded in relations of power that challenges traditional models of symbolic domination which serves to both legitimize and reproduce structural inequalities.

Conclusion

We have been talking about issues such as those raised in these case studies for many years. Histories, while always social, are also distinct enough to merit closer attention to the details that contribute to significant differences in learners' ways of being and choices or lack of choices across the fields they inhabit. This is a time when the gap between the richest and poorest has grown to its widest for several generations (Dorling, 2015), and the impact of policy reform is biting the most vulnerable that have often been cut off and silenced in the national conversation on poverty and its impact. Instead, images in the media often pathologize people in poverty which take a hold on perceptions that people living in poverty are not working hard enough. Indeed, we live in a culture that blames individuals for their social exclusion. It pathologises poor people for being poor; as a society and in the research we carry out we need to look at the big picture, the structural inequalities and individual intersectionalities that shape people's lives. Policymakers often minimize the social justice implications of poverty, such as the complex interrelated issues which include chaotic housing situations, nutrition, liveable wages and literacy. Learners in the study often arrived in further education from situations of ongoing poverty that had blighted their lives and their families and community. Many faced the challenges that stem from low pay and precarious incomes and lived under continuous threat of hardship because of this.

We need acknowledgement of the importance of this research in the policy arena. We also need further research and action to ensure children and adults are given a voice and have the resources, including literacy, they need to navigate through life with agency, dignity and hope. As educationalists and community members, we also need to look at the violence and trauma, such as that identified in Duckworth's study (2013), not as isolated accounts but as phenomena related to the structural inequalities in people's lives. Violence and trauma, including the fallout of austerity, have an impact on learners and their families and communities in many ways which include mental and physical well-being, economic and social capitals or lack of capitals. It offers an indicator of the relationship of the learners to the state and the social values which underpin it. It shapes their experiences and continues to do so in many communities whereby structural inequality is being paid for by families and communities in vulnerable circumstances; many of those who are most in need of support are bearing the brunt of austerity politics. Transformative teaching and learning which include critical pedagogy offer a model of education with social justice at its heart and against education structures that marginalize women and men and their families and communities. As highlighted by Duckworth and Smith (2018a, 2018d) education and research are both enabling tools that can promote a more equitable and socially just society; they can have the potential to offer resistance against structures that reproduce marginalization – the research process mirroring the focus on social justice that sits at the heart of critical pedagogy.

Socially just research in literacy (and beyond) which is dialogical and participatory offers a bridge for learners to generate a personal connection with the historical, social, economic and political structures privileged by the dominant ideologies. It empowers the learners and their families and communities. Empowerment is the strength and will to resist oppression and inequality, to have agency over one's own life and the will, motivation, self-belief and hope to contribute to the needs of oneself, family and local and wider community. A vital drive in this is an awareness of the structural inequalities oppressing people and, where possible, challenging and changing these conditions (Duckworth and Smith, 2019b).

Further reading

Ade-Ojo, G., and Duckworth, V. (2015), *Adult Literacy Policy and Practice: From Intrinsic Values to Instrumentalism,* London: Palgrave Macmillan Pivotal.

Duckworth, V. (2013), *Learning Trajectories, Violence and Empowerment amongst Adult Basic Skills Learners*, Research in Education, London: Routledge.

Hamilton, M. (2012), *Literacy and the Politics of Representation*, London: Routledge.

Nind, M. (2014), 'Inclusive research and inclusive education: Why connecting them makes sense for teachers' and learners' democratic development of education', *Cambridge Journal of Education*, 44(4): 525–40.

Robinson-Pant, A. (2016), *Promoting Health and Literacy for Women's Empowerment*, UNESCO Institute for Lifelong Learning (UIL). http://uil.unesco.org/literacy-and-basic-skills/focus-women/investigating-relationship-between-literacy-health-and-womens. Accessed 30 July 2017.

Street, B. (1984), *Literacy in Theory and Practice*, Cambridge: Cambridge University Press.

CHAPTER SEVEN

Global perspectives on researching for equity and social justice

Introduction

This chapter draws on five extended case studies of different forms of research concerned with social justice conducted across the globe in Armenia, Barbados, Ireland, Pakistan and South Africa, with children and adults accessing different forms of education from Early Years to Higher Education (HE). Thus, the chapter explores a wide range of research methods which can help us to understand how research can form socially just practice or result in outcomes which promote social justice. These examples are drawn from multiple different contexts, and the studies offer examples of attempts to frame social justice in ways that can help to explain and understand the practices of those working across and within diverse and often challenging education settings. We have presented the case studies as 'stand-alone' texts. We gave our contributors guidelines on structure, and these have been interpreted slightly differently. Within the ethic of respect we consider fundamental to values of social justice, we have therefore forgone consistency in favour of what we believe is the strength and authenticity of the unmediated voices of our colleagues. Following the case studies, we present an extended discussion on the implication of the various approaches for socially just research practice.

We live in a world of increasing complexity, in which in/equalities have become increasingly evident, for example, between and within local communities at a micro level and the global north and south from a macro perspective. Living in 'liquid' and uncertain times (Bauman, 2007), in which the impact of the 2008 banking crash still resonates internationally (Dorling, 2015), we see political upheavals (and their consequences for people and their communities) and an increase in conflict across the globe leading to mass migration. Within this context, education – especially in developing and conflict contexts – often forms a response to or an intervention in a particular set of circumstances. These complexities are compounded in many respects by the interconnectedness of the world today and the implications of that for individuals' lives. For example, Atkins (2016a) has argued that contrary to policy rhetoric, in advanced economies such as the United States, Europe and Australia, globalization is 'redistributing employment opportunities and incomes' (Spence, 2011) and that the impact of this is different for different groups within individual economies. The implications of this in terms of education and social in/justice are profound. In Western countries young people with more restricted access to the symbolic capitals associated with education, and thus have particular constraints associated with their socio-spatial positioning, find the school-to-work transition more extended and challenging. Having local outlooks in a globalized world, their employment opportunities will be limited to those in a small geographical area, yet dependent on historic and contemporary global economic developments and changes which influence multinationals' investment – or lack thereof – in particular geographical areas. These issues of changing (and mobile) multinational investment have even more profound impacts in some global contexts, where the transfer of production from one site to another will result not only in loss of income for families but, in countries without universal access to free education, also in education being denied altogether for children whose families can no longer afford it.

Other implications of interconnectedness relate to the dominance of particular social, cultural and political perspectives and the ways in which these can now be reified through online interconnectedness, as well as other forms of globalization. In relation to educational research, and as some of our case studies highlight, there are particular issues in doing research from a dominant or colonial perspective which bring specific issues of power relations with them. However, in addition, educational research concerned with social justice has an added set of debates and issues to contend with: where practices are culturally situated but widely regarded as negative or oppressive, to what extent is it appropriate or inappropriate, moral or socially just, to undertake research and interventions which seek to change those practices? These are problems that two of our case studies had to grapple with. In both cases, they sought to recognize that 'ways of knowing' are not Western bound and homogenous, reflecting a shift from what Freire (1996) describes as 'cultural invasion', in which invaders penetrate the cultural context of another group, in disrespect of the latter's potentialities, imposing their own view of the world upon those they invade and inhibiting the creativity of the invaded by curbing their expression (Freire, 1996: 133). Resistance to this invasion includes challenging what Smith (1999) describes as the dominant Western frameworks of knowledge. This dominant framework shaped by notions of 'Orientalism' (see Said, 1978) is challenged in the recognition of indigenous research which includes indigenous methodologies that align to their world views and histories. This approach moves from the colonizer's lens which presents a dehumanizing gaze of objective research. Instead Smith positions research as a driving force to reclaim the history and identity of Indigenous peoples. Indeed, her research with Maori communities and the methodology it ignites, which includes writing, is an important role of decolonizing methodologies as it offers a representation of a very powerful need to give testimony to and restore spirit, to bring back into existence a world fragmented and dying (Smith, 1999: 28) and, in doing so, a catalyst for reclaiming community voice and 'fight back against the invasion of communities by academic, corporate and populist researchers' (Smith, 1999:39). Moving to an African perspective, Chilisa (2012) also critiques the Euro-western methods of conducting research and positions it as a methodical subjugation of other ways of knowing and 'othering'. She proposes that when the researcher is an outsider, issues of how to frame the research are vital to avoid objectification. As such, for Chilisa, postcolonial indigenous research methodology is a culturally responsive methodology that requires researchers to develop relationships, have a commitment to the community and importantly be accountable to that community which includes its dissemination and what the participants play in this process which is responsive to their voice and agency.

In both case studies, participants were offered the opportunity to be actors of their future and active members of their communities, through the utilization of emancipatory practices to encourage autonomy and critical thinking, opening up spaces where the community could ask questions, analyse and subsequently work through effective and meaningful strategies for development.

Case example

A community-based participatory action research project in South Africa
Mary McAteer

Overview

Mary McAteer discusses one aspect of work undertaken with the support of a British Academy Newton Fellowship grant for Professor Lesley Wood, North-West University, South Africa (the applicant), and Dr Mary McAteer, Edge Hill University, UK (the co-applicant). The focus in this case example is the way in which they conceptualize and enact their roles as university academics in a community-based Participatory Action Research (PAR) project in South Africa. They explore issues of power and privilege and the ways in which their project was able to support democratization of knowledge and positive, sustainable outcomes for the participants and their community.

Introduction

The project was undertaken in a school–community partnership in a disadvantaged, peri-urban area of Western Cape, South Africa. The school has for a number of years engaged in self-driven, externally supported community development work in an effort to improve the life chances of the children and the local community members. This specific project arose following the identification of a group of teachers, and volunteer teaching assistants in the school, that parents needed more support from the school if they were to better support their children's education.

As academics holding the funding, and the (perceived) power in the project, we were conscientious that full democratic participation is not easy to attain in situations where there is a deep and embedded power differential operating at multiple levels. For this reason, our epistemological and ontological positions were based on notions of inclusion, democracy and respect for local knowledge as essential elements in seeking social justice.

Research goals

The project was undertaken as a community development endeavour, in which we hoped that we would, along with the participants, co-construct new knowledge which might be made available to and be useful for the community. We did not want to come as outsiders 'bearing gifts' and imposing university-generated concepts on a community that we felt should find their own solutions to the problems that they had identified. In this way, we hoped to enact what Biesta (2007) refers to as the 'civic' role of the university, contributing to the development of a knowledge society, rather than the more commodified knowledge economy.

As an action research project, we had, as our central aim, the practical outcomes that might support the development of parenting skills for the parents in the community. It was agreed with the participants that this would take the form of a parenting programme, accompanied by a manual for them as trainers and a separate one for parents. A further aim was to enable the project participants to build a set of transferable skills, which might support longer-term sustainability of their work. For this reason, the participants, after the initial set-up period, became basically self-managing, arranging and booking meetings, completing costings and budget reconciliations, undertaking their own collection and recording/transcribing of data, and providing three-way translation in the work between English, isiXhosa and Afrikaans.

Finally, as researchers, we had personal goals relating to the building of democratic and democratizing processes. We recognized the fact that top-down (Western) knowledge transmission was unlikely to lead to community transformation (Mahlomaholo, 2013) and hence an aim for us was to successfully resist the urge to work directively, and non-democratically and develop new insights into participatory and democratizing methodologies.

Methodology and methods

Our chosen methodological framework was PAR, allowing us to recognize knowledge as a means to create more socially just and democratic conditions. Drawing on Gavanta's (1991) work on Knowledge Democracy, we wanted to particularly support the involvement of our participants in producing their own knowledge and chose our practical strategies and methods accordingly. The project implementation phase consisted of a set of workshops conducted over a three-day period in the participants' own school, with the two researchers in attendance. Following this, the participants were to meet on a regular basis (every 1–2 weeks) over a period of several months to explore more fully and respond to the identified needs of their school and community. These meetings were self-managed, with occasional visits from one or both of the researchers and occasional visiting 'experts'. Because of the self-managed nature of most of the project, in our set-up workshops, we undertook a number of exercises designed to fulfil a number of key criteria:

● Trust and relationship building
● Establishing 'operating principles' for the group of participants
● Modelling a range of procedures for conducting and recording data from workshops

We were conscious that as outsiders to the community, the full and meaningful participation of the participants would mean that their agenda would have to drive the process, and thus, the knowledge produced would be fit for purpose, benefit the community and support the possibility of sustained change (Burns and Worsley, 2015).

There was a further matter also to consider, that of language. While the participants spoke English, they were often more fluent, and more comfortable and confident, in isiXhosa. Some also were Afrikaans speakers.

This informed not only the methods that we used in the set-up workshops but also the procedures that we used and the time we made available for activities. It was important that there was space and time for translation where required; the use of visual methodologies was also a supporting structure. A further strategy was the ability to say without embarrassment, 'I do not understand that.' This mechanism emerged from within the group itself – as we report in our article (Wood and McAteer, 2017: 257):

> We found a humorous way for anyone in the group to indicate they did not understand something. One of the participants said something in isiXhosa, and when we asked for a translation, she said '*I have just left the room to have a cup of tea*', meaning that she might as well go and do this, since she does not understand what is going on. After this, we all used the term 'just gone for a cup of tea now!' when we did not understand what was being said. This made a potentially threatening situation into a fun one, and allowed participants (and us) to admit they did not understand without feeling exposed or embarrassed.
> *I was able to say 'I am going for a cup of tea' – we laughed and I did not feel stupid.*

Full ethical clearance had been granted by the two universities concerned and ensured that we adhered to the principles of voluntary, informed consent and confidentiality of participants' identity in publications. As part of this process the benefits to participants were deemed to outweigh any risk of participation.

Theoretical framework

Our theoretical stance therefore draws on the concepts of power and privilege and their relation to the development of ecologies of knowledge and the democratization of knowledge. We draw heavily on the work of Freire, Fals Borda and de Sousa Santos for their relevance to work in contexts of significant power imbalance and social injustice. Friere's (1968) *Pedagogy of the Oppressed* (republished in 2005), introduces us to 'critical pedagogy' as a means of promoting social and epistemological justice and knowledge decolonization. Through it, we questioned and troubled notions of educational hegemony and what de Sousa Santos (2007) describes as "Abyssal Thought" which gives dominance to (usually) Western thought and, by extension, renders indigenous knowledge 'invisible', thus removing agency from those who hold such knowledge. Cautioned by Hall's (1992: 25) claim that society has 'created an illusion and we have come to believe in it – namely, that only those with sophisticated techniques can create knowledge', we were particularly concerned not to 'stimulate popular knowledges' (Fals Borda and Rahman, 1991) in order to preserve the epistemic inequalities that the context embodied.

Throughout the operation of the project and in the ongoing data analysis, we were mindful to foreground these concepts, continuously asking how we could understand the ways in which knowledge is produced, disseminated and translated to action. We hoped to establish an ecology of knowledge, valuing the knowledge and the *ways of knowing* brought by both the participants and the researchers. Using dialogic and critical pedagogical process throughout helped us recognize the rich and varied epistemic ecology in which we were working and provided a structure through which we could seek knowledge democratization.

Project outcomes

During the two-year project period, a number of significant outcomes were realized. In relation to the three core aims of the project, we now report on the first two of them – those relating to (i) the development of the parenting programme and manual and (ii) the development of transferable skills for sustainability. The third aim, that of our own personal and epistemic growth and development, will not be reported on here, as we continue to reflect on that experience.

By the end of the second year of the project, the participants had successfully developed, piloted and refined their parenting programme, with an accompanying manual produced in both isiXhosa and English. They had decided, along with the community members, that there was no need to produce an Afrikaans manual, as the Afrikaans speakers were comfortable with the other languages, and the small amounts of translation required would be easily and informally managed. In addition to this, they had developed a range of transferable skills including project management, budgeting, word processing, leadership, mentoring and presentation skills.

What was of particular interest to us, as academics, however, was an observed change in the ways in which the participants interacted with other staff in the school. There was a noted and clear increase in their confidence levels. One young Teaching Assistant (we will call her Asande) who had not felt comfortable to speak at all during the early project meetings, by the end of the project, was voicing opinions on ways in which the school leadership needed to be more proactive in working with parents. On the last full project meeting, the volunteer Teaching Assistants organized, hosted and catered for a ceremony to celebrate the fact that a group of eleven parents had undertaken the training programme. Asande led the ceremony, presenting each of the parents for recognition in front of the school staff and invited community guests. While the tangible outcomes of the programme were highly significant, arguably, the more developed skill sets of each participant along with the attendant increase in confidence are more likely to have a lasting impact.

Case example

The multilingual literacy practices of Mirpuri migrants in Pakistan and the UK
Tony Capstick

Overview

Tony's research was located in a challenging context: an area which has particular security issues and one where the communities often have limited access to education and consequently to the literacies they need in order to enact their personal agency in a global context. His work highlights the importance of different forms of literacy in engaging with a global society and contests the common Western assumption that access to English (or, indeed, other dominant European language) can be conflated with integration in a new community.

Introduction

The multilingual literacy practices of Mirpuri migrants study was carried out in Pakistan and the UK from 2008 to 2013. When Tony carried out the study, Pakistan was in the news across the world due to increased militancy and the US-led war against the Taliban in the northwest of the country. Azad Kashmir, a disputed territory also in the north of Pakistan, has its own security issues which emerged at the time of independence from Britain and which are explored in the wider study. Hence the portrayal of both country and territory is often dominated by political and military issues. Many Mirpuris, from the Azad Kashmir region of Pakistan, leave school having been unable to access literacy in Urdu, the national language, or English, the official language, which then makes their goal of migrating to Britain more challenging. At the same time, they are more determined as England is seen as a land of opportunity. Conversely, the British government no longer requires cheap labour from South Asia and has moved towards tighter controls on migration from non-European Economic Area (EEA) countries.

Five months after the start of my data collection in Mirpur, in November 2010, the British government introduced English language testing for migrants which was aimed specifically at spousal migrants from non-EEA and therefore, in terms of social justice, resulted in unequal access to migration procedures for many thousands of families. This had immediate consequences for the participants in this study, their language learning and their literacy practices, as individuals turned to their family, friends and wider communities in order to access the literacies that they needed to migrate. These are the literacies that they needed for filling in visa forms as well as those for maintaining ties with their families and friends before and after migration.

Research goal

The goal of my study was to explore what language and literacy practices Mirpuri migrants draw on in their migrations and to identify the role of access to English in Pakistan prior to migration.

Methodology and methods

The methods chosen included Critical Discourse Analysis and New Literacy Studies. New Literacy Studies are social approaches to literacy. They offer a multifaceted view of the nature of literacy which challenges the dominance of the autonomous model, recognizes how literacy practices vary from one cultural and historical context to another and thus could be argued to be more consistent with social justice.

The main ethical and methodological issues I encountered related to 'being critical', by which I mean the way in which I 'make the implicit explicit' in the analysis of discourse, following Chilton et al. who suggest that this means 'making explicit the implicit relationship between discourse, power and ideology, challenging surface meanings, and not taking anything for granted' (2010: 491). Chilton et al. also highlight a further aspect of the critical enterprise which I used to orient my study, that of being reflexively self-critical. This is also captured in Heller's (2011: 6) critical sociolinguistics which she defines as 'informed and situated social practice, one which can account for what we see, but which also knows why we see what we do, and what it means to tell the story'. What I took from Heller here is that, as a researcher researching discourses, my critical project must include a critical examination of my own discourses. I see this as part of the way that ethnographers think about reflexivity when addressing the ways the researcher and the conditions of the study affect knowledge production in the field and my awareness of this. In light of this, I explored my own research journey through a reflexive account of how my positionings impacted on the production of research (McCorkel and Myers, 2003). This meant that once I had carried out participant observation and interviews in settings across Mirpur town in Azad Kashmir and in Lancashire, UK, I analysed the way in which my own biases about language and migration were discursively constructed.

Theoretical framework

Building on the central claim that some literacies are more dominant and visible than others, I argue that a focus on how these processes have occurred over time can lead to a more fruitful understanding of power relations and literacy practices. This can lead to challenging the power relations that make some literacies more powerful than others. With this in mind, it was an aim of this study to examine how migrants do not go as far as challenging the power relations that make their migration from Azad Kashmir to Lancashire difficult, but rather how they go about appropriating the literacies that make their migration successful. Castells (2009: 10) argues that 'power is exercised by means of coercion (or the possibility of it) and/or by the construction of meaning on the basis of the discourses through which social actors guide their action'. Thus, according to Castells, these relationships play out by threats of violence or through discourses that constitute social action. I therefore developed a theoretical framework that combined Critical Discourse Analysis with New Literacy Studies.

Project outcomes

The findings from the study provide evidence to help challenge the common-sense opinion that standard English facilitates 'integration'. Quite the contrary in fact, as all of the languages in migrants' repertoires are drawn on when developing ties and the presence of English in the multilingual repertoires of the participants in my study did not ensure integration with non-Mirpuri communities.

Ethical issues

Verbal informed consent was sought from all the research participants, though my research ethics went much further than this. I informed all participants that they were free to withdraw from the study at any point and assured them that the research would remain confidential. In other words, I told the participants that I would not reveal details of what they told me to other people, other than in anonymized versions of the study. Whereas my role as a participant observer was marked out when writing notes while others were involved in activities such as literacy events, my role as an interviewer had greater potential to arouse suspicion as I was asking questions about people's personal circumstances as well as details of their visa applications. I assured these participants that I did not judge their decisions about migration but was rather interested in documenting and recording their practices. When writing up the research notes it was important to give each participant a pseudonym so that they could not be identified. For the same reason, I have given the town in northwest England that the family have migrated to the fictional name Hillington. I did not ask participants to sign a written consent form as I was told at the beginning of the research that this could make people feel as though they might be traced. I therefore chose to offer the participants verbal consent and they told me that they preferred this.

Case example

Opening up the 'black box': Biographical research on working-class students' experiences and Higher Education in Ireland

Fergal Finnegan

Overview: Social justice and research

Social justice, Nancy Fraser (2013) persuasively argues, requires not only the redistribution of social goods but also the recognition of diverse social needs and identities and a meaningful participation in decision making in political processes. Achieving this will require enormous changes in how we produce knowledge, organize education and do research (Wainwright, 2009). I think one small, simple, but necessary step we can take towards this is presenting research in a more realistic and less grand way. In that spirit, I want in this brief case example to capture some of the processual, flawed and context-bound nature of doing research which is orientated to social justice.

Mind the gap! Identifying a departure point

When I began looking at research and policy on working-class access to HE in Ireland what struck me, with some force, was what was missing. There were decades of reports and articles – manly using quantitative methods – which had demonstrated how deeply rooted class inequality is in Irish HE. Much of this research is useful but it is remarkable just how little of it began by asking working-class students how they viewed HE or, for that matter, how to best widen participation. There are almost no working-class voices in acres of text. In sociology more generally, research which explores how class and education is understood, experienced, culturally mediated and resisted on an everyday level by working-class people is very rare (Lynch and O'Riordan, 1998; O'Neill, 1992). This is true even of most of the radical, usually Marxist-influenced work on class in Ireland.

Biographical methods, critical realism and radical doubt

This lack of concern for lived experience seemed to me, as an egalitarian adult educator, extraordinary but unfortunately not surprising. To begin to address this I conducted a qualitative research with working-class students in three different HE institutions. At the heart of the research are eighty-one in-depth biographical interviews done with fifty-one people (the research included a longitudinal dimension). My choice of biographical methods was a very conscious intervention in a research field based on my commitment to social justice; I saw this as an attempt to bring voice and agency into a field dominated by 'top-down' systemic perspectives. Here the participant, their story and how they tell this story *on their own terms*, is central to the research (Merrill and West, 2009). The aim is to gather through participant-led interviews and complex, rich accounts of lifeworlds.

From a critical realist perspective (Sayer, 1992) we understand very little about the social world if we fail to attend to how people think, feel and act. But careful thought also has to be given to how a topic is framed and conceptualized in academic and popular discourses. It also means cultivating what Bourdieu called 'radical doubt' about the adequacy of these discourse (Bourdieu and Wacquant, 1992: 235).

But radical doubt cannot be just limited to the concepts and assumptions dominant in the research field. It is also about being reflexive about how one positions oneself in the research process within a wider institutional and political context. For me there are three key things related to this: I came from a more advantaged background than most of the people I was interviewing; the research was produced in an academic field with all its rules and rituals; and class and education is a highly charged, often ideological, yet poorly understood topic. These factors made me determined that in the design, analysis and presentation of the research I would seek to avoid a mode of social science which claims authority for itself by claiming people 'know not what they do'. I worked hard to avoid effacing diversity or forcing the findings. To do this I grounded myself in the stories by listening and re-listening and by going through them very slowly and carefully. As general themes emerged through analysis I would return to the audio or a clean transcript to connect me to what a particular person said as a whole. Here the longitudinal aspect of the research was crucial as it allowed me to check in with people on emerging findings. A recursive spiral – between self, interviewees, field and literature – created space to discern knots and contradictions which I think leads to empirical and theoretical discoveries.

Troubling tidy stories of class, education and human capital

When life stories are put at the centre of education it shifts the centre of gravity in a way that challenges many of the tidy and trim assumptions of policy and research. For example, the biographies of working-class people suggest we cannot treat class solely in relation to income, wealth or types of employment. It has cultural and affective elements – linked strongly to misrecognition and disrespect – which are integral to many people's experience. Some of this can be grasped by Terry's discussion of growing up in a working-class area in a rural town:

> I remember feeling embarrassed, less than, basically having . . ., having less worth than other people, not being listened to and not being taken seriously, condescended to, looked down upon, frowned upon- people expecting you not to understand.

These life stories also challenge deficit accounts of working-class participation in education. HE was very highly valued by participants not least because it proved one's worth as a learner (something which had been badly undermined in schools for many, but not all, students I met). This certainly had been the case for James, a man in his thirties from Dublin's inner city who said of university:

> I have learnt all these things-these things that have enriched me so much. . . It has] opened up all sorts of things, I'm aware of a bigger world out there [. . . I'm doing it for the piece of paper that says I can.[. . .] I wanted to find out more. I wanted to develop my language. It was always in the back of my head to start the reading and the writing and stop being afraid of that. I wanted to learn more about that. I wanted to, you know, I just wanted more. I wanted more for myself. I wanted, and I don't mean like. I didn't want a big car; I didn't want that, I wanted to be educated. You know I wanted to be educated and I wanted to be able to stand to an argument.

The stories I heard also trouble the functionalist and human capital fantasies about seamless transitions and easy upward mobility supposedly facilitated by access to HE. The long-term impact of class inequality creates all sorts of difficulties wealthier students simply do not face in, and after, university. Significantly, the burden to *adapt* to middle-class institutions fell on the shoulders of individual students. This creates challenges and psychic conflicts in HE and it involves risky transitions to uncertain destinations afterwards. Elaine, a thoughtful woman from west Dublin, loved being in HE but wondered if this now meant she was moving away from her community and mused on the depth and force of class inequality:

> It is like there is a river flowing in between. [. . .] the doers and the ones that tell the doers to do, [. . .] and thinkers and non-thinkers. I want to be a thinker and so like that's getting wider and I'm just so lucky that I might jump it, I might jump it but I didn't say I will. I don't know.

Reflecting on the research: The value of a sense of possibility and an awareness of limitations

My expectations of what could be achieved through a single piece of research were modest and the impact has indeed been minor. The research addressed a gap in research and therefore offers an alternative basis for thinking through working-class access to HE (Finnegan and Merrill, 2017; Fleming et al., 2017). Initiatives in terms of pedagogy and institutional collaborations and the institution where I work have also flowed from this project. These are small but not insignificant things. In so much as the research has value, I think it flows from holding on to the truth of what people said in all its richness and diversity. It is also buoyed by something less commonly discussed as part of the researcher's toolkit: a sense of the enormous potential of human lives and how a different type of education might help people flourish. In this regard, I should mention before I became an academic I worked in adult education for many years in Dublin's inner city. This shaped me in many ways and was one of the richest learning experiences of my life. It informed the research in multiple ways especially a sense of what might be possible if we choose to organize education differently.

I am acutely aware of the flaws in the research. There are three, I think, other researchers might learn from. First, while I was very cognizant of power issues in the conduct, analysis and presentation of the research I did not plan carefully enough around non-academic modes of dissemination. Second, I had the desire to do research which alters from where and how we look at education. I took on a great number of interviews as I thought this would help amplify the point. But I believe now a smaller number of interviews would have opened up space for further collaboration with the participants. Thirdly, and this is the most significant one I think, I did not link the research to social movements and politics as I found much of the research in Ireland done so far too concerned with ideological narratives and not enough with lived experience. While I still think this judgement is correct I now think I should have given more thought to how the project could have been linked more tightly to wider collective work and social action.

Case example

Supporting parents of children with developmental disabilities in Barbados
Julie Sealy

Overview

Barbados lies south of the Caribbean chain of islands between the Atlantic Ocean and the Caribbean Sea; it has a total population of

287,000 with a surface area of 166 square miles. A former British colony, Barbados gained independence in 1966 and became a sovereign state within the British Commonwealth. Today, Barbados has a stable economy and is ranked as a 'high-income' developing nation (World Bank, 2016). However, a recent in-depth analysis of living conditions found that while policy developments have been implemented to address poverty, vulnerable groups such as disabled people still experience gaps in the provision of vital services along with social exclusion and discrimination (SALISES, 2012). As a small island state, Barbados is exposed to global and neo-liberal policies promoted through global institutions such as the World Bank and the International Monetary Fund (IMF) that have political, economic and social implications (Ramsaran, 2004). Barbados, like many Caribbean nations, still faces deep socio-economic injustices – a legacy of their colonial past. Many social institutions cling on to neocolonial models and structures and this is particularly evident within the education system that is affected by what Hickling-Hudson (2014) calls 'neo-colonial educational structures of privilege, elitism and deprivation'.

A recent study assessing living conditions in Barbados revealed rising poverty levels and a 5 per cent increase in the individual poverty rate (CALC, 2012). According to Margaret and Kas (2015) developing countries experience a disability–poverty cycle and in developing nations this is more pronounced and particularly impacts children with disabilities. While Barbados ratified the United Convention on the Rights of the Child (UNCRC) in 1990 and the United Nations Convention on the Rights of Persons with Disabilities (UNCRPD) in 2013, to date no national disability legislation has been enacted, and children with disabilities, and their families, remain a largely neglected group. According to SALISES (2012), 86 per cent of homes in Barbados are single-female-headed households, with families more likely to be living in poverty and mothers experiencing an increased burden of care.

Introduction

As a social worker and education practitioner I have worked in the Caribbean for 30 years, running non-government organization (NGO) and privately funded early education programmes and advocating for improved policies and services as a director of the Barbados Council for the Disabled. In 2007, I sourced private sector funding and implemented an early intervention centre for children with developmental disabilities and their families. Over the past ten years working closely with parents, mainly mothers, of infants and children with developmental challenges I observed their resilience and strengths as they navigated a system devoid of services and support. This case example presents an ethnographic account of a research project implemented to support parents. According to Jones and Lyons (2004) case studies generally focus on specific issues that give insight to the system being investigated, and Cronin (2014) suggests that ethnographic case studies can take the reader to places that they would probably never experience and should present the story through the eyes of the researcher. The case study narrative also needs to be embedded within the political, cultural and socio-economic context in which the research took place. Within all social settings during ethnographic research the researcher is engaged in 'a culturally constructed dialogue' as a participating actor balancing the explicit and the implicit actions and behaviours expressed throughout the interaction (Spindler, 2014: 2).

Research goal

In 2015, having worked for many years with parents of children with developmental disabilities I undertook a research project to evaluate a relationship-based intervention that aimed to support parents to feel connected to their children. Over the years during parent education and parent support workshops and meetings, many parents shared how they felt unsure of how to manage their children. Difficulties included those associated with 'hidden disabilities', such as those children with autism spectrum disorder who generally do not present with physical challenges, but which were often viewed and misinterpreted as behavioural problems. Extensive research literature also exists on specific Caribbean socialization practices that have been identified as detrimental to healthy child development such as authoritarian disciplinary measures in schools and at home (Barrow, 2003, 2008; Roopnarine et al., 2003; Williams et al., 2006). While identifying cultural practices such as the harsh, authoritarian disciplinary measures used by Caribbean parents, researchers also caution the imposition of a Eurocentric lens, and Roopnarine (2006) suggests that cultural practices can often be mediated by the perceived normalcy of the practice. However, Brown and Johnson (2008) conducted research in the Caribbean and stated that the cultural normativeness of authoritarian disciplinary practices employed in homes in the Caribbean cannot overshadow children's right to protection from violence and abuse. Baradon and Joyce (2005) stated that it is important to consider cultural practices when working with parents and children but it is also critical to be mindful of the infant's core developmental needs and global advocacy to end child violence which lends a voice to the call to address cultural practices that adversely impact child development. To this end, the goal of the research conducted in Barbados was first to listen to parents and to design a project that addressed the issues that they identified in their narratives. Many parents did not want to use traditional methods and worked tirelessly to do what they could to support their infants and children, but would resort to cultural practices characterized by traditional, authoritarian methods of child-rearing. To meet the needs identified by parents, the goal was to implement an intervention that strengthened the parent–child relationship by helping parents to accurately read their child's communicative intent and respond in a sensitive and contingent way, with the aim of mitigating the risk factors associated with adverse cultural child-rearing practices. A broader aim was to empower parents to be able to engage with their children in ways that they intrinsically felt they should and to feel empowered to challenge current social structures and advocate for social change for their families.

The theoretical framework that underpinned the research was a transactional model (Sameroff, 2009). The Transactional Model addresses the complex interplay between dynamic systems. The individual or group under study cannot be seen as distinct from the experience and the social context and the 'emphasis is on the multidirectionality of change' (Sameroff et al., 2005: 13).

Methodology and method

Yin (2009) stated that case study research can include multi-method designs and is not restricted to qualitative approaches common in ethnographic research. Research can be exploratory, explanatory or descriptive and has as its main focus the goal of researching a phenomenon within its real-life context. Within the current research forty parents and their children with neurodevelopmental disabilities agreed to participate in a study to investigate if a relationship-based, twelve-week intervention could support parents to feel more confident reading and understanding their child's behaviour and ultimately enhance the parent–child relationship. The study used a pre-test/post-test design with twenty parents randomly assigned to a group who received the intervention and twenty parents to a 'wait list' group who received the same intervention after the study period ended. The study was guided by the following research question:

Q.1 Would the quality of the parent interaction and the parents' reflective capacities be enhanced after a twelve-week, relationship-based intervention?

Parents attended sessions for two hours per week with their child where they were supported by play therapists to engage with their child in a natural play interaction. The therapists coached parents on how to affectively attune to their child and how to enrich the parent–child interaction. The parents were helped to develop a greater understanding of their child's behaviour looking at what supports and disrupts the dyadic interaction. The parents were encouraged to tune in to their child's emotional cues to support their emotional regulation and to develop a rich engagement. The interactive sessions were video recorded; at the end of the session the parent was engaged in a reflective session where they reviewed the video recording and discussed the interaction. Video biofeedback has proved to be a successful method to help parents to engage in reflective practice with the goal of strengthening the parent–child relationship (Beebe, 2003; McDonough, 2005; Schechter et al., 2006), and strengthening parents' reflective capacities has been associated with stronger parent–child attachment security (Fonagy et al., 2007; Slade, 2005).

Before and after the intervention sessions all forty parents were video recorded in a natural play interaction with their child and all parents engaged in a forty-five-min semi-structured interview (the Parent Development Interview, PDI) schedule to explore parents' reflections on their relationship with their child. The video recordings were assessed using the Parenting Interactions with Children: Checklist of Observations Linked to Outcomes (PICCOLO) (Roggman et al., 2007). The PDI interviews produced an in-depth understanding of parents' thoughts, feelings and beliefs about their relationship with their child and the video recordings showed parents in live interactions with their children. Both of these measures were scored using the assessment manuals and produced quantitative data that indicated a statistically significant increase in both parents' reflective capacities and the quality of their play interactions after the twelve-week intervention. The PDI interviews also produced rich qualitative data from parents' reflections on their relationship with their child.

Project outcomes

Quantitative analysis of the scores from the PDI and the PICCOLO revealed a statistically significant increase in both the quality of the interaction and the parents' reflective capacities after the intervention. There was a greater difference in the scores of the parents in the intervention group at time 2 compared to time 1 and when compared to the scores of the parents in the 'wait-list' group. This type of design measures the degree of change after an intervention by obtaining a baseline score at the beginning of the study and a post-intervention score on completion of the project (Kazdin, 2003). While these data gave validity to the intervention, the rich qualitative information gathered through the interviews provided insight into the parents' journey throughout the study period. Research on parental reflective functioning explores how parents' narratives and 'mentalizations' about their child can influence the parent–child relationship. Fonagy and Target (2007) have suggested that when parents accurately reflect on their own and their child's mental states, particularly in early childhood, this nurtures the child's internal representations of the world and shapes the quality of the parent–child attachment relationship.

In their post-intervention interviews the parents were better able to read their child's behaviour. Their narratives were richer and there was an element of 'thinking in the moment', a sense of wondering about how their child was feeling and what may be impacting their relationship. When reflecting on the video recordings of their sessions with their child, parents gradually became more confident reading and commenting on the interactions. Initially parents had great difficulty trusting their own intuition and their ability to read their child's behaviour; however, as the sessions progressed and the parents were supported to reflect on the sessions they began to trust their own interpretations of their child's actions and relied less and less on the professional guidance of the therapists. The parents appeared more confident in their ability to read and respond to their child's communicative intent and there was a 'shift' in parents' reflective thinking that seemed to coincide with richer reciprocity in the parent–child interaction.

Research has revealed that parents of children with developmental disabilities can experience disruptions in communication (Kalmanson, 2009; Sayre et al., 2001), and Slade (2009: 10) suggests that these parents often struggle in a 'sea of confusing and chaotic communications'. The results of the current study suggest that the intervention, particularly the reflective video-feedback, enhanced parents' capacity to navigate the parent–child relationship and to feel more confident engaging with their child. Janssens, Rosemberg and van Spijk (2009) have suggested that early intervention programmes are on the increase in the Caribbean; however, the majority of these are privately funded and are often out of the reach of many families due to disadvantaged economic circumstances. Although there is clear evidence that increased investments to provide enriched early childhood learning environments promote healthy outcomes for children and families (Engle et al., 2011; Heckman, 2013), Bornstein et al. (2012: 19) have stated that 'Around the globe, children and caregivers in developing countries tend to suffer deprivation of economic capital; specifically, there is a lack of general economic infrastructure and families have access to only limited choices of goods and services.'

The current study provides an example of a cost-effective intervention to support parents of children with developmental disabilities; however, like many developing countries, Barbados experiences social and economic deficits that impact the provision of policies and services for at-risk children and families. Supporting parents to connect with their child is the first step in mobilizing and empowering parents to be involved in care planning strategies. This type of support can empower parents with children with disabilities to actively create equitable opportunities and outcomes for their children and families. Using a framework of social justice, researchers can raise questions regarding policy provision and reform and can engage in social action research in partnership with children and families (Wight-Felske, 2003). Listening to parents' voices is the first step to developing research agendas that value their participation and that begin to change the power differential and inequalities that impact their lives (Guberman and Maheu, 2003).

Ethical dilemmas

The cultural relevance of measures used in research is often a source of concern for Caribbean researchers. Williams, Brown and Roopnarine (2006) suggested that the appropriateness of many research measures has not been tested on Caribbean populations and future research is required to test the validity and reliability of these tools. Krishnakumar, Buehler and Barber (2004) stated that definitions of meanings and constructs ought to be examined within a cultural lens. For example, the Caribbean family and Caribbean relationships have specific cultural nuances that may not be captured in Eurocentric measures and models. In addition, further research in the region is required to understand the culturally constructed ethno-theories that shape the parent–child relationship.

My motivation for the research was clearly influenced by the many years I have spent working with families and observing their struggles and the social injustices that they endured. Cunliffe and Karunanayake (2013: 365) caution that, 'immersion in the field often means that ethnographers become implicated in the lives of research respondents'. Ethical practice requires researchers to be conscious of how they situate themselves within the research context, mindful of issues of power and privilege. In Barbados issues of power and privilege are historically and complexly enmeshed in race. Economic power is held by a national elite of European heritage and, although making up only 3.2 per cent of the population, whites in Barbados occupy a position of privilege and power – a historical legacy of the Island's colonial past (Ramsaran,

2004). Although I had studied, lived and worked in Barbados for over 30 years I was conscious of how my presence as a white researcher may be perceived within the research space. To address this dilemma, I reflexively scrutinized how issues of race, power and privilege may be affecting my interactions with the parents and impacting the study. Proudfoot (2015) states that it is important to adopt a reflexive approach throughout the research process to evaluate issues of positionality and identity, and I suggest that awareness of the historical context and an understanding of the cultural nuances of the field of study are also vital to informed, ethical practice.

Case example

Perceptions of children with autism in Armenia
Fiona Hallett

Introduction

This research was underpinned by the recognition that lay perceptions of people with autism are an under-researched area (Huws and Jones, 2010) with conceptualizations being influenced by cultural context (Perepa, 2014). In response, the study utilized social comparison theory (Huws and Jones, 2015; Locke, 2014) as a lens with which to analyse views of disability in Armenia, a national context that is currently under-represented in the literature. In addition, the research aimed to address broader concerns expressed by the United Nations Educational, Scientific and Cultural Organization (UNESCO, 2015: 3) that, [Armenian] 'Societies' misperception of different forms and types of disability and the limited capacity of social actors to accommodate special needs often place these people on the margin'.

Research goal

The primary objective of this research was to apply and develop existing theory in a unique national context and across a broader respondent group than in previous studies.

Methodology and method

When conducting research across different cultural groups, it is necessary to utilize culturally and linguistically appropriate instruments to ensure that results and conclusions are not compromised by ineffective methodological choices. In order to capture the lived experiences of the three respondent groups in this study – individuals with Special Educational Needs and/or Disabilities (SEN/D), parents of individuals with SEN/D and members of the public – a number of research techniques were piloted including: questionnaires, individual interviews and focus group interviews. In each case, a lack of awareness about different types of disability rendered the technique ineffective. In order to overcome this challenge, a vignette was produced to represent a young person who exhibited some of the characteristics associated with Asperger's syndrome.

Vignettes have a long history in qualitative and quantitative research on social judgements (Seguin and Ambrosio, 2002) and, when designed in collaboration with local communities, can elicit the views of 'hard-to-reach' sectors of society. Vignettes should also provide enough contextual information for respondents to clearly understand the situation being portrayed, yet be ambiguous enough to ensure that multiple solutions exist (Seguin and Ambrosio, 2002; Wason, Polonsky and Hyman, 2002). Thus, in order to minimize translational disturbance, the research participants in this study were presented with a vignette that portrayed a school-aged individual with Asperger's syndrome. Given concerns about attitudes towards persons with disability in Armenia, as 'sick defective people' (Save the Children International, 2012), we felt that a description of autism that included more complex difficulties would negatively prejudice responses.

Project outcomes

This study highlighted a complex web of discourses that require a more nuanced understanding of social comparison theory than is often reported. Individuals with SEN/D, and their parents, drew upon aspirational and normalization discourses in order to face the pressures of society; normalization was viewed as a crucial aspect of functioning and both groups sought to find connections with behavioural norms. Thus, normalization and aspirational discourses were framed as a defence of upward social comparisons (e.g. the gifted and talented individual is identified, or presented, as an admirable characteristic).

Ethical dilemmas

It has been argued that the views articulated by members of the public in Armenia demonstrate worrying levels of prejudice and rejection (UNICEF in 2012), whereby marginalized groups live an uncertain life in a society that struggles to recognize them as equal members. Karapetyan et al. (2011) identified unequal economic opportunities, and differences in regional development, as the next important challenge in the implementation of inclusive social policies for people living in small towns and villages in Armenia, arguing that unemployed youth, women and people with disabilities are much more vulnerable if they do not live in Yerevan (the capital city).

In response, studies of this nature enable a more comprehensive understanding of the utility and wider applicability of models of social comparison. Secondly, the reported attitudes and perceptions of the three respondent groups who engaged with this research offer a unique insight into perceptions of Asperger's syndrome across an under-researched post-Soviet national context. Finally, research of this nature has the potential to inform debates around the development of culturally sensitive research methodologies.

Approaches, strategies, challenges and responses, and their implications for social justice

Each of the examples of socially just research in this chapter has drawn on different theoretical and methodological perspectives, reflecting the way in which concerns about social justice extend beyond particular paradigms. It is not possible to say with authority that a particular method, methodology or theoretical framework is more or less likely to be successful in facilitating research which is socially just. This socially just research is highly contextualized, demands a situated approach and must be continually reflexive and considerate of other perspectives. We can, however, draw 'broad-brush' lessons from the examples in this and other chapters, always with the proviso that any method or approach can become inequitable and unjust if used in a way which is exploitative or fails to respect the individual and their communities (e.g. see Ollis et al., 2017).

In research which is concerned with social justice, the process of data collection provides researchers with a unique opportunity to engage with global communities in intimate and meaningful ways. However, it is possible that ethical researchers who otherwise consider themselves to be multiculturally experienced can build barriers shaped by unintentional injustice (Denzin and Lincoln, 2005; Duckworth and Ade-Ojo, 2016). Unintentional injustices are often subtle and prevent the data collection process – or indeed other aspects of the research process – from being one that has the integrity of reflecting the communities and individuals who participate in the research. Such injustices can, in particular, find their way into the discourses arising from and within research. Marginalized children, young people and adults globally are subject to discourses of blame and deficit: issues of power and unintentional injustice can lead to those discourses being rehearsed in research, particularly during dissemination, thus reifying historical oppressions. This illustrates the importance of thoughtful use of language: it also follows that socially just practice is an essential component of valuing and respecting the other.

The issue of having a different cultural positioning and the implications of that for research are significant. Recently, scholars such as Ladson-Billings and Donnor (2005) have advocated Activist forms of Critical Race Theory (CRT), while others have moved beyond this to advocate an endarkened feminist epistemology which 'articulates how reality is known when based in the historical roots of global Black feminist thought' (Dillard and Okpalaoka, 2013: 308). These theoretical and activist approaches are particularly concerned with addressing the multiple oppressions facing Black women, who are positioned in the context of a white, as well as a male, hegemony. Like other forms of critical theory associated with social justice, CRT and notions of an endarkened feminist epistemology raise multiple issues, not least that of representation. In what Lincoln and Denzin (2002: 1049) refer to as a 'crisis of representation and legitimation' researchers are increasingly struggling to find ways of locating themselves and the other in reflexive texts, which consider the authority the researcher has for the text. These issues are evident in Julie Sealy's work as she wrestles with being a privileged white woman – albeit one who has lived and worked in the community she is researching for 30 years.

The related issue of power is also a recurring theme in each of the case studies, not only from a methodological and ethical perspective in which the researcher is located in a more powerful position than the researched but also in terms of the relations of power that restrict people's lives, as discussed by Fergal Finnegan in relation to working-class university students and by Mary McAteer in relation to the South African communities she was involved with. Power relations are central to all social research and, whether we are conducting research on a global or a local basis, these are issues which are pertinent to all of us who are concerned with social justice and equity. Issues of power can be subtle. Griffiths (1998: 57) argues that since knowledge depends on human interpretation and values, research methods need to take account of the unequal power of different social groups, pointing out that meanings and interpretations are developed in social groups which are themselves structured by sociopolitical power relations. Power relations are also influenced and mediated by research relationships and by the possibility of 'unintentional injustices' which can be enacted at any point in the research process. For example, Fine (1992) points to the possibility of the misuse of participants' voices, perhaps by making assumptions that voices are free of power relations or failing to acknowledge the researchers' own position in relation to the voices. Even where unintentional misuse does not occur, how to make 'voices heard without exploiting or distorting those voices [remains a] vexatious question' (Olesen, 2000: 231).

The case studies in this chapter draw largely on two strategies in response to these difficulties, these being collaboration or participation, and reflexivity. Participation and collaboration have long been seen as possible responses to issues of power in research concerned with social justice and equity (see Chapter 8). It is worth noting that collaborations for local and global change go beyond the academy. They also include community stakeholders such as NGOs. One project which brought stakeholders together was the BAICE (British Association for International and Comparative Education)-funded *Building Capacity and Networks Project* organized by the UK Literacy Working Group and the Literacy and Development Group at the University of East Anglia (2016). The project brought together literacy policymakers, researchers and practitioners to consider issues around developing adults' literacy learning, and women's literacy learning in particular. The project acknowledged that many NGOs and international NGOs are involved in initiatives, programmes and projects that embrace or include women and men's literacy learning in diverse ways and that are informed by their extensive work in the field, which positions them as trusted intermediaries.

However, whilst as Nixon et al. (2003: 94) acknowledge, 'collaboration is . . . ethically desirable', it is also worth noting that collaboration in itself does not address issues of social justice, human value or power relations, despite consideration of these issues being of fundamental importance: does a study pay lip service to the notions of dialogue, equality and collaboration or does it try to find a means to negotiate the issues arising from the research with the participants in the context of an equal relationship? Does it acknowledge any difficulties arising from this? Clearly, where researchers are concerned with social justice, their response will be one of reflexivity and negotiation.

Pragmatically, irrespective of the approach taken to reflexivity, the *degree* of reflexivity and relative openness to the data can, perhaps, only be judged by the reader, as there are obvious difficulties in objectively assessing the extent of one's own reflexivity and readiness to have one's perspectives challenged. Essentially, reflexivity leads us to consider what is moral, as well as confronting our own prejudices and assumptions. In this respect, Sikes and Goodson (2003: 48) advocate the use of interior reflexivity, arguing that this is a better 'anchor for moral practice' than any external guidelines. All discussions around reflexivity emphasize the importance of the researcher being introspective, taking responsibility for their own practices through articulating their positionality and acknowledging their understanding and values (e.g. Griffiths, 1998; Wellington, 2015). One of Griffiths's own responses to the challenge of reflexivity appears in her 2003 book where she addresses issues of power by inviting others to 'answer back' at the end of each chapter.

Finally, each of the examples contributed to this chapter uses a form of storytelling to a greater or lesser degree. The use of storytelling, narratives and biographical research enables researchers to explore the lived world and to reveal how people experience their everyday life (for a practical example, see Johnson et al. 2010).

They facilitate researchers to study how experience is given meaning by the individual and embrace a variety of methods, such as the exploration of life stories, the development of life histories and case studies and oral histories. As such, they are central concepts in interpretative social research. Griffiths (2003: 86) argues that good storytelling is an art, which is dependent not only on the teller but also on the context and the listener, and it is essential to get all these right if the researcher is to avoid ventriloquizing and/or finding listeners whose intention is to exploit or silence the story. Despite this caution, she goes on to say that even imperfect stories can be powerful in how and what they communicate.

Conclusion

Considering research on a global scale brings into sharp focus the extent of in/equalities and divides across the world and highlights the importance of research which aims to promote equity, address in/qualities and facilitate 'little voices' (Griffiths, 2003: 81) to be heard and empowered. Inequality and its impact is a critical economic, social and political concern. Educational researchers are uniquely positioned to bringing together global research communities to co-develop research agendas around some of the most important issues in the twenty-first century. This means collaborating across disciplines and with stakeholders to address the multiple consequences of inequality and how they affect different groups of people and communities. We conclude this chapter with a quote from bell hooks, which eloquently symbolizes the possibilities that can arise from research which is conducted within an ethic of social justice.

Moving from silence into speech is for the oppressed, the colonized, the exploited, and those who stand and struggle side by side a gesture that heals, that makes life and new growth possible. It is that act of speech of 'talking back', that is no mere gesture of empty words, that is the expression of our movement from object to subject – the liberated voice.

(hooks, 1989: 9)

Further reading

Chilisa, B. (2011), *Indigenous Research Methodologies*, London: SAGE.

Freire, P. (1990), 'Conscientizing as a way of liberating', in A. T. Hennelly (ed.), *Liberation Theology: A Documentary History*, pp. 5–13, Maryknoll: NY: Orbis Books.

Freire, P. (2005), *30th Anniversary Edition, Pedagogy of the Oppressed*, New York: Continuum.

Heller, M. (2011), *Paths to Post-nationalism*, Oxford: Oxford University Press.

Piketty, T. (2014), *Capital in the Twenty-First Century* (first published in French in 2013), Cambridge, MA: Harvard University Press.

Smith, L. (1999), *Decolonizing Methodologies: Research and Indigenous Peoples*, New York: Zed Books.

Wood, L., and McAteer, M. (2017), 'Levelling the playing fields in PAR: The intricacies of power, privilege and participation in a university-community-school artnership', *Adult Education Quarterly*, 67(4): 251–65.

Yasukawa, K., and Black, S. (eds), *Beyond Economic Interests: Critical Perspectives in Adult Literacy & Numeracy in a Globalised World (International Issues in Adult Education, Volume 18)*, Netherlands: Sense Publishers.

PART THREE

Research methods for equity and social justice

CHAPTER EIGHT

Collaborative and participatory methods for social justice

Introduction

The words collaborative and participatory have slightly different meanings, and participatory research is perhaps better understood and generally taken to mean research in communities which emphasizes the participation of, and action by, members of that community. It has its origins in the work of Paulo Freire in developing communities and in action research, although, as Kemmis and McTaggart (2000: 567) note, they originally used the term *collaborative* action research in several different fields 'to emphasise the interdependence of the activities of university academics and educators in particular' but now refer to participatory action research 'in recognition of practical and theoretical convergences between our work and the activities of people engaged in "participatory research" in several different fields'. Education is significant in the 'several different fields' as participatory approaches are extensively utilized by researchers concerned with issues of social justice and/ or of power relations, something which is reflected in Kay Heslop's case example later in this chapter.

Collaborative research, however, is more difficult to define. It has multiple meanings in different contexts which lack consistency; added complexity arises from the different levels at which collaboration occurs, including groups, individuals, departments, institutions, sectors, disciplines and countries and the extent to which the collaboration is formal or informal (Smith and Katz, 2000: 4). Hatch (2002: 32), however, distinguishes it from action research on the basis that the principal aims of collaborative research are the generation of knowledge, rather than action. Two of the case examples used in this chapter refer to collaborative research. In each case it is self-defined, with one researcher, Joanne Clifford-Swan, collaborating with a school and university partnership and a second, Francesca Bernardi, collaborating with other teachers in her practitioner research in a special school. These examples reflect pragmatic, as well as ethical and methodological, reasons for undertaking collaborative research. Teaching is collaborative by its very nature, whether between a small number of individual teachers working to develop curriculum in a single school or between groups and partnerships of institutions working together for their mutual benefit. However, what the case examples in this chapter have in common is that all are concerned in some way with emancipatory and critical forms of pedagogy such as those espoused by Freire (1970/1996) as a means of working towards and enacting social justice.

The philosophy and values arising from Freire's work – around praxis which is values based and linked with social action (and see Habermas, 1974: 113) – have had a significant influence on academics and education internationally as have his rejection of the 'banking' model of education and his proposals for more critical, democratic forms of pedagogy (Freire, 1970/1996). Participatory paradigms, have, as Kemmis and McTaggart argue, converged. Erickson (2013), however, argues that education led the way in many of the paradigm shifts which have taken place in qualitative research over the past two decades. In terms of collaboration, he points out that from the earliest qualitative inquiry in education, pupils, teachers and parents were able to read what had been said about them and respond to this using the 'researcher's own terms'. Further, he suggests that 'The "gaze" of educational researchers – its potential for distorted perception and its status as an exercise of power over those observed – had been identified as problematic in qualitative educational inquiry before critics such as Clifford and Marcus (1986) had published on these matters' (2013: 112). Thus, notions of participation and collaboration have been significant in educational research for generations (e.g. see Stenhouse, 1975), and these have related both to sociological and ethnographic work on the hidden curriculum and subject-orientated work on the manifest curriculum. For this reason it is possible to observe significant 'overlap' between studies which might variously be described as ethnographic, insider or participatory research.

Irrespective of paradigm, however, and for the reasons articulated above by Erickson, much educational research tends to be participatory. It may also be argued that much research conducted within an ethic of social justice is participatory as this provides a means of situating the research socially and culturally within the researched population and addressing some of the issues of power relations which are so significant in research for social justice. Methodologically, therefore, providing the research design and implementation is rigorous, and this approach can offer a meaningful, if partial, picture of the group and/or phenomenon. Also in relation to social justice, and as we have alluded to elsewhere in this book, most educational research is concerned with (in schools) improvements and developments for children and young people who have unequal and inequitable positioning in education and (in adult and informal education) marginalized groups and communities.

Thus, we view participatory and collaborative approaches to research as a framework that can transform any research method into a socially just endeavour, particularly where the research is concerned with developments and/or social change in groups and communities who experience educational disadvantage. It is a form of research which is values based (Atkins and Wallace, 2012), emphasizing the moral imperative for social change. Within this context, we recognize ourselves as culturally situated and have reflected deeply on the attitudes and biases related to our own cultural positioning as well as others. With this in mind we understand the importance of framing research in ways that legitimize differing cultural knowledge, driven by an awareness that researchers should understand the importance of framing social justice research with the needs and desires of, and benefits to, the groups and communities being studied.

Collaboration and participation for social justice

The ideologies, attitudes, biases and world views of researchers infuse their work, and the approaches chosen have the potential to reproduce existing social inequities or to drive social and educational change for social justice. Across discipline areas and in many settings research and knowledge generation is a hierarchal concern, based on unequal power relationships, for example, between researcher and participant. However, the inequity may also be between researchers: in a large, funded project, for example, more senior researchers often exercise the power, perhaps by leading on the research questions, shaping the research design, taking precedence in the publication process and taking credit for research. In contrast, the more junior researchers who may have carried out data collection, analysis and done much of the writing remain on the sidelines, and their contribution receives minimal acknowledgement. This state of affairs is often an unquestioned, 'taken-for-granted' working in academia, but it is demonstrative of un/equal power relations and of broader societal and educational inequities and hierarchies which reflect, rather than challenge, dominant injustices in society. As such, the *conduct* of research *managed* within the context of a traditional hierarchy, is, we would argue, contrary to the ethic of social justice, irrespective of the outcome and purpose of such a study. Issues such as this can be addressed through utilizing more collaborative (and collegial) approaches to the conduct of research projects, such as the case examples utilized throughout this book.

Collaborative and participative approaches mean that all those involved in a particular project – community members, researchers, practitioners and activists – are engaged in democratic research communities, recognizing, as Griffiths (1998: 12/13) in the second of her three principles for social justice argues that 'each individual is valuable and [should be] acknowledged as such by wider society'. This has particular implications for relationships within the project, which are predicated on notions of equity and equality. This implies building empowered and empowering relationships based on trust, negotiating roles and boundaries, learning from others and striving to contribute to the field of study. Much collaborative research is based on forms of co-inquiry, which rejects traditional research approaches that create clear distinctions between the researcher and the researched and where research is carried out *on* the researched. The co-inquiry approach includes researching *with* people throughout the research stages and attempting to achieve equality between participants in relation to their contribution to the research focus, design, methods and analysis of results in forms of 'joint theorizing and action' as part of different forms of collaborative relationship which can offer a means for developing empowerment, voice and ultimately social justice (Griffiths, 1998: 114/115). We have both drawn on these methods in our own attempts to undertake research which is socially just (e.g. see Atkins, 2009, 2013a; Duckworth, 2013; Duckworth and Smith, 2018a), and we both have found that building collaborative research takes time and commitment. Much of this is associated with developing effective relationships with co-researchers. This is underpinned by critical reflection, critical dialogue and other activities geared towards building a community, as well as effective communication is accessible to and understood by people from different fields, whether these be other disciplines, cultures, work environments or communities, and which places explicit value on the different perspectives offered. In relation to this, Reason (1994: 324) draws on a participative world view whereby he positions human beings as engaged in 'co-creating their reality through participation'. Here we can see that relationship is key to the generation of reality and, importantly, that a methodology which separates the researcher from the researched denies that relationship. This may be viewed as what Reason and Heron (1995) pose as a question of power and politics in the research setting. As such it seeks to establish partnerships which may include community groups and outside researchers throughout the research journey, in relation to, for example, sharing power, resources, credit, data ownership, results and dissemination. This also addresses what the priorities and aims of the research are. In socially just collaboration the research may have social justice outcomes which include transformative impact on community life and aims towards community agency, self-determination and empowerment. Therefore, it can be a lever for anti-oppressive research methodologies. For example, Hines (2012) draws on anti-oppressive social work practice and its work with oppressed populations to inform work which specifically seeks to probe how the approach can be applied to lesbians as an oppressed group who are dealing with issues of heterosexism, homophobia and internalized heterosexism. This includes working in 'coalition with other agencies in each state to ensure that all lesbian parents and their children are afforded the legal protections that all families have and need' (Hines, 2012: 34). A catalyst for this can be collaborative participatory research projects that engage community members and community-based organizations that serve lesbians (Harper et al., 2007, cited in Hines, 2012).

There are, however, potential barriers to co-enquiry research. It is time-consuming and can be personally demanding. The investment in time and commitment, however, can be repaid with interest in terms of the ways in which people from researched populations and other professionals engage with research and the resulting outcomes in terms of the richness of data and the longer term impact. This has been the experience of Kay Heslop, whose participative doctoral study on intergenerational activity within the urban Forest School environment has resulted in not only valuable research outcomes but also changes in practice and personal development for those engaged. Kay's project – in which she was, to some extent, an insider and in which she used ethnographic methods – also reflects the difficulties in framing any individual study within a single paradigm or approach.

Case example

Intergenerational engagement: A participatory action research study investigating the inclusion of older adults in the lives of young children
Kay Heslop

Context

Having worked formerly as an Early Years practitioner, and more recently as a University lecturer specializing in Early Years, I am acutely aware of the dedication of Early Years practitioners and the importance of the work they undertake. This often goes unrecognized. Commencing my doctorate in Education presented an opportunity to work alongside such practitioners, as co-researchers, to plan for, implement and analyse a participatory action research project, which would offer mutual benefit to those involved. The project involved me working alongside Early Years practitioners, older adult volunteers and young children within a forest school environment. Despite me not belonging to the Early Years setting, some practitioners knew me professionally. All individuals involved were aware of my identity and I had a good understanding of the ethos of the group.

Goal

This negotiated research project aimed to investigate the importance of the inclusion of older adults in the lives of young children. The research explored interactions and knowledge exchange between the participants and aimed to determine the benefits of intergenerational involvement.

Methods

Forest School activity (Knight, 2011) was a regular experience within the urban day nursery in a disadvantaged urban area in the north-east of England which was the site for my study, supported by trained and enthusiastic practitioners. These practitioners, through reflective practice, had recognized the scope for further development of their practice. Once trust was established and access was gained to the setting, the implementation of Research Circles (Persson, 2009) enabled open discussion, planning for and critically reflecting upon this research project. These Research Circles ran prior to, alongside and in the months after the research.

Throughout the research we all (me as lead researcher, co-researcher practitioners and older adult volunteers) kept field notes. While I wrote up my notes as observations, the recordings from the older adults informed their interview responses. Practitioners (co-researchers) shared their thoughts in recorded Research Circles, along with the responses from the children, which were collected at nursery, during play or in floorbooks (Anthamatten et al., 2012) at reflection time. Floorbooks were initially introduced to 'encourage oracy in the early years' (Warden, 2015) by introducing a child-centred approach which set out to motivate and engage children and which allowed children to think in an unpressured way. Now known as 'Talking and Thinking Floorbooks', they have been used to support child-initiated planning and to 'develop higher order thinking skills' (Warden, 2015: 1). The co-researchers and I adapted them for use as a method in this project. They were familiar to the children and offered opportunities to understand the children's experience of the project from their own perspective.

The development of a Floorbook allowed the children and their key adult to work together in collaborative learning, in this case about the forest school experiences. The adults would usually sit in a circle around the Floorbook; children sometimes drew, adults sometimes scribed for the children and photographs were included. Warden (2015) describes how features of a talking and thinking Floorbook included children's ideas and thoughts, as unedited genuine responses. The Floorbooks were available at all times, so children had ownership of them, and they were revisited and added to over time. The Floorbooks were also an integral part of planning, as well as being used for reflection upon activities and documenting achievement.

The Floorbook approach links well to the Reggio Emilia philosophy (Barr and Truelove, 2015: 45). Within Reggio Emilia settings, the curriculum is flexible and emerges from children's ideas, thoughts and interests. This inspires each child to gain a passion for learning. Early Years Practitioner and co-researcher Diane Gregory writes (about Floorbooks), 'children have the opportunity to see their theories, plans and strategies put into words. It brings importance to the child in that they have been listened to and that their ideas are valued. It builds their self-esteem as well as confidence and skills for life.' Diane goes on to explain, 'working with Floorbooks allowed the opportunity for groups of children to work alongside their practitioner as their co-researcher, and peers, to enquire, reflect and problem solve. The practitioner's deep knowledge of each child allows for differentiation of approach. For example, the less vocal child could produce a photo as their contribution and be presented in words by the practitioner's scribing. Alternatively the whole group could create a mini story based upon their experiences and/or produce artwork.' The Floorbook resulted in strong evidential documentation of children's learning and abilities, demonstrating their competence in all areas of learning (see outcomes, below) and of some of the wider benefits of the project.

Outcomes

Currently removed from practical Early Years activity, in this real-life situation I was invited into the world of others, where food and experiences were shared, trust was developed and mutual benefit was determined. Practitioners enthused about having extra support for the recording of observations, they reflected upon the personal learning gained from the older adults and they valued the time allocated to discuss research and practice. Children developed relationships very quickly. They were observed seeking out the older volunteers to share learning experiences, to engage them in play and to learn new skills. Finally, the older adults' initial anxieties, about patience and physical restrictions, just evaporated as they immersed themselves in the woodland activity, with one volunteer commenting, 'It was much more brilliant than I expected it to be.' They had initially volunteered to help the children, yet had learned new skills, realized a new energy and felt satisfaction at their achievements. Since the completion of this research project, and on recognizing the benefits, the nursery setting has continued the intergenerational theme with an allotment project.

Ethical and methodological dilemmas

Although initial access to the nursery setting was agreed in principle, consideration had to be given to the potential disruption to usual practice and safeguarding of children due to volunteers attending. The manager required reassurance that benefits were mutual, not just for the researcher, and that ethical procedures were robust. The researchers needed to ensure that the volunteers were aware of the physical demands of the research and were safe to work with children.

Young children, by their nature, are inquisitive. They interact with others and make sense of the world around them. As the children were already familiar with the environment and practitioners, it was clear that having new older volunteers and a researcher in their midst would invite questions and perhaps alter play, especially as the fieldwork spanned six weeks. It was therefore ethical and respectful to introduce the children to the volunteers prior to their attendance, to explain to the children why they were there and to ensure that they were comfortable.

Developing and sustaining relationships with all involved was essential from the start, as power dynamics between various practitioners, manager, children, volunteers and university researcher could have been problematic. During early Research Circles, practitioners discussed their strengths and preferences and so, when tasks were identified, roles were chosen. Practitioners remained responsible for the children while I was the main contact for the older adults. This pre-preparation was time-consuming but essential. Trust continued to build and reflections were open and honest. By the third forest school session, the reduction in anxiety was highly apparent, with friendships blooming and trust secure.

The participatory action research process – observing, talking, drawing on the children's floorbooks and then critically reflecting in Research Circles, then observing and talking again – has been fundamental to the richness of the data Kay has collected, although that has presented challenges in terms of collating and interpreting the data (see Figures 8.1 and 8.2 as examples).

The importance of relationship building is highlighted in Kay's account, as are the significance of power relations. While it is evident that Kay's research was participatory and collaborative, the fact that she was undertaking a doctoral study made it imperative that she remained clearly identified as lead researcher. Together with her positioning as a university lecturer (who had taught some of her co-researchers), this had significant implications for power relations within the study. In this context, however, other, more subtle issues of power come into play: the role of the nursery manager in granting access, for example, and the position of the co-researchers as experts in their own setting. Following Griffiths (1998: 57), Kay has utilized research methods which not only take account of the unequal power of different social groups but also acknowledge that the different adults involved could be argued to have a strong intrinsic motivation for participating in the study (Johnston, 2000). In addition, and from a participatory perspective, the design, data gathering and interpretation of the data has been produced with the co-researchers (see Griffiths, 1998: 35/43; Stake,

FIGURE 8.1 *Collating the data.*

FIGURE 8.2 *Ready for interpretation.*

2000: 450). In terms of social change, the nursery now involves older people with its allotment project. The health and social benefits of exposing older people to young children have been advertised on popular media as well as in research literature (e.g. Hedd-Jones, 2017; Skropeta et al., 2014; Teater, 2016), but projects such as these have significant implications in terms of learning and access to capitals in a group of young children who are socially situated in a disadvantaged, urban area.

This project also illustrates the different forms of collaborative relationship which can exist in a research project. Joanne Clifford-Swan's collaborative research was originally driven by the need to develop a more equitable relationship between a university Education department and the local primary schools it needed to host trainee teachers. This developed into a long-term primary literacy project which is subject to ongoing, collaborative, review and evaluation and which has significant outcomes in terms of social justice for the children involved. In this case example, Joanne emphasizes the values-driven approach to the development and implementation of the project.

Case example

Primary literacy project
Joanne Clifford-Swan

The primary literacy project was born out of both a renewed vision for initial teacher education at Northumbria University, England, as well as experience to find a solution to the ongoing challenge of finding schools to host students on placement. Many schools in the partnership remained fully committed to an ongoing programme of student placements and felt them to be integral to the school's own development. However, by 2013 there was a shared sense that the partnership between schools and university was not an equal one, with some schools increasingly reluctant to commit to student placements, as well as some cohorts clearly perceived by schools to be more problematic than others. The 'middle child syndrome' seemed to have crept in, with the year 2 primary undergraduates emerging as the cohort who were most likely to be overlooked by schools (the last to be picked for the Rounders team, and sometimes even left on the sidelines). It was clear that this largely unloved cohort, neither fresh faced and malleable nor experienced and almost flying, were at times being compromised in a highly competitive placements market. With schools under increasing levels of external accountability and the stakes becoming ever higher, who would blame a school for taking less of a risk with a final placement student coming to the end of his or her training than someone needing much more of a leap of faith?

It was against this background that I brought my own core values to play. Having spent all of my career in state education, I had joined the university's initial teacher education team two years previously and was struck by the missed opportunities there were in terms of developing genuine partnerships of mutual benefit with schools in the region. The placement model was very much based on schools doing us a favour, a model which had managed itself successfully enough in simpler times. But life in school was no longer simple. The increase in external scrutiny over the previous 10 years and the relentlessness of policy shifts had made schools much less risk averse. And the days of 'having a student', meaning putting your feet up in the staff room for six weeks, were now a distant, memory. Having a student meant more work for the teacher, not less, and the benefits were not always clear to a teacher with already excessive demands on his/her time.

However, as a university, what we had at our disposal was a huge resource in the form of large numbers of trainee teachers. It became clear that the very thing that was our problem was also our solution. Instead of thinking of these students as a burden, requiring schools to do more, I felt that we needed to rebrand our students as an asset to a school, individuals who could make a difference to the people who mattered the most across the education system – the pupils. While our students continued to need to be guided, mentored and supported to develop the skills of an effective class teacher, they were in a unique position to give something back and impact on the progress of identified pupils.

The Primary National Strategies in England (1997–2011) had seen a change in approach to English and maths teaching. The Strategies addressed the pedagogy and content of whole class, mixed ability teaching as well as introduced the concept of additional layers, or waves of targeted intervention to specifically identified pupils, who would receive more input than their peers to accelerate their progress over a limited time period. Programmes such as Springboard in maths, Early Literacy Support (ELS), Additional Literacy Support (ALS), Every Child a Reader (ECAR) and one-to-one tuition were all part of the suite of layered support designed to be delivered as well as, not instead of, the quality first teaching that all pupils were expected to receive. The interventions were largely designed to be delivered by qualified teaching assistants (TAs), though some specialized interventions, such as one-to-one tuition and reading recovery, were delivered by qualified teachers, the latter requiring training by teachers who had undertaken specialized masters-level study as part of a national initiative.

Alongside this, research was showing the impact that poor attainment in literacy, and in particular reading, could have on pupils' overall educational opportunities and ultimately life chances (Clark and Dugdale, 2008; Warren, 2015). Literacy is a particular problem in the north-east, an area which shares with London the unfortunate distinction of having the lowest literacy levels in the UK (DBIS, 2012: 65). These combined contexts provided us with the opportunity to contribute to the wider social justice agenda of improving access to education through improving the attainment of pupils within partnership schools. A reading intervention was chosen by the university primary education team, in consultation with a small number of partner schools, as being the key to having a wider impact on pupil progress, potential engagement and ultimately life chances. However, subsequent to the end of National Strategies, a huge number of interventions had come onto the market, many requiring the acquisition of expensive resources and many also being labour intensive. A reading intervention called 'Boosting Reading at Primary' (BR@P), though a commercial product like many others, was selected by the primary literacy team as it addressed many of the core principles about the teaching of reading that research suggested made a difference to the successful development of effective reading strategies, namely that 'reading is a message getting, problem solving activity' (Clay, 1991).

Building on these principles, BR@P also based its programme on reading materials already in school, rather than prescribed texts; therefore, it required investment in almost no specialist resources, a critical issue for schools facing ongoing government restrictions on spending. Instead, the programme focused on developing the expertise of the person undertaking the training via a two-day intensive programme. This equipped participants with an understanding of the principles behind reading for meaning, as well as the practical skills required to identify pupil reading strategies and address and improve these during a series of twenty one-to-one sessions spread over the course of half a term. Once accredited training of the year 2 undergraduates had taken place, they were deployed into schools to deliver the intervention to up to four identified primary pupils over a ten-week period.

In the first year of delivery, challenges arose over the accurate identification of pupils who would most benefit from the intervention and the skills of the students to accurately measure progress. In the second year, both of these were addressed, resulting in a more accurate data set which suggested measurable and accelerated progress of the identified pupils. When the programme commenced, only a handful of partnership schools were familiar with BR@P as an effective reading intervention. By 2017, most schools had built this Autumn Term reading intervention, delivered by students, into their cycle of school improvement. Annually more than 500 pupils now undertake the intervention delivered by the undergraduate students. We have continued to work with students and partnership schools to systematically evaluate and develop the project as it has progressed. Our findings suggest that the perception of these students by schools has changed significantly. These students have, in some small way, become agents of change providing expertise in a very specific discipline and raising the profile of reading skills acquisition across schools, at a time when there has been a significant focus on systematic synthetic phonics. Our research also indicates that the project has had an impact on students' own understanding of how children learn to read. Looking to the future, we are currently planning a more comprehensive longitudinal study in order to establish the extent to which the intervention has a sustained impact on individual pupils, students and the schools in which they are placed.

Joanne's decision to develop the primary literacy project was initially driven by the imperative to find training placements for her students. However, her approach to this was very much values based and predicated on meeting other needs and responsibilities – concerns not only about literacy in the region and about the wider responsibilities of the institution as a leader in learning but also about building meaningful collaborative partnerships with local schools which were mutually beneficial. In terms of collaboration, the willingness of schools to host the students and participate in ongoing evaluation of the project are both indicative of more collaborative and collegial relationships, despite the historical legacy of a relationship in which the university was very much the senior partner, with all that entailed in terms of power relationships. The intervention itself led trainees to have a greater awareness of the conditions and processes necessary for children to learn to read, a form of 'consciousness-raising' (Freire, 1970/1996) and praxis. The praxis was linked with social action (see Habermas, 1974: 113) and change, now formalized in the context of school improvement plans, with the students acting as agents of change. In terms of social justice, however, literacy has particular importance, since it offers access to the wider curriculum, meaning that the child who is supported to acquire literacy at an early stage is less likely to experience negative outcomes in the context of 'an education system that uses assessment to rank and segregate people for unequal opportunities' (Ecclestone, 2004: 133). It is also foundational to facilitating individuals to become citizens who are able to engage in the dialogical process which Griffiths (2003) argues is essential within a society which claims to be working towards a state of social justice.

Joanne's project surrounds an intervention for children with literacy difficulties, a group with the potential to become excluded and marginalized if those difficulties are not addressed. Similarly, Kay's research is focused on, in her case, a group of children and elders from a traditionally socially and educationally disadvantaged area. Research (e.g. Atkins, 2016a; Avis, 2016; Avis and Atkins, 2017; Bourdieu and Passeron, 1990; Duckworth, 2013; Reay, 2012) demonstrates that children born into disadvantage are subject to forms of educational, labour and social reproduction which profoundly impact on their life chances. Disadvantage is, however, multifaceted and more problematic where intersectional issues come into play. These issues are of particular concern where they relate to children and young people with silenced voices – those with learning disabilities and difficulties who are unable to speak for themselves. Francesca Bernardi is an art teacher in a Special Educational Needs (SEN) school whose collaborative research was undertaken as an insider and as a practitioner. She has been influenced by research by Mottron et al. (2013), which suggests that individuals with Autism Spectrum Disorder (ASD) have exceptional visual ability. Mottron et al.'s study includes an evaluation of the impact of using art practice in engaging pupils with autism in a variety of learning contexts in the SEN school, and this became the inspiration for Francesca's research and practice. Through practical art experiences and observations she gathered information from her school, working collaboratively with other teachers and support staff, to measure the effects on participation in learning when art materials and resources are used to promote engagement for pupils with ASD in a segregated SEN school. The school comprises primary and secondary classes in which pupils are grouped according to social and educational ability and, where possible, age and Key Stage.

Case example

An arts-informed pedagogic model: Supporting self-expression of individuals with autism
Francesca Bernardi

During the preliminary period of the case study, which was part of my master's thesis, I developed an arts-informed pedagogic model extending art activities to literacy and numeracy tasks for my own learner group: a Key Stage 3 class of five pupils with minimal verbal or signing skills (four individuals with a diagnosis of ASD, one with a diagnosis of foetal alcohol syndrome with features of ASD). I reflected on the benefits and the limitations of this process through observations and my own participation in pupil-led creative processes. Having provided detailed feedback from my observations to the school's leadership team and to parents, I was given the responsibility to develop and deliver the art curriculum across the secondary department: a good opportunity to focus on art, creativity in autism and person-centred learning; working with colleagues to directly evaluate the impact of art practice on learners and practitioners. The secondary department comprised small groups of pupils, and each individual had a diagnosis of ASD.

I conducted daily observations in the secondary classes, initially in art lessons, then searched for evidence of use of creative materials beyond the art lessons to study the relationship between the deployment of basic art materials and the engagement of the learning potential of visual learners such as individuals with ASD. My findings included reflections on how art practice is affected by the availability of art materials and the confidence of practitioners in using such materials in the special school. The project intrinsically lent itself to observe the tendency of practitioners (teachers and TAs) to use art materials in a variety of learning contexts with their pupils, beyond dedicated art lessons.

The scope of the research was to experience and evaluate *how* art practice facilitates learning for pupils with autism, driven by the (evolving) scientific research on the visual capacity of individuals with ASD (Mottron et al., 2013). The original question generated subsequent lines of enquiry, relating to the role of the teacher (or practitioner) and the constraints and demands of the context, in this case, the special school. My interest in the subject originated from my prior experiences in special education and art education for pupils with autism, as well as from my own specialist education in the Arts and the encouragement of creative freedom for social justice in education. Hoping such an affirmation is not considered a limiting feature of the study, but merely its 'philosophical assumption' (Creswell and Plano Clark, 2011: 415), I argue, in fact, that while aware of the potential that art has for pupils with autism, the evidence produced through this research must extend beyond the evaluation of teaching art in the context of autism education. The imperative to validate the role of art in improving learning experiences in autism education, across the curriculum, has always been one of the most significant considerations throughout my professional development and represents the axiological lead of this study. My intent was to measure the impact of art practice on the engagement in learning for pupils with ASD, using a mixed-methods approach to study the specific evidence from my teaching setting, during a period of focused participant observations within it.

Findings

The findings elicited and included critical sociological characteristics of the school's culture. The expectations and delivery of learning in the school appeared to be strongly driven by curriculum demands and structured teaching, focused on intervention and outcome. From the initial, informal observations and conversations on the delivery of art (and use of art materials), I found that art-teaching followed the same rigid approach of 'instruction for completion' observed in other lessons, rendering outcomes indistinguishable from those produced in other subjects delivered through similar means. From responses in interviews it became evident that the suggestion of a seemingly unstructured approach to learning, associated with the spontaneous use of artistic tools, is considered synonymous of lower standards of achievement and diminished opportunities to gain measurable outcomes.

My intention to render the ecological conditions necessary to implant a culture of independent, inquisitive and explorative learning (in the scheme of this study) was initially forestalled by the critical views of teachers and TAs. Such initial perceptions, expressed through comments and actions, were indicative of defensiveness around habitual practices and curriculum influences. For example, early in the study during a session with a Key Stage 3 (age 11–14) class, I asked pupils and TAs to sit together at the main table (usually pupils would sit in separate learning spaces for practical tasks). I presented the materials to each pupil: a sheet of sugar paper, a palette with acrylic paint (two colours) and an easy-grip brush. Pupils readily began to manipulate the materials with their hands, one pupil started mixing the colours using the brush and collectively all showed intent as they commenced mark-making on the sheet of paper (using their fingers, hands and the brush). At this point a TA commented, '*He will need help to do it properly . . . I need to help him hold the brush if you want it done properly.'* Soon after, another TA said, *'If I don't hold his hand he'll eat the paint. . . He'll pour it.'* The disposition and gestural address that followed, towards pupils performing and making art, appeared to be the physical extension of TAs' preoccupations, and the enjoyment and engagement of each pupil were overlooked.

I continued to observe each pupil and the experience which was unfolding in a very productive, comfortable and safe setting; my endeavour was gradually corresponded by the others in the team. Occasionally, pupils emerged from their activity to assess their surroundings (and my reaction) and returned to mark-making, unprompted, possibly surprised about the freedom they had been given. At this point, it became apparent that TAs were beginning to join me in observing the processes of expressive mark-making and evidently felt less compelled to instruct or steer pupils' actions. *'I have never seen the class so calm, this must be what they need. It was so nice for us to watch, I hope it's like this every time we have art with you. They should have more lessons like this, I think it's what they need'*, indicating the positive effect art practice had on learners. In the course of subsequent observations, this type of activity evoked a similar (gradual and in some cases rapid) change of perspective from the support staff in relation to independent, pupil-directed learning. The preliminary reactions to what TAs considered to be the unconventional deployment of their skills, in relation to pupils, their learning and engagement, were gradually replaced by conscious attentiveness towards the authentic outcomes that pupils were producing in the conditions fostered in the art lessons. On each occasion pupils and staff were encouraged to sit together, often on the floor space (which was cleared from furniture) where materials I had prepared would be presented in accessible and appealing individual *resource sets*, ready for independent use and exploration; this encouraged all (adults and pupils alike) to proceed without requiring assistance or approval. The environmental adjustments and the attitudes of the adults present in the creative space, in a non-hierarchal capacity, fostered autonomy and creativity and enabled adults to observe different facets of their pupils' character through personal and autonomous creative processes.

Conclusion

It is essential to recognize the contribution that autism interventions make to education, care communities and families. These strategies provide a necessary frame to support teachers (and carers) in adapting environments, materials and language to set the conditions for positive learning experiences for individuals with ASD. Consciously, or accidentally, educators allow for the visual abilities of their pupils to be exercised by adopting visual supports, colourful materials and making effective adaptations to environmental structures: visual cues assist individuals in organizing, clarifying and understanding their environment and what is expected in certain activities (Sandberg and Spritz, 2013: 147).

Art practice can complement structured teaching, providing self-directed, errorless learning experiences that allow pupils to leave concrete marks of individual and spontaneous quality. Art practice, in the learning environment, can create the habitat for individuals with ASD to develop spontaneous and personal means of participation. Observing and facilitating learning in these conditions is the driving motive of my research, thus moving towards creative pedagogical models critical in socially just research and practice.

The research findings emphasize that using art practice provides independent learning opportunities that in turn promote engagement and self-discovery in pupils with autism. Observing pupils, manipulating and using art tools, has shown evidence that intuition and intention are gradually developed through spontaneous, self-directed learning that involves the visual ability and interests of individuals with autism, without anchoring the significance of their visual strengths solely on symbolic recognition or structured instruction, thus improving access to expressive freedom, emotional self-regulation and communication through independent visual expression. While the latter was just one of the skills observed in pupils' learning in art, it would be beneficial to explore communication development, in detail, as it is argued that the engagement of motor-cognitive skills and art practice as a means for deploying such skills could lead to authentic self-expression and language development.

One of the things I have learnt is that accommodating and fostering the need for self-expression (through art) enables pupils with autism to participate in learning with a more vivid sense of self. The art room, while in isolation from other learning contexts, became the place where it was possible to secure such processes away from other forums where assessment is prioritized.

Allowing expressive needs to develop in an environment where visual skills can flourish through experience and self-definition, separated from the tendency to measure and assess, was crucial to the success of this project. However, what also emerges is that current assessment demands for art remain unchallenged because the subject is marginalized: policies and actions belie a lack of respect for, or perhaps mistrust for, the value of arts experiences and the effectiveness of artistic training in education, special education in particular (Lazuka, 2009: 6).

This calls for the development of an accountability model that validates the learning principles, outcomes and language of art (and thus of art practice). If learning *in* art is to be measured and thus valued, in the context of the 'broad' curriculum, it is crucial to recognize the skills that are intrinsically gained in participating in art; alongside the bank of practical and holistic benefits it contributes to cognitive development.

> This is how art-making works: problems arise and are solved. While the artist rejects and selects media, meaning, and voice, there is a personal uncovering of style, multiple and shifting, manifested in a self-talk or personal performance.
>
> (Grube, 2009: 6)

Francesca's study has significant implications in terms of social justice. It also reflects some of the challenges in undertaking practitioner research which aims to be collaborative, as well as some of those associated with being an insider researcher. Like Kay Heslop's work, Francesca's overlaps a number of perspectives and could have 'sat' in a number of different chapters. However, we have chosen to use it as an example of the way in which collaborative relationships can change and develop over time. Collaborative or participatory approaches are ideal for many researchers. Yet, establishing relationships which are truly collaborative or participatory is challenging at many different levels. In Francesca's case this was not about establishing relationships – these were pre-existing – but about perceptions of the changes she planned to make as part of her project, which led to initial resistance, an issue raised by Garrido et al. (1999). Resistance from others challenged her ability to address an issue of social justice and develop an approach (in her case, art practice) which could lead to the 'flourishing of individual persons and their communit[y]' (Reason and Bradbury, 2007). Relationships with others were fundamental to overcoming this resistance by encouraging other teachers to observe her work and then discussing it with them on 'an open and honest basis' (Stenhouse, 1975: 144).

Francesca's study raises other issues in relation to social justice: debates about inclusion and segregation (e.g. see Atkins, 2016b; Graham and Slee, 2008), about the privileging of 'academic' subjects within the curriculum, about differential and differentiated access to a curriculum which remains 'divided and divisive' two decades after Tomlinson's (1997, 2001) excoriating critiques, but primarily about voice, and how young people who literally, as well as figuratively, had silenced voices in terms of their minimal verbal and signing skills were facilitated to express themselves and their feelings spontaneously. Much research for social justice emphasizes the importance of voice: this case example demonstrates that voice can be given and expressed in non-verbal forms. Similarly, empowerment is a word which is, perhaps, somewhat overused in the context of participatory and collaborative research, but we would argue that this study reflects meaningful empowerment, albeit in the form of what may often be viewed as small, incremental steps which are no less significant than societal change at an individual and in terms of social justice.

Conclusion

This chapter has highlighted some of the differences and similarities between participative and collaborative research in education. In the examples we have provided, Kay's work is clearly participative, in that her nursery colleagues acted as co-researchers and producers of knowledge. Joanne's project was more clearly collaborative. Francesca's study might be seen on a spectrum, becoming increasingly collaborative as she overcame initial scepticism and participative as others gradually adopted the same approach. Each of these projects has significant value and has made an impact on children and on their teachers. However, we note that while recent developments in teacher research have led to more teacher-researcher studies, there remains a divide between notions of the teacher as researcher and the university academic. This divide is often based on hierarchical assumptions that privilege Higher Education (HE) scholarship above school-based scholarship. We would argue that collaborative research between HE and schools has the potential to form a catalyst to rupture traditional and contentious theory/practice rifts between academics and teachers.

Further, and as reflected in the examples in this chapter, we would argue that in terms of social justice it is imperative for teachers and teacher educators to collaborate with one another to produce studies, such as Joanne's, that expand educational research in and out of the classroom. Collaborative teacher research provides a way for teachers to participate in examination of classrooms and schools in order to shape policy as well as practice. The relationships forged are also a means to make educational research more accessible to teachers and, thus, help redress some of the unequal power dynamics marginalizing teachers in educational research. Collaborative research between teacher educators can support classroom teachers to navigate the complexity of practice and theory. Thus, collaboration not only offers the potential breakdown of historical divisions between universities and schools but also offers future teachers useful models for participation and engagement in educational research. Teachers, student teachers and academics can begin to see themselves as collaborators engaged in educational research, the scholarship produced on teaching and learning can reflect a wider array of voices, ideas and perspectives and contribute to the development of research-based partnerships based on democratic, empowering and inclusive values.

Finally, in terms of collaborative and participatory research more generally, it is important to be cognizant of the fact that research has the power to oppress or to empower marginalized groups and individuals. In doing so it can either lead to an experience that blames people for their victimization or one which transform their lives. It is not the method or methodology alone that determines the outcome, but rather the *intention* behind and the practical application of that method/methodology which has the capacity to support social justice aims. Contributions from the researched community throughout every stage of the research, development and dissemination process ensures participation, stewardship and intentionality. In this sense, collaborative and participatory research can form a transformative catalyst for promoting equity and social change.

Further reading

Atkins, L. (2013), 'Researching "with," not "on": Engaging marginalised learners in the research process', *Research in Post-Compulsory Education*, 18(1–2): 143–58.

Duckworth, V., and Smith, R. (2019), 'Research, criticality & adult and further education: Catalysing hope and dialogic caring', in M. Hamilton and L. Tett (eds), *Resisting the Neo-liberal Discourse in Education: Local, National and Transnational Perspectives*, Bristol: Policy Press.

Griffiths, M. (2003), *Action Research for Social Justice in Education Fairly Different*, Buckingham: Open University Press.

Kellett, M. (2010), *Rethinking Children and Research*, London: Continuum.

Kemmis, S., and McTaggart, R. (2000), 'Participatory Action Research', in N. Denzin and Y. Lincoln (eds), *Handbook of Qualitative Research*, 2nd edn, pp. 567–605, Thousand Oaks, CA: Sage.

Persson, S. (2009), *Research Circles – A Guide*, Malmo: Centre for Diversity in Education.

CHAPTER NINE

Ethnographic approaches for social justice

Introduction

'Ethnography involves an ongoing attempt to place specific encounters, events, and understandings into a fuller, more meaningful context' (Tedlock, 2000: 455). The primary aim of ethnography is to understand the sociocultural contexts, processes and meanings of a cultural system from the perspective of the members of that system and is an approach which has been used to good effect in education, uncovering the ways in which societal structures impact on particular groups and constrain and enable them in different ways (e.g. see Ball, 1981; Duckworth, 2013; Skeggs, 1997; Willis, 1977). Ethnography as an approach to explore learners' life experiences offers the opportunity to provide rich description and, in terms of enacting social justice, has the potential to provide a 'space for the articulations and experiences of the marginalised' (Schostak, 2006: 23). This chapter draws on a range of ethnographic approaches to illustrate different ways of driving forward socially just research.

There are a range of different genres of ethnography, utilizing a variety of ontological and epistemological positionings. Different philosophical lenses will often direct the choice of methods used in social research, how those methods are implemented and the strategies for dissemination of the work. This is particularly significant in terms of ethnography which is concerned with enacting social justice or with addressing issues of in/justice and in/equality. Ethnographic researchers may also differ in their ontological orientations in terms of whether they adopt the idea that what is being studied exists as some exact phenomenon (a positivist orientation) or that the nature of the phenomenon varies when considered in relation to, for example, structural influences (cultural, social, economic), as well as political and personal experiences. For us, the belief that an objective truth of what is just exists and waits to be discovered has not been a helpful stance in our own lived experience where we have encountered a myriad of diverse perspectives of what is socially just (Duckworth, 2013; Duckworth and Smith, 2018a). We have found it more helpful to explore social theory for alternative ontologies about ways of being and lenses for viewing social realities and for making meaning of what is un/just (Atkins, 2016a and b), and this is consistent with the case examples – both classic and contemporary – that we draw on in this chapter.

Ethnography: Origins and examples

The term 'ethnography' stems from the Greek *ethnos* which relates to race and culture and *graphein* which relates to writing and refers to a methodological approach which draws on the older disciplines of anthropology and sociology and is characterized by the use of particular methods. Early anthropological ethnographers such as Boas (1966) and Mead (1930/2001) researched primitive cultures and their rituals, practices and beliefs, while sociologists from the Chicago school adapted anthropological approaches to undertake examinations of American culture, using the city of Chicago as their site of investigation.

Ethnography is a complex term with some ambiguity (Walford, 2009): it is a process and a product (Tedlock, 2000: 455, and see also Pole and Morrison, 2003), is used in large- and small-scale research, and overlaps with many other approaches. It is important to make the distinction between 'true' ethnography, in which the researcher(s) are members of the researched community (as in many 'classic' ethnographies such as Laud Humphreys's *Tea Room Trade*), and research using an ethnographic approach, which may be any investigation of a community which utilizes those methods widely recognized as being associated with ethnography. Key among these are participant observation and ethnographic interviewing which seeks to explore people's lived lives. Apart from interviews and observations, other methods that anthropologists and ethnographers have traditionally used include the physical mapping of the study setting, conducting household censuses and genealogies, and evaluating community links in order to understand group and societal structures.

An early sociological study, now considered a seminal work in this area, which attempted to do this was that conducted by William Foote Whyte (1955/1943) on gang culture in an Italian slum (*Cornerville*) in Boston, United States. Whyte used participant observation to reveal the organizational structures and social worlds that existed within the community (e.g. between 'corner boys' who hung around particular areas and 'college boys' whose focus was to use education as a mechanism for their own social mobility). Up to this point in time, ethnographic studies had always positioned the researcher as the *other* and examined face-to-face interactions in a variety of locales, often using a symbolic interactionist frame of reference. Whyte's study was a departure from this approach. He established close relationships with the gang in their own urban setting, living with one of the gang member's families and becoming immersed in the culture. He also used his main informant to check whether his interpretation(s) were correct and to seek clarification. Other seminal works in America include Laud Humphreys's *Tearoom Trade* (1970), and, in the UK, the publication of classics such as *Beachside Comprehensive* (Ball, 1981) and *Two Cultures of Schooling* (Hargreaves, A., 1986) as increased importance was placed on ethnography in the study of teachers and teaching.

Forms of ethnography

Tedlock (2000: 459) has argued that discussion around different styles of ethnography has been 'rather general and superficial'. She notes that because researchers 'can and do inscribe the same material in many different ways', and for audiences with different expectations, the parameters of ethnography relate to what is read, as well as what is authored. This reflects the significant overlap between different forms and genres of ethnography. However, in relation to social justice and equity, there are a few which are worth mentioning. For example, Institutional Ethnography was an approach first developed by Dorothy E. Smith and, reflecting the position of women at that time in the twentieth century, it was designed as a method 'for women' rather than 'about women' in which ordinary daily activities formed the site for investigation. Since then, 'it has developed as a form of ethnographic enquiry which is used across disciplines to explore textually-mediated social relations and the way in which they shape everyday lives. In other words, how the every-day world of the institution works and how it is represented through the discourses it creates' (Atkins and Wallace, 2012: 153/154). This form of ethnography has significant implications for social justice. As Atkins and Wallace go on to argue:

> All discourse is powerful: it communicates and embeds ideology from powerful groups (e.g. policy makers) in a cascading process, reflected in the policy, procedures and institutional practices followed by those within an institution. These practices impact most on those who are most marginalised in an educational context and profoundly shape the experiences of generations of students and teachers. Representation and institutional practices reflect the lives of the elite group who creates them: therefore, the reality that is presented to the world is one in which an elite is represented but the lives and experiences of others are not. Effectively, this denies the experiences of those who differ from the elite, for example in terms of race, gender or class. The emphasis that institutional ethnography places on relationships between sites and situations in the contexts of policy, professional practice and working life make it useful in exploring such relations across sites within an institution in order to explain how they shape the working lives of those within it, for example in (re) producing and legitimating elite groups and marginalising others. Within this context, notions of power and power relations are of critical importance and form an important theoretical aspect of institutional ethnographies.

Institutional ethnography is significant in terms of its influence and its implications for equity and social justice. Other forms of ethnography include, for example, life history, which Tedlock

(2000: 461) dates to the early twentieth century; multi-sited ethnography, which attempts to establish clear boundaries to the social world under investigation, something which is not addressed in many ethnographic studies. In any social world, the actors or members are multiply situated; their world exists in spaces beyond the immediate site of study and may be virtual as well as real. Networked technologies have disrupted any simple notion or indeed construction of a field site. Early internet culture tended to draw on social groups gathering around topic or activity; indeed this still happens today but has reached out to further virtual tools which, for example, include Twitter and blogs. Social technologies have changed the dynamics of how fields are positioned across time and space. Hine (2009) suggests that 'just as some people argue that mobile ethnographies are just ethnography dressed up, so others will doubt that they are ethnography at all' (p. 18). This contested methodology has fuelled a developing body of internet-related ethnographic literature which aims to address the fluid nature of our information ecology (e.g. see Burrell, 2009; Hine, 2007) that has been and remains a shifting field. Hine (2009) recognizes that ethnography is 'an adaptive methodological approach' (p. 18) and that learning to do it is a lifelong process. By probing different ethnographic projects, she also reveals the diversity of approaches that researchers take in undergoing an ethnographic study; Kozinets (2010, 2015) discusses the use of 'netnography', a form of ethnography which draws data from virtual social worlds. Similarly, Beddall-Hill et al. (2011) highlight how with the fast technological development of Social Mobile Devices their methodological use is an important task that will enable researchers to take advantage of the future applications they provide, while being aware of their impact upon the research process.

Another example is bricolage, which refers to multi-perspective research and, in relation to social justice, is an 'emancipatory research construct [which] is ideologically grounded, [reflecting] an evolving criticality in research' (Kincheloe et al., 2013: 349). The term 'bricoleur' draws on the French for handyman, implying 'the fictive and imaginative elements of the presentation of all formal research'; it is an approach utilized by many critical theorists who seek to confront and contest their own assumptions, which they acknowledge do not lead to emancipatory actions (Kincheloe et al., 2013). As such, it is an approach which critical ethnographers might draw upon. Critical ethnographers apply a critical theory to ethnography, which they undertake for political purposes and in which they focus on the implicit values expressed in ethnographic studies. The political nature of critical ethnography and its concern for equity and justice mean that it is a significant form of ethnography for researchers concerned with social justice. Indeed, in relation to this, Madison (2012: 4/5) articulates five central questions relating to critical ethnography and its conduct:

1. How do we reflect upon and evaluate our own purpose, intentions and frames of analysis as researchers?
2. How do we predict consequences or evaluate our own potential to do harm?
3. How do we create and maintain a dialogue of collaboration in our research projects between ourselves and others?
4. How is the specificity of the local story relevant to the broader meanings and operations of the human condition?
5. How – in what location or through what intervention – will our work make the greatest contribution to equity, freedom and justice?

Madison's points also relate to many of the issues all forms of ethnography seek to address: the ethical understanding of the lived experiences of communities and cultures, in which assumptions are put 'on the table' and problematized, consideration of lives in their widest context, reflexivity and our contribution to equity and social justice. Addressing these issues successfully relies on rigorous research, which pays particular attention to the philosophical and theoretical underpinnings of the project, the methods utilized to gather data and, more importantly, the ways in which those methods are used, as well as the ethical and methodological framework of the study.

Ethnography: Theory, method and methodology

In order to generate authentic insights into the lives of individuals, and understandings of the structures that variously constrain and enable them, all ethnographies adopt a complex theoretical and methodological orientation towards culture. In this context, culture is positioned against different landscapes, such as educational institutions, student communities, teacher communities, classrooms or groups and is explored through a lens that is heterogeneous, conflictual, negotiated and importantly changing; this contrasts to a homogenous lens whereby culture is perceived to be unified, fixed and immobile. Thus, in contrast with a relativistic view of cultures as different-but-equal, critical ethnography explicitly assumes that cultures are positioned unequally in power relations. In order to explore their chosen community from a critical perspective, ethnographers are committed to seeking a deeper immersion in others' worlds in order to understand what they experience as meaningful and important. To achieve this, Goffman (1989: 125) argued that field research involves 'subjecting yourself, your own body and your own personality, and your own social situation, to the set of contingencies that play upon a set of individuals, so that you can physically and ecologically penetrate their circle of response to their social situation, or their work situation, or their ethnic situation'.

To achieve the kind of immersion Goffman discusses may require the ethnographer to draw upon a wide range of methods. However, ethnographies are generally characterized by extensive interviewing (often unstructured) and participant observation. Participant observation is a method in which the researcher spends considerable time observing and interacting with a social group: in a 'true' ethnography this is likely to be as a complete participant, although in research using ethnographic methods the observer may be less embedded in the population they are interested in (see Wellington, 2015: 169 for a helpful spectrum of observation). In either case, the observations will be carefully recorded as field notes and/or journal entries. In doing this, the ethnographer is 'suspending judgement until there is evidence to make one' while actively seeking out contradictory evidence, a process which involves 'systematically generating data and [recording] those data for future analysis' (Walford, 2009: 273).

In addition to interviews and observation, there are multiple methods that the ethnographic researcher can draw upon to develop narratives which reflect the multidimensionality of the participants' experiences. The methods of data collection may include – but are certainly not restricted to – written documents; the researcher's own field notes (observational notes, diaries, journals; communications, chance conversations); art in its many forms, such as images, photographs, audiotapes and videotapes; work products such as meeting minutes, lesson plans or artefacts such as students' work; or visual maps of, for example, location of students' homes. Quantitative data may also be included (see Walford, 2009: 272), particularly in large ethnographies, and might include methods such as surveys or experimental findings. The key determinant of the choice of methods should be their fitness for purpose in terms of eliciting useful data in ways which are respectful of the lives, understandings and cultural practices of the participants. Contemporary research which adopts ethnographic methods often tends to utilize a wide range of methods, and although some early ethnographies drew on large quantitative data sets (e.g. Hargreaves, D., 1967) other classic examples, such as those discussed below, relied largely on the traditional methods of observation and interview.

Classic ethnographies in education

Conducting an ethnography in an education setting presents significant ethical, methodological and practical challenges. These include time, negotiating access and undertaking research with individuals deemed to be vulnerable as well as a whole host of related problems. For this reason, despite their capacity to illuminate the lives of particular groups and contribute to social justice by uncovering and confronting inequalities, only a handful of true ethnographies in education have been completed. Two of these, conducted in the UK two decades apart, shine a light on the educational experiences of working-class youth, illustrating the ways in which education acts as a process of reproduction for classed and gendered identities.

Paul Willis's (1977) seminal book *Learning to Labour* argues that the function of education in society is to satisfy the demands of capitalism and prepare working-class children for a life of labour-intensive jobs. It is an ethnographic study which included extensive participant observations of classes, career activities and leisure activities, as well as extensive unstructured interviews. He spent eighteen months following twelve working-class 'lads' in their non-selective secondary school in Birmingham, then a further six months following them into the labour market, and his data resulted in an in-depth, descriptive and often brutally honest understanding of their lives. The study was conducted between 1972 and 1975 and aimed to answer the question of how and why 'working class kids get working class jobs' (1977: 1).

Many sociological writers believe the unintentional purpose of education and schooling is the (re)production of class and labour (e.g. see Avis, 2016; Avis and Atkins, 2017; Duckworth and Smith, 2018a; Skeggs, 1997; and, for an early example, Bowles and Gintis, 1976). Therefore, by rejecting their schooling it may be argued that the boys in Willis's study have inadvertently placed themselves in the 'working class', thus reproducing the social class and of their parents, as well as eventually engaging in similar types of occupation. However, while Willis recognized the tensions within the educational system he refuted the notion that education is an entirely successful agent of socialization as suggested by Marxists such as Bowles and Gintis (1976). Willis also rejected the view that there is a simple deterministic relationship between the economy and the way the educational system operates.

Two decades later, in 1997, Bev Skeggs published *Formations of Class and Gender: Becoming Respectable*, her longitudinal, ethnographic study of white working-class women in the North of England. Skeggs first met the young women while she was teaching them on a community care course. Initially, she 'hung around' with them, but they eventually became the focus of her PhD study, and she followed them for twelve years, utilizing formal interviews as well as observation and tracking their families and life stories. The study explored subjectivity across learners' lives as they moved from their caring courses, to work and family, negotiating their class positioning as they did so. Skeggs found that complex class structures were 'absolutely central' to the lived lives of these young women and the ways in which they understood their place in the world. Many of the women in her study did not see themselves as working class, but disassociated from it (explored in detail in chapter 5 of her book). She considered that this was not related to a lack of awareness, but formed a strategy for survival in the face of a culture which equates working-class (and underclass) women with derogatory labels such as 'slags'. Skeggs believed that her participants sought to avoid being pathologized by derogatory and gendered labels and instead looked at ways (such as developing a caring self) they could find value in and which positioned them as 'respectable' in the class system. This led her to argue that '[Class] representations . . . are not straightforwardly reproduced but are **resisted and transfigured** in their daily enactment' (Skeggs, 1997: 6, our emphasis).

Similarly, Skeggs found that subjectivity was (re)produced through class, gender and sexuality, explaining that:

> Categories of class operate not only as an organising principle, which enable access to, and limitations on social movement and interaction but are also produced at the intimate level as a 'structure of feeling' (cf. Williams, 1961, 1977) in which doubt, anxiety and fear inform the production of subjectivity. (1997: 6)

She also explored the related notion of respectability in relation to class and gender, demonstrating the relationships between caring and respectability and offering new insights into how working-class women are constructed through classed and gendered power relations and societal structures. These issues were later also explored by Colley (2006) and Colley et al. (2003) in work on processes of 'Becoming' in vocational education as part of the ESRC *Transforming Learning Cultures* project and Duckworth and Smith (2018b) in the Further Education Transforming Lives project. Skeggs's study and work such as that by Colley, Colley et al., and Duckworth and Smith, which builds on it, provide examples of theoretical and empirical approaches which can explore structural power positioning, revealing who has power and value in society and who does not (see also Chapter 5 for another example).

Ethnography: Challenges, ethics and social justice

Both Skeggs's and Willis's work are classic examples of education ethnographies, and both have had a significant impact on scholarship in education over the past four decades. However, they also reflect some of the challenges in undertaking ethnography.

First, the field work for both studies took considerable amounts of time: while Willis's fieldwork was much shorter than Skeggs's it still took two years to complete, and a further two years to write. Secondly, undertaking ethnographies of this nature in the current climate would present issues in terms of ethical approval. For example, during Willis's research he observed behaviours such as fighting, 'bunking off' and vandalizing property but did not intervene (see Willis, 1977). Today, constrained by safeguarding requirements around research with people deemed to be vulnerable, he would have had to intervene, and yet, to have done so would have affected the relationship with his participants, potentially impacted on his data collection and possibly resulted in a less rich and nuanced understanding of the 'lads' experience of their school-to-work transitions. In turn, limiting our understandings of in/equalities in people's educational lives would leave us less able to take action to make a more socially just education system.

Skeggs's work presents the challenge of knowledge. This is a major focus for her, in terms of not only the knowledge she generates, and its theoretical and methodological underpinnings, but also her concern that 'the practices of working class women have usually tended to be read through normalized knowledge which has been produced from the situated bourgeois knower (female and male)' (Skeggs, 1997: 20). In making this argument, Skeggs highlights the impact that education can play in creating a socially just and equitable society.

Thus we can see that the scholarship on social justice and education tends to align to relations and dominations of power and the legitimization and distribution of knowledge (Allan and Duckworth, 2018; Apple, 2004; Atkins, 2009; Avis and Atkins, 2017; Duckworth and Smith, 2019a,b; Freire, 1970/1996). It is important to consider that domination occurs not just through economic forces, but through access to privileged forms of dominant knowledge and to valorized capitals that perpetuate the cycle of inequality and maintain the status quo. For this reason, educational ethnographies such as those by Willis, and more particularly by Skeggs, explore power and knowledge by unpicking and confronting structural inequalities, such as class, gender and ethnicity, and exposing how through the circulation and legitimization of knowledge certain groups dominate over others.

Thus, one value of ethnographies lies in their ability to allow us to identify in/equalities by exploring cultural norms, assumptions, beliefs, social structures and other cultural patterns. To do this ethnography facilitates the researcher to 'become' a member of the group or culture under study and establish positive relationships within the group. To make meaningful relationships ethnography requires researchers to be fully prepared for the very significant time investment that such research demands. Within this challenge also, paradoxically, lies a key strength of ethnography in that it allows the researcher to position themselves as an 'insider' (see Chapter 4) and as such facilitates close proximity between researcher and the researched. Methodologically, it enables researchers to observe, document and monitor their own impact on the situation they are researching. As such there is a need for ethical norms to frame the researcher's position and agency, especially when working with marginalized and vulnerable groups: there should also be a focus on context and the particularity of the relationship between the researcher and participants: indeed, as Tedlock (2000: 455) argues, 'ethnographers lives are embedded within their field experiences in such a way that all of their interactions involve moral choices'. In particular, ethnography offers an approach at the micro level providing insights into lives and relationships in a way macro-analyses cannot.

Understanding those lives and relationships, particularly from a more meaningful and critical perspective, means addressing power relationships in the context of the ethnography. A central aspect of this is addressing the researcher's social location, political commitments and personal values to make overt how power relations permeate the construction and legitimation of the generation of knowledge. It also involves attempting to 'move beyond the objectifying and imperialist gaze associated with the Western anthropological tradition' (Kincheloe and McLaren, 2000: 297). Vitally, the methodology employed needs the capability to resist fading *into* the processes of individualization it is struggling to understand. Ethnographers concerned with issues of social justice need to address the symbolic and material processes and consequences of how the inscribing of structural inequality, including classed and gendered subjectivity, is a specifically personal, sometimes private, highly emotional phenomenon. And indeed, as touched on earlier, Sheller (2013) highlights how mobilities research offers a route for 'revisiting a diverse range of historical and contemporary sociological issues, mobilities research re-casts some of the classical concerns of social stratification theory and urban ecology, expanding the notion of social mobility to wide-ranging spatio-temporal contexts and multiple scales' (Sheller, 2013: 51). Indeed, it has the capacity to what Urry (2007) highlights as social analysis that shifts beyond the stationary to expose social structures that affect the social, economic and political life.

Significantly, in ethnographic research concerned with social justice there is a strong realization that participants, particularly those from marginalized groups, should have a role in all aspects of the research, especially when the research has specific relevance for these groups. Indeed, when people of different cultures are involved in the research, their ways of knowing should be embedded in the research process. This is of particular significance in Bally Kaur's ongoing research, which explores the educational trajectories of people in the multicultural Aston area of Birmingham, England.

Bally's research is structured as an ethnographic study to allow insight into the lived experiences of her participants and also adopts a participatory approach, reflecting the way in which ethnography can overlap with other approaches. She is exploring how the geographical location impacts on lives, particularly in terms of the lens with which it is projected by policymakers, and the implications this has in terms of social justice. Initial encounters and a review of the grey literature available on the area point to a stark mismatch between the imagined space of Aston perceived by policymakers and the actual lives of communities that access it. The former adheres to the dominant but deficit discourse promoted by policymakers. The data generated by the local council is problematic, and the policy depiction of Aston as a place of worklessness, with high proportions of ethnic minority residents and above-average numbers of Jobseeker's Allowance claimants, is limiting. (Jobseeker's Allowance is the benefit paid to help with living expenses while someone is unemployed but looking for work and is administered through the JobCentre Plus. To claim, you must be over 18 but below State Pension Age, available for work and not in full-time education.) This is, perhaps, in line with assumptions and expectations of the area for any outsider. However, what the data doesn't tell us is who these individuals are. It does not demonstrate respect for their differences nor does it contribute to developing a more socially just approach to learning in the area. These are issues which have concerned Bally in the design of her study.

Case example

The lived experience of informal education: An ethnographic study
Bally Kaur

Co-constructing meaning-making

An approach that sets out to co-construct meaning-making and knowledge *with* participants is important. There is something deeply empowering and enabling about co-construction; it removes an egoic pursuit of martyrdom on the part of a researcher seeking to ascertain the authentic voices of a place. Pursuing this line of inquiry is deliberate; the study is not about uncovering a single truth. It is about individuals engaging with their own stories and becoming consciously aware of structural inequalities. The study seeks to provide individuals with the opportunity to voice their narrative and to reflect on it in order to gain validation. There is an anticipation here of multiple truths: realities that are diverse in experience and the everyday while commonalities may emerge in other ways.

This study is central for individuals to voice who they have *been*, who they have *become* and are *becoming* as a result of reflecting on their life narrative. Story-telling is a powerful tool in giving permission and validating personal experience. In addition, being listened to affirms to an individual that they are worthy of being heard (Ledwith, 2007). It is anticipated that this may be the catalyst for more critical consciousness that prompts either action or a shift in mindset. Essentially, by becoming aware of structural inequalities, individuals and communities have a foundation for taking ownership of what happens to them and perhaps in the physical space too.

Our expectations and our egoic attachment to outcomes can block creativity and experiences that lead to transformation.

(European American Collaborative Challenging Whiteness, 2005)

Setting the intention to research with both humility and authenticity has prompted an explicit recognition of my researcher positionality. I grew up near the area and returning to 'research with the neighbours' was a significant driver in undertaking this as an ethnographic study. However, moving to a more affluent place and having had a 'successful education' is my privilege. Researching with humility is rooted in understanding that I am no change-agent for the lives of the participants. Past experiences remind me that the sharing of a story can be a deeply vulnerable and sensitive experience. To receive this as a researcher is a privilege. It is probable that participants may undergo changes through this process though my claiming this as a personal victory would be short-sighted. Any shift requires a readiness and being a research participant may be one (powerful) contributory factor. This study seeks to provide a safe space for participants to voice their narrative and to reflect on it. Using an ethnographic, participatory research approach stems from my belief in adopting practices that are egalitarian.

Methods

The rationale for ethnographic, participatory research is to capture the lived experiences of non-formal education in a way that is empowering and dialogic. My research is *with* participants rather than on them (Atkins, 2013a), hoping for the co-construction of meaning to be mutually beneficial. Using a range of methods is consistent with the nature of participatory research (Bergold and Thomas, 2012). I have adopted a narrative methodology through conceptual mapping, walking tour interviews and a series of photographs. This provides the flexibility to accommodate data that is complex (Greene, 2008); narratives are unique to each individual and their circumstances.

Recognizing the potential power relations involved between myself as researcher and the participant has impacted on the shaping of the research design. Meeting with participants in a location that is familiar to them means that I am the one who is being invited to step into their world. I have avoided 'traditional' interviewing or techniques that involve face-to-face questioning which might position me as being the authority or frame a situation that feels confrontational.

The walking tour interview is deliberate; walking literally 'shoulder to shoulder' assumes equal footing on the part of both the participant and myself, the researcher. Walking through places of significance shifts the power relations; the participant is in control of the direction and any commentary given. This becomes a space in which experiences can be visually and spatially narrated. The walking tour will provide a material base for the conceptual map, perhaps connecting the past to the present. During this tour, I will be taking photographs to complement the participants' commentaries. These photographs will then be offered to the participant to select, edit and caption as a visual representation of their walk and, indeed, trajectory.

Ethical and methodological challenges

I am working closely with a third sector organization in order to identify and get to know potential participants. However, outside of this space, access has been especially challenging. Key gatekeepers have demonstrated a high level of mistrust and suspicion, speaking a 'well-rehearsed script' of defence and caution. This is unsurprising given that this neighbourhood has been subject to a series of external interventions in recent years. I soon discovered the extent of the damage done by objectifying a space and its inhabitants – resulting in an often hostile reception from custodians of the area. Establishing trust and setting conditions for safe and egalitarian environments is, therefore, a priority.

There are clear ethical issues associated with researching individuals of this neighbourhood. My role as the 'well-meaning researcher' raises questions about the power and authenticity of researching with humility. Is my language, conduct or methodological approach in any way dismissive or dishonouring in any way? This is not another intervention and this has to come across in my approach.

Bally's case example raises a number of issues in terms of conducting ethnographic research in a way which is consistent with principles of social justice. In particular, she highlights the importance of respect, ensuring that her methodological approach is not 'dismissive or dishonouring'. She notes difficulties of access and recruitment, briefly alluded to earlier in this chapter. Negotiating access and recruiting participants can present difficulties even as an insider, given that a significant majority of people engaged in education are children, young people, and/or from marginalized communities. In addition, the researcher is asking individuals – who may have complex and difficult life experiences – to open up their personal space in order to participate in the study. This is a big 'ask' in any circumstances, but the problem is compounded in Bally's case by the number of interventions 'on' this population which have taken place in the past – why would they open themselves to another, privileged, outsider?

Acknowledging one's own privilege, as Bally does, in a reflexive manner and taking a caring, respectful, informal and participative approach to data collection are key strategies for undertaking ethnographic work which might be described as socially just in its processes, as well as its outcomes. Reflexivity is particularly important in ethnographic research, given 'it's potential to examine the impact of position, perspective, and presence of the researcher' (Finlay, 2002: 532), which are significant throughout all stages of the research and essential in critically exploring and negotiating the complex power relations in the field. Reflexivity – in this case meta-reflexivity – was a significant aspect of Janet Lord's ethnographic work. Meta-reflexivity is consistent with concerns about social justice and critical forms of ethnography, as it refers to a form of reflexivity in which the social order is problematized, rather than normalized, and in which the individual has a deep concern for the excluded and marginalized.

Case example

Agency and structure: The lived realities of teachers' lives
Janet Lord

Goal

I wanted to investigate the lived realities of teachers' lives, in particular how they negotiated the links between agency and structure. Part of my work was about acknowledging and recognizing issues relating to caring and to social justice, and how there were sometimes tensions between local or personal agendas and various discourses in education, such as performativity, that caused issues for teachers.

I was interested in teachers' reflexivity, their inner conversations or what Archer (2012: 1) refers to as 'the regular exercise of the mental ability, shared by all people, to consider themselves in relation to their (social) contexts'. Archer proposes that reflexivity mediates the link between structure and agency. She suggests that individuals have preferred modes of reflexivity; their 'inner conversations' take different forms, and hence the relationship between structure and agency is mediated differently. I drew on Archer's work in order to consider the variety of ways in which teachers' thinking mediated the links between their agency and structure, and hence what teachers purposefully do.

Methods

Ethnographic research is research which aims primarily to describe what is happening in a particular setting together with the participant's perspectives on these events (Church, n.d.). It was key to the nature of the work that I took an ethnographic approach to get a picture of the participants' 'ways of life'. The true value of ethnographic approaches comes from developing an understanding of the relevant contexts, individuals, processes, goals and context(s) of use. In my case I was using it as a process to facilitate the research by observing and interacting with the four teachers in their real-life environment.

I presented four case studies, one for each of the four teachers, as written portraits (Lawrence-Lightfoot, n.d.). To generate data, I used timelines, concept maps, lesson observations and interviews with the teacher participants. One of the key features of portraits is that the person being depicted is usually set against a background, and this is one reason why using an ethnographic approach was key. I was able to see the teachers in the contexts where their daily professional lives were set (their schools); I watched them teach and interact with their colleagues; and I talked to them about the intersecting contexts and discourses with which they interacted, thus developing an understanding of the views of their 'beings and doings'.

Outcomes

Because of my beliefs about caring and about teaching being a 'moral profession' (e.g. Campbell, 2008), I was particularly interested in how meta-reflexivity, a particular form of reflexivity, is evident in teachers' lives. According to Archer (e.g. 2003; 2012) individuals who use meta-reflexivity as their dominant mode or reflexivity share certain characteristics. They show a deep concern for the underdog, oppressed and deprived. Also, meta-reflexives are idealists – this makes them social critics. They seek a better fit between the person who they wish to be and a social environment that permits their expression of it. It's not a surprise to me that it feels as if many teachers seem to fit this description, and in my work with my four teacher participants, I found that meta-reflexivity was fundamental to the way that three out of the four of them operated.

We discussed notions of gender, power, ability and disability and, most particularly, of disadvantage. For example, one teacher had been concerned about a newspaper report that suggested that many children went hungry over the school holidays, as they didn't get their free school meals. She said of the children in her classes that she was glad when they came back to school in September:

They're waking up hungry but at least if they [parents] can send them to school they know they will get something . . . kids have come in and not had lunch . . . all I've got is cereal bars or an apple . . . My cereal bars went, my apples went and in one day . . . three or four apples, they just all went . . . I think to me that's a big part.

Another teacher was teaching cookery in a disadvantaged area of a large city. Her school, of necessity and because of its commitment to community, provides a lot of food for the children, in various ways (e.g. breakfasts, lunches and food to take home from cookery lessons). She shared her concern that students should have skills for life; a recognition of the disadvantaged area in which the school is situated is clear.

They can choose to do catering from year 7 it's about doing quick – stir fries, things that are cheap.

When I asked whether they could take home the food they cooked, she replied:

Yeah, that's one of the reasons we always make sure that we don't order in from an industrial supplier. We get stuff from the local supermarket; and it's 'smartprice' and it's the basics . . . I think that is . . . really important.

These quotes exemplify the essence of the daily work of the teachers I worked with and reflected an intersection of personal biography and the situational structures and cultures of schools in which they operated, which brought about differences in professional thinking and doing. Teachers demonstrated different ways of dealing with the world depending on their dominant way of reflexive thinking as well as the situations of their schools. Caring and social justice were key concerns for all four of the teachers.

Issues/Dilemmas

I already knew from my own experiences that the consequence of teachers' beings and doings being located in a set of uncertain contexts is a risk to individual teachers of ontological insecurity, the fear of uncertainty which in turn threatens identity (Mitzen, 2006). I feel strongly that in such complex, challenging and changing contexts, social action perhaps demands a greater reflexive competence in individual teachers than perhaps it might do in less complex situations. Meta-reflexivity was the dominant mode of reflexivity for these teachers as it embodies their concerns with social justice.

When, after the event, I consider the portraits of the teachers, there were evident tensions; for some teachers these were in relation to the type of school in which they were employed being at odds with their values; for others, issues of disadvantage affected the way they worked with the children. These tensions were sometimes felt very keenly as being examples of how social injustice plays out in the lives of the pupils in schools and of how unjust life can be – both in terms of recognition and redistribution, to use Fraser's 'folk paradigms' of justice (Fraser and Honneth,

2003). And there was a sense in which teachers sometimes felt that they might only be able to deal with issues of redistribution (such as ensuring that children had enough food), rather than of recognition; or perhaps they prioritized this on a practical level. Issues of recognition were, although important, perhaps less manageable for teachers to contend with in their daily lives.

The case studies presented by Bally and Janet reflect different ways of doing and understanding social justice in ethnographic research. Janet's work has revealed the importance of social justice in the agency and daily labour of teachers, highlighting their role in confronting issues of inequity and social injustice. In contrast, Bally's work is concerned (for the present) with the design and implementation of a methodology and of research methods which can be seen to be respectful of individuals and their differences within a community and thus to reflect a way of enacting social justice in the research process.

Conclusion

Ethnography offers a meaningful, innovative and exciting approach for probing the relations and forces that legitimize certain forms of being. As such, ethnography for social justice and equity involves examining the social, historical and political contexts in which social justice appears as a main tenet or goal of the participants and their families and communities. In this vein contemporary ethnography provides a rich emancipatory framework that has the potential to give voice to the silenced and offers a critical and dialogic space for empowering learners and their communities. Socially just ethnography has a strong praxis agenda and the potential to be used as a tool for change and field of social struggle.

This is reflected in each of the cases we have drawn upon in this chapter. Willis's and Skeggs's classical works underpin our understandings of the ways in which education systems and social structures can reinforce and enable privilege and constrain those with more limited access to valorized capitals. Both Bally Kaur and Janet Lord are concerned with giving voice: Bally to a marginalized and mis-represented community, and Janet to teachers who are trying to make social justice within the constraints of managerialism and performativity. This reflects the fact that, despite all being defined as ethnography, they have very different aims, approaches and outcomes.

In relation to this, each study has raised different issues in terms of the research process. For example, in respect of sampling, Willis's study was limited to twelve 'lads' and criticized in relation to sample size, and Bally Kaur has reported on her difficulties with recruiting participants. The common theme in relation to data collection is that of time – twelve years in the case of Skeggs's study – and the degree of participation of both the researcher and the researched. For example, Skeggs was a member of the community she researched, albeit in the privileged position of teacher rather than student, while, as part of her commitment to undertake research that is socially just, Bally Kaur is seeking to make her study participatory as well as ethnographic. All the cases discussed in this chapter also reflect the significance of voice, even where this is not made explicit. Creating meaningful understandings of social and cultural phenomena is only possible when the actors involved in that phenomena are able to make their voices heard.

Finally, a note on dissemination. Where ethnographic research claims social justice as part of its aim or purpose, the usual forms of dissemination such as conference presentations and journal articles are insufficient. For social justice to be enacted, the research needs to inform policymakers and others involved in education: pupils, parents, students, teachers and others. This means being mindful that dissemination implies an active approach which is specifically targeted at a particular audience and giving consideration to the means by which the ethnography can be communicated. Technology has presented us with a whole range of new approaches, such as websites, video and social media, but other forms of dissemination might include ethnography as a performance, drama, music or exhibition (e.g. see Buckland, 1999; Frith, 2004; Knowles, 2010; Magnat, 2012). These present new and multiple opportunities in which to inscribe the narratives of lives and social practices and consider their implications for social justice.

Further reading

Atkins, L., and Wallace, S. (2012), 'Ethnographic research, Chapter 8', in L. Atkins and S. Wallace (eds), *Qualitative Research in Education*, London: BERA/SAGE.

BERA Blog series, Transformational Education, Transformational Further Education: Empowering People & Communities 23 January 17. https://www.bera.ac.uk/blog/transformational-further-education-empowering-people-communities.

Foley, D., and Valenzuela, A. (2005), 'Critical ethnography: The politics of collaboration', in N. K. Denzin and Y. S. Lincoln (eds), *The Sage Handbook of Qualitative Research*, 3rd edn, pp. 217–34, Thousand Oaks, CA: SAGE.

Pole, C., and Morrison, M. (2003), *Ethnography for Education*, Maidenhead: Open University Press.

Tedlock, B. (2000), 'Ethnography and ethnographic representation', in N. Denzin and Y. Lincoln (eds), *Handbook of Qualitative Research*, 2nd edn, pp. 455–86, Thousand Oaks, CA: SAGE.

Walford, G. (2009), 'For ethnography', *Ethnography and Education*, 4(3): 271–82. https://www.ncrm.ac.uk/research/PASAR/.

CHAPTER TEN

Methodological creativity for social justice

Introduction

In this chapter, our case studies emphasize the use of the visual in terms of creativity and innovation in their methodological approach. However, it is important to note that creativity can be applied at any stage of the research process and that many of the case studies elsewhere in this book could equally well have been located in this chapter. For example, Liz's research with low-attaining young people (see Chapter 5) utilized a range of creative *methods* (in addition to interviews and observations and as part of a creative *methodology*) which facilitated the participation of the young people. She is using similar methods in an ongoing project (see Atkins and Misselke, 2018), this time including the construction of visual, map-like 'transition plans' by young people as they begin to understand how they will achieve their career ambitions, as well as strategies such as personal profiles and small group ideas recorded on flip charts. The methods are all designed to be respectful of the young people and to facilitate their engagement while acknowledging that many have very low levels of functional literacy.

Other creative approaches are designed to address issues of social justice in other ways. For example, Mark Vicars's research (Chapter 4) involves both children and Initial Teacher Education (ITE) students in the development of new approaches to pedagogy in Myanmar, designed to promote social justice and equity. Similarly, but in a UK context, Deborah Herridge is concerned with access to outstanding science teaching at primary level and notes that excellent primary science pedagogy is not only limited but most frequently located in 'good' schools in more affluent areas. Her doctoral research draws on video recordings of outstanding pedagogy. These are then observed by the teachers concerned, who are recorded reflecting on their teaching. The lessons drawn from this process are subsequently integrated into Deborah's own teaching of ITE students undertaking a primary science specialism. Her aim of widening access to outstanding primary science pedagogy is being enacted through the preparation (and follow-up) of her students. In terms of the fact that Deborah is drawing on her data to inform and improve her own teaching, and more particularly that of her students, her approach is more akin to photovoice (e.g. see Strack et al., 2004; Wang and Pies, 2008) than to the photo-elicitation (e.g. see Dixon and Hadjialexiou; Oliffe and Borroroff, 2007; Bates et al., 2017; Malloy, 2007) which is the focus of the following two case studies. While photo-elicitation is a strategy which involves using photographs in interviews, photovoice is an approach developed by Wang and Burris (1997) which is derived from the work of Paulo Friere and seeks to 'engage research participants and researchers in a process of social learning, analysis, and empowerment, in the hope of eventually changing the social situation itself' (Rose, 2016: 315).

While the approach to each of the studies explored in this chapter may differ, all are united by their desire to create new and critical knowledge which can inform both policy and practice in education. Knowledge production, including methodology, can be creatively re-imagined in shape and purpose as a lever that drives local, national and international efforts to move towards a more just and equitable society. Part of this drive includes interrogating processes of knowledge production and finding creative (and democratic) ways of being and acting as researchers.

Creative methodologies are driven by a number of considerations which include the following:

- Ways of thinking and 'being'
- How the research questions are shaped

- Methodological approaches
- How the results are communicated

The case examples in this chapter reflect a range of different responses to each of these considerations.

Images

The use of photography can be drawn upon as a methodological tool and the use of photographs as a means of presenting and disseminating social research. Visual anthropology was the first field to experiment with the use of photography and film 'in a discipline of words' (Mead, 1995). Together with Bateson, Mead led the way in the use of extensive photography data of another culture, which is captured in Balinese Character (1942); both subsequently continued using photography in their research. Why use photography? In a nutshell, we would argue that the visual world offers researchers across disciplines a holistic approach. In ethnographic research (see Chapter 9) we see how photography can be a sensitizing tool to facilitate as a multisensory experience (Pink, 2013) as the researcher becomes immersed in a community. Photographs are an easily accessible artefact to share and can be used, for example, to capture and follow important events in people's lives (Barton et al., 2007; Barton and Hamilton, 1998).

Photography, like other visual data, also offers the opportunity for collaboration around the data material with participants in the study which includes providing a critical space to challenge imageries and biases. Duckworth's (2013) use of photographs in the ethnography of adult literacy learners and their communities in the north-west of England recognizes that the images offer multiple perceptions and interpretations. Pink (2013) explains that meanings do not exist in photographs but are attached to them as part of the analysis. Information is not extracted from the photograph or from the participant, rather photographic interviewing is 'informed by the ideas of inviting, co-creating and making knowledge with photographs rather than the notion of eliciting knowledge from respondents through them' (pp. 92–93). Indeed, it is important to recognize that every image does embody a way of seeing (Berger,

1972), this embodiment is not deterministic but relational and it is that relationality that adds depth to the analysis. Pink (2007) positions video as a product of social encounters in the field which we suggest has real implications for how digital visual research is experienced and made meaningful in the field, including from the point of view of children, young people and adults.

Case example

Research in Special Education (RISE) project
Clare Woolhouse

Introduction

This case example outlines a research project that utilized a photo-elicitation methodology with children and young people to explore diverse understandings of inclusion. Photographs were taken and annotated by the children; these were then anonymized and shared with other children and young people to stimulate discussion with them and then with further groups of student teachers, serving teachers, teaching assistants and academics. In this case example I describe the project and the rationale behind the methodological framework employed in this study.

The researchers involved with the Research in Special Education (RISE) project developed the study in order to explore how children and young people, their teachers and other adults who work in education feel about inclusion. We wanted to look at inclusion as a concept and inclusion as a process that is enacted within educational settings. This approach arose for social justice aims because a range of UK government policies have been introduced that explicitly require educationalists to 'include' children (i.e. Children and Families Act, 2014; DfE, SEND Code of Practice, 2014). However, inclusion remains a disputed concept that refers to opaque practices (Allan, 2010; UNESCO, 2015). As has been pointed out repeatedly, inclusion cannot be 'reduced to a set of strategies or inspection criteria' (Atkins, 2016b: 8); otherwise control is divested from those who are included or who work with children, emasculating those who are the subjects of such practices (Hodkinson, 2012; Whitburn, 2016).

To explore the concept of inclusion, a method was needed that was participatory, actively involved children and young people, and met appropriate ethics and codes of practice (e.g. see Flewitt, 2005; Pope et al., 2010). While there are a number of approaches that could be used, photo-elicitation (Boxall and Ralph, 2009; Prosser and Loxley, 2007) was chosen. This method offers a framework for drawing meaning from photographs and is designed to create a comfortable, visual space for the sharing of experiences and views between researchers and participants. This is particularly useful when respondents are young or have learning or other needs, since photo-elicitation can particularly engage children of all ages in a fun activity that they are familiar with (taking photographs and selfies) and be accessible for children who might have language, communication or physical impairments that might make methods such as interviews or focus groups problematic.

Initially, cameras were given to children and young people in four schools: one primary special, one primary mainstream, one secondary mainstream and one secondary mainstream with specialist provision that were all part of an existing University–School network in north-west England and the Isle of Man. In each school a member of the research team worked with the teachers and pupils of each class in order to explore why we were interested in their opinions and ensuring that they felt comfortable about doing so. This time was also used to discuss the concept and practices of inclusion and exclusion in a style that was accessible and age appropriate, that is, 'do you like to be asked to join in a game with your friends? Can you say why you feel like this?' We did this because we really wanted the children and young people to understand the intentions for the research. Following detailed discussion about ideas of inclusion and gaining informed consent from the individuals as well as their parents and teachers, they were asked to take photographs from around their schools that represented inclusion or exclusion to them. From the original sixty-three photographs a database was created of around 30 anonymized images that could be shared more widely. This dataset was shared and discussed with children and young people in matched schools and with groups of adults working or training in various educational settings between 2014 and 2016. In both phases, individuals were asked to annotate the images describing whether they felt they represented inclusion or exclusion and give reasons for their views. In cases where it was primary-aged children discussing the images we hoped to access a 'window into their worlds' by asking if their image was of inclusion or exclusion and why they had taken this picture. We used this terminology in order not to lead the participants. The children and young people also provided a small amount of demographic information. One example of how this information was recorded is shown in Figure 10.1 (originally published in Dunne et al., 2017: 6).

Image	Child Photographer
	12-year-old girl without SEN in mainstream secondary school. 'Exclusion – using your mobile phone to leave other people out. Secrets.'

Responses for PGCE Secondary group: 19.12.14:

Inclusion as both those pictured are engaged in activity/excluding others as only two involved in small, close, activity.

Exclusion: girls together sharing something on screen of the mobile. Looks to me like they are finding amusement in something not particularly nice on the 'phone'. Perhaps a bit of cyber-bullying going on.

Exclusion – excluded from the class or disengagement.

Inclusion – friends interacting with each other. Don't know what they are doing on 'phone', could be bullying, could be asking more friends to come out.

Inclusion – girl with 'phone' is including her 'friend' or peer in the message on her 'phone'. Both girls appear relaxed and happy in each other's company.

Here the act of sharing is portrayed. This, therefore, is an image of inclusion. An alternative view is taking the image as the viewpoint from pupils every day on the playground. Pupils sharing things on a 'phone' inherently exclude those who they do not share the information with.

Neither inclusion nor exclusion; just an image of friendship.

Dependent upon surroundings – inclusion between the two but if surrounded by other people this would be exclusion as it is an intimate moment between the two.

Mobile 'phones' – exclusion for poorer children.

Inclusive – they are friends. Exclusive to the person they are messaging – are they being 'cyber' bullied?

FIGURE 10.1 *Expanded dataset*

The aim of using this two-phase method was to draw out a range of views from different groups, not to reify one or the other definition of inclusion, or to establish a right or wrong way to 'do' inclusion, as the four researchers in this project would argue that there isn't one. Indeed, in order to discuss the analysis of the images and comments there has been a need to redefine terminology. Hodkinson (2012: 680) argues 'inclusion and exclusion [have] been constructed as a false dichotomy' and for this reason, we have developed and used the term 'in(ex)clusion' to highlight that they in part define each other and can exist simultaneously. As such, we are seeking to move 'beyond the binary' (Dunne et al., 2017) in order to explore the complexity of notions of inclusion, exclusion and in(ex)clusion.

Throughout this project, our overriding intention was to provide a safe space for individuals to voice their concerns, including those who too often go unheard, such as young children or those with learning needs or disabilities. Each comment offered was treated with equal value and worth, since inclusion is viewed as being about how an individual subjectively experiences an event rather than something that is 'done' in a way that is right or wrong. In taking this approach, the project was designed to access different types of data, such as emotional responses that 'evoke a different kind of information' connecting 'an individual to experiences even if the images do not reflect the research subject's actual lives' (Harper, 2002: 13). The intention was to create an interesting, maybe even troubling, dataset of anonymized photographs that could be used with children and young people to invite honest and open discussion about their understandings of inclusion and the impact practices have had for them.

FIGURE 10.2. *Exchange Gallery at Tate Liverpool*

The dataset is being used with professionals who currently work with children and trainee teachers to invite reflection upon the impact policy might have in practice, and we have recently hosted a week-long event in June 2018 at the Exchange Gallery at Tate Liverpool in which twelve photographs were shared (see Figure 10.2) so that comments and views could be garnered from the general public, the analysis of which will inform the next stage of this study that involves workshops for school and community groups.

Taking a creative approach to using a visual methodology (Moss et al., 2007) such as photo-elicitation might be deemed 'non-traditional', but this can be the most appropriate choice when the aim is to create a safe, non-judgmental space within which the 'opening up' of experiences, ideas and interpretations can be facilitated.

Acknowledgements

The research detailed here is part of a larger collaborative study and involves five researchers: Linda Dunne, Fiona Hallett, Charlotte Hastings, Virginia Kay and Clare Woolhouse.

Like Clare, Garth Stahl is concerned with forms of exclusion in education. In his case, his interests lie in class and gender as sites for in/exclusion, and he has also drawn on the power of photo-elicitations in his study of working-class masculinities. In this case, the symbolic images are drawn upon to identify broader patterns in relation to their emerging levels of awareness concerning gender and class.

Case example

Working-class masculinities
Garth Stahl

Context

Within the field of sociology, the study of working-class masculinities has remained of persistent fascination for the last forty years. Such scholarship has employed a variety of approaches to show the relationship between masculinities and class, and recent research has sought to embrace new methodologies in order to understand the identity negotiations of working-class boys where conventional identity markers of class and gender are being reconfigured (Ingram, 2011; Stahl, 2015). Boys can be 'uneasy and monosyllabic' (Francis, 2000: 20). In her research on working-class boys, McDowell (2000: 209) notes many 'were not verbally adept, perhaps unused to exploring their views and feelings with a stranger'. She further explains how a persistent level of shyness required her to adapt her methods in order to engage her participants and privilege their voice. In considering my own research, which comes from a social justice standpoint, I have used photo-elicitation to investigate the conceptualizations and constructions of gender and class within a specific youth subculture of white working-class boys in south-east London (Stahl, 2015).

Goal

Using photo-elicitation. the aim was to differentiate aspects of youth cultural identity in order to understand how these young men perceived their social environments, specifically the community and the school. Asking direct questions about gender identity, what constitutes masculinity and social class/social hierarchies would not have been productive. Photo-elicitation offered a tool to open up spaces between the participants and me where the norms associated with gender and class could be destabilized and interrogated theoretically. In the discussions of photographs I presented of different types of classed masculinities, it became clear what the participants considered to be acceptable and not acceptable forms of working-class masculinity. Arguably, working-class youth often negotiate powerful pathologizing discourses which bring conceptions of respectability in terms of gender, class, race/ethnicity and sexuality to the fore (Skeggs, 2002). Skeggs (2002: 1) argues respectability is one of the most 'ubiquitous signifiers of class' where it is a key mechanism by which subjects are 'othered' and pathologized informing 'how we know who we are (or are not)', as well as what is valued and what is de-valued. The conversation that the photographs stimulated formed the central means through which I came to understand the personal meanings the boys attach to certain class and masculinity signifiers concerning respectability.

Methods

I was aware that the standard semi-structured interview format would not be conducive for all participants, and I wanted to explore ways to break down hierarchical tensions and power imbalances. It was important to consider how my participants would possibly respond 'more easily to visual, rather than lexical prompts' (Prosser and Schwartz, 1998: 123). I considered a variety of methods and methodologies and was sensitive to how any form of written communication (short newspaper clippings, surveys, mind maps) may make participants with low levels of literacy anxious and uncomfortable. As an ethnographer who lived and worked in the area for five years, I felt I had a solid knowledge of the visual repertoires the boys experienced, a 'sense of the visual and technological cultures' of my participants (Pink, 2007: 45). This knowledge was important when planning the use of photo-elicitation as it influenced the photographs I chose. In some ways I had a hunch concerning the images of classed masculinities the boys might respond to. The use of photo-elicitation broke up the semi-structured interview format and the participants could become more relaxed simply responding to the stimuli.

Outcomes

As an exploratory study, the intent was not to provide a detailed analysis of young men's responses towards symbolic images but to instead identify broader patterns in relation to their emerging levels of awareness concerning gender and class. The methodology privileged student voice and enabled me to step aside as interviewer, allowing for a co-construction of knowledge. As a methodology, photo-elicitation provided an entry point to understanding 'identity work' as the ongoing processes through which people come to understand 'who I am' as well as their positionality within the parameters of certain social, cultural and economic context. Furthermore, I found the use of photo-elicitation allowed for diffusing the hierarchical dimension, allowing me to build better relationships between me and the boys and also placing student voice as central (Stahl, 2016).

Ethical and methodological dilemmas

The aim of the visual images was to trigger discussion of certain representations of masculinity, while enabling me to probe the participant understandings around the making of gendered and classed bodies. Croghan et al. (2008) found that interviews using photo-elicitation enabled young people to talk about race and culture and to 'introduce aspects of their lives that they felt might appear obscure or abstruse to their audience' (p. 353). Photo elicitation allowed me to unearth a deeper understanding of the boys' identity negotiations as it was not dependent on language (Daniels, 2008).

It is important to acknowledge there were limitations to the photo-elicitation approach. The data gathered was constrained by the photographs I chose and – if I chose different photographs – it may have been elicited by other responses depending on the 'cultural events and symbols' presented (Connolly et al., 2009: 222). Furthermore, while this methodology did open up spaces in order to discuss class and gender representations, some boys enjoyed the methodology more than others.

Clare and Garth have both made use of photo-elicitation in creating knowledge about the lives and experiences of young people in diverse, and often marginalized, educational communities. Film-making also offers a methodologically creative approach to research, particularly that utilizing ethnographic methods to investigate lived lives and communities. However, it is an expensive, technically challenging and skilled process, so this approach to research is limited to those few scholars who have access to those skills and equipment. Ethnographic documentary film-making is generally regarded as having begun in the 1950s and 1960s when sound recording had become easier, although silent film was used as early as the 1920s to document the lives of the Kwakiutl people in north-west Canada (Erickson, 2013: 100). While still focused on ethnographic studies, film-making has recently also been utilized in the making of alternative documentaries and 'video terrorism' associated with performing gender (Plummer, 2013). Ethnographic work represented as film presents a valuable opportunity to inform policymakers through the use of an accessible medium. Indeed, Thieme (2012, cited Rose, 2016) deliberately shortened her film, her decision driven by her desire to screen it to 'busy policy makers'. Hadfield and Haw (2012) discuss different film-making modalities researchers use to capture different types of knowledge shown in a research project. They argue that 'researchers need to understand these modalities and be clear in which their use of a particular video method fits before they can consider its epistemological fit' and start to consider how they might analyse the video artefact that they have produced' (ibid.: 312).

Curtis Chin is a Hollywood film-maker and New York University visiting scholar who presents his research as documentary films in order to disseminate the issues of social justice and equity he raises to policymakers, the academic community and wider audiences. Exploring access to elite schools in New York, but in this case with a focus on in/equalities associated with Race, Curtis outlines his film *Tested* (2016) and some of the issues and dilemmas which arose from it.

Case example

Tested
Curtis Chin

Introduction

I wrote, produced and directed a full-length documentary called 'Tested'. The film follows a dozen eighth-grade students in

New York City as they prepared for a single standardized test called the Specialized High School Admissions Test (SHSAT). If the student scored high enough, they would be offered a seat [place] at one of the city's three elite public high schools.

The film begins at the start of eighth grade, as the students have just returned from summer break. All of the students are enrolled in some type of preparatory program in advance of the one-day test. The programs range from expensive private programs to free programs run by non-profit community-based organizations.

The film follows the students as they continue to study and take SHSAT practice exams until October, when the test is administered. After the test, the students continue with the high school application process where they must find alternate schools, in case they do not score high enough to gain an offer. The film ends when the students receive the results of the test. Some are offered a seat, while others are not.

Throughout the film, the students and their parents experience a wide range of emotional experiences. Some students gain momentum while others lose focus. Due to the amount of stress, a couple of the students drop out of their prep programs, even before the test day.

Interspersed, with the cinema vérité of the families, the documentary features interviews with educational experts and politicians. The experts discuss such issues as generational poverty and the 'school-to-prison' pipeline that exists in America for Black and Hispanic students.

As someone who has spent my entire educational career in public schools and someone with a keen sense of social justice, I was particularly drawn to the alarming demographics at these schools. While the New York City public school system is 70 per cent Black and Hispanic, at the top-scoring school, Stuyvesant High School, that number drops to 1 per cent Black and 3 per cent Hispanic. It was important for me to understand the issues behind educational equity and whether or not all students, regardless of race, class or gender, are given an equal opportunity to succeed. The students we followed represented African American, Hispanic, Asian, White and Jewish families of various class backgrounds. Specifically, I wanted to look at how stereotypes and racism impacted the students' sense of opportunities and their results.

After an extensive casting process that included reaching out to various schools, prep programs and teachers groups, as well as utilizing our personal social network, we ended up following twenty students over the course of the school year, with twelve of them being featured in the final cut of the film. There was a lot of consideration that went into this casting process.

A few key takeaways

The twelve students in our film all possessed certain advantages. For instance, they all had engaged parents who were active in their educational experiences. This was a function of needing the parents' legal approval to participate in the film.

The students also had to be familiar with the existence of these high schools and the admission process. This was a story development decision as we found the students all needed to have a similar goal in terms of following their different stories.

In coming up with the final list of students to follow, we wanted to make sure we didn't fall into the situation of the single story where an individual is reduced to representing all students from their particular background. Because of that, we needed to include several students from each racial group and we needed to show a variety of class backgrounds. We also tried to have a gender balance representative of who takes the test.

As we followed the families during the school year, we discovered how much the issues of race and class were discussed in their daily lives. For the economically disadvantaged, these issues seemed to be natural points of conversation for their peer group. These students were very comfortable talking about these issues and seemed to have formulated opinions prior to our filming.

For the more affluent families, these issues seemed to be new and undiscussed topics in their lives and among their family and peer groups. With economic privilege, they were able to avoid these discussions. These students often seem to be formulating their ideas as we went along with filming.

To gain the trust of the participants for filming, it was important that our crew represented the diversity of our cast. After all, these families were allowing us into their homes and permitting us to film them in their private moments. Because we had a pool of diverse students, to help create a level of trust, I hired a diverse production crew. This immediately put the subjects at ease, particularly after they learned that some of my crew members had actually gone through this process themselves and attended these specialized high schools.

As reflected in this case example, racial inequalities are deeply embedded in America, but mediated by access to economic capital. Methodologically, this raised issues of intersectionality in relation to sampling, and the importance of the comprehensive approach Curtis and his team took is reflected in the outcomes. The film shows young people from affluent homes accessing the best private preparation, side by side with interviews illustrating that many young people and their parents are not even aware of the SHSAT process and are, therefore, excluded from it and the opportunities it potentially presents. This not only reflects the inequitable approach to High School in America but also raises issues around the process of preparation for and actually undertaking the test, and the stress that that imposes on young teenagers. Like Deborah Herridge's work (see p. 254), *Tested* offers significant opportunities for teaching and raising awareness of the issues addressed in the film. However, this should be undertaken with caution. As Rose (2016: 346) notes, little research has been undertaken into the impact of ethnographic film upon its audiences, but that the research which has been done suggests that such films can sometimes affirm stereotypes rather than increase understanding. It is possible, therefore, that utilizing strategies to interpret the film, rather than leaving that to the audience, may help to address issues of understanding, as may taking a collaborative and participatory approach to film-making (Franzen, 2013: 417/418), itself an approach consistent with social justice. Franzen also argues, citing Yang (2012), that participatory video techniques 'involve engagement between researchers and participants but shift the purpose to participant authorship and participant control of the production'.

Multimedia

The notion of participant authorship and control has been central to the project *Transforming Lives* which explores the role of the teacher, and the wider further education (FE) sector, in social change at the level of the individual accessing FE. In addition to film, it draws on a full range of new technologies, including social media, to help interpret the films and tell the stories of the individual participants. The advent of the internet has, ultimately, led to the development of netnography (Kozinets, 2015) which offers significant opportunities and challenges in terms of using the internet as a platform for ethnographic research, as well as new opportunities for dissemination via social media, blogs and other online platforms. As a consequence, many research methodologies – large and small scale, qualitative and quantitative – now include an online component. Duckworth and Smith (2019c) draw on methodological creative technologies which include video and audio presentations and web blogs allowing for a multi-sensory approach. Multimedia offers a platform for learner, teacher, family member and employer narratives. The virtual narratives have the potential to transcend traditional narratives. These methods are about reflecting different social realities and projecting them into spaces where they are not often acknowledged or heard and about creating opportunities within this process itself for critical dialogue about the power of FE to empower learners and their communities.

Case example

Further education: transforming lives and communities
Vicky and Rob Smith

The University College Union (UCU) FE transforming lives and communities virtual website (http://transforminglives.web.ucu.org. uk/) has developed into a virtual and physical community concerned with social justice and mirrors our deep commitment to engaging learners, educationalists, policymakers and the wider public. The research has resulted in the building of a democratic virtual space. Relationships based on trust have been built, for example, working with educationalists, researchers and policymakers on issues of education and social justice. From the outset, the project used a digitally orientated research methodology. The interviews for the project (65+) were video recorded, many with a digital SLR, others with hand-held smartphones. The prevalence of smartphones meant that some participants were able to record their own contributions and subsequently forward them to us to be edited. The editing process made us acutely aware of ourselves as creating narratives from the videos.

Our aim was to draw on film what was true to the participants' voices, with coherence and accessibility. We did not want the lens to objectify the participants. The videos were hosted on a dedicated YouTube channel and embedded on the project website. The digital platform fed into the ethical way in which the project and its democratic aims progressed. In order to gain further approval that they were comfortable with the video narrative, the videos were shared with participants by email prior to being placed in the public domain.

In several cases, the videos were re-edited in accordance with the wishes of participants. This was not surprising as many of the narratives were of an intensely personal nature and, indeed, the lens provided learners, teachers, family members and their communities with the opportunity to tell their stories through voicing their experiences and trajectories in education and the impact of this in the personal and public domains of their lives; each narrative exposed the distinctiveness and power of FE. The narratives also expose how transformation and the construction of positive educational identities allow for the reclaiming of spoilt identities based on agency and hope.

A further aspect of the digital scaffolding that supports and enhances the project is the use of a dedicated Twitterfeed (@ FETransforms). This has enabled us, our participants and the wider community to share the participants' stories and further contributions in the form of written narratives, photographs and artefacts garnered as the project evolved. The digital platform is becoming a dialogical tool for building a virtual community which includes learners, educators and policymakers.

The voices in the study clearly illustrate transformative learning and teaching. The use of videos is an illuminating and powerful tool for disseminating the emerging findings from the study to draw on the experiences of students, teachers, family members, employers, college leaders and the local and wider community. The aim is to provide a 360° perspective of the impact that FE can have on individuals and their families and communities. For teachers, transformation evolves by discovering new knowledge, creatively using that knowledge and self-confidently facilitating action by taking responsibility for what one learns. Because teaching always involves action, learning can become a flow of discovery, a transformational process of lasting and positive impact and change. For example, in Jimmy's case, treating young and sometimes disaffected people with respect while providing firm boundaries is key.

Jimmy recognizes that simply recreating a school environment in college isn't the way forward. Instead, FE has to offer a distinctive learning experience that includes a well-defined pastoral aspect. Students' background stories need to be taken account of while a new educational identity is constructed, one that is positive, engaged and forward looking (hyperlink to Jimmy's story: http://transforminglives.web.ucu.org.uk/2016/07/15/jack/).

Importantly, the learner is central to the process of transformation. However, the juxtaposition of being poor and having little social capital to support them to break out of their conditions can mean many of the learners feel anxious, have low self-esteem and a belief they were stupid and failures. The narratives in our study have exposed the contradictions, complexities and ambivalences they experience in their daily lives and how they try to make sense of them from their structural positioning as learners in a society based on inequality of opportunity and choice. As illustrated by the voices of the participants, the learners had to re-discover agency in their learning process before transformation could occur. The challenge for teachers and policymakers is, therefore, to establish the conditions in which learners are empowered to take agency within the field of education. This has implications for curriculum and for funding. The curriculum needs to connect at an important level with learners' lives and experiences. The funding has to support small step progression. Some learners from our project have been facilitated by colleges to take a series of small steps and achievements leading to full engagement with a mainstream qualification. Claire, for example, found in her Access course a new world in which for the first time she was listened to and was also able to find her own voice (hyperlink to Clare's story: http://transforminglives.web.ucu.org.uk/2016/09/23/claire/).

This led to her positioning herself differently in a world she could see from a fresh perspective. This change in her view of herself in relation to the world was integral to her transformation and to her success as a learner.

The research illustrates that transformative learning includes dealing with the political, social and economic factors that have interacted to marginalize these students. Transformative learning is successful because it engages with students in a holistic caring way, as people with families, experiences and histories that are all significant and meaningful in their lives. Challenging inequalities in students' lives and communities, adult and 16–19 education at its best mobilizes a critical pedagogy and provides a curriculum that is culturally relevant, student driven and socially empowering. It unites people and communities in hope for the future.

From this perspective, it's important that teachers and policymakers establish the conditions in which students are empowered to take agency within the field of education and beyond. This has implications for curriculum and, inevitably, for funding. The curriculum needs to connect with students' lives and experiences. Funding can facilitate this by recognizing the value of informal and formal education, step-by-step progression rather than uniform linear progression. Indeed, a number of students from FE *transforming lives and communities* have been facilitated by colleges to take a series of small steps and achievements leading to full engagement with a mainstream qualification; some have gone on to fulfilling and affirming employment.

The methodology sought to enact a democratic approach to research. Participants engaged with the project because they had a positive story to tell (Duckworth and Smith, 2019b and c). The research approach itself became a part of the affirmative practice that aided the creation of conditions for the transformative learning that participants had often experienced. In that sense, taking part in the research reinforced the positive learning identities that the participants talk about having achieved.

> The digital platform was the catalyst to what we describe as *virtually enhanced engagement,* driven by the connection between a digital, organic research methodology and critical pedagogy in an attempt to model a democratic and dialogical approach to knowledge generation and dissemination (Duckworth and Smith, 2019c).

Collection, collation, analysis and writing of data

Each of these case studies raises issues in terms of the collection, collation, analysis, writing up and dissemination of data. We use the term 'writing up' loosely, including the visual representation of research via film as being 'written up'. In terms of the collection of data, the processes used in each study referred to in this chapter were, to a great extent, idiosyncratic to that project. However, there were also significant similarities, which might also be seen in other case examples elsewhere in this book. First, for example, the approach to ethics in each study is woven through every stage of the research process as each researcher sought to ensure that what they were doing in terms of generating knowledge was moral and ethical at that moment in time. In each case, this required an advanced degree reflexivity, something which is integral to all research for and about social justice. Reflexivity describes the ability of individuals and communities to reflect knowingly upon the social conditions of their existence. It has an important part in socially just research as individuals – researchers and participants – reflect on and question the nature of the topic they are studying. Indeed, Hertz (1997: viii) suggests that reflexivity 'permeates every aspect of the research process, challenging us to be more fully conscious of the ideology, culture and politics of those we study and those we select as our audience'.

In relation to ethical and reflexive concerns about researched individuals and communities, it is important to note the centrality of the voice of the participants in each study in this chapter. While each project addressed different concerns and utilized different methods, each methodology was underpinned by concerns about social justice and (lack of) equity and sought to address this, at least in part, by enabling small or previously silenced voices to be heard and validated. Thus, each of these diverse studies collected data in ways which emphasized the importance of respect, care and inclusion – underpinning values in research which claims social justice as part of its aim and/or purpose – and utilized methods designed to draw out and illuminate participant voice. In each study, participant voice was central to the collation and analysis of data, although different approaches were used: for example, Clare Woolhouse offers an example of the process of analysis in her study, while the voice-over in Curtis Chin's documentary leaves the viewer to consider the implications of what they have seen. Both approaches, however, are consistent with Wellington's (2000: 99; 2015: 177) argument in respect of case study that determining the value or 'truth' of a study is a 'function of the reader as much as of the researcher'. Another strategy used by Clare Woolhouse, and also by Vicky Duckworth and Rob Smith, was the continual checking of data and its interpretation by participants. Both took different approaches to this (and there is a further example in Chapter 5). This approach to analysis, in which the participants undertake analysis or check that the interpretation of data accurately reflects their views and attitudes, is favoured by many social justice researchers as a means of enabling voices to be heard while addressing concerns about how to avoid the 'vexatious question' of 'exploiting or distorting those voices' (Olesen, 2000: 231). In addition to these advantages, it also provides a form of methodological triangulation (Wellington, 2000: 24/25), thus supporting the validity and credibility of the study from a methodological perspective.

Forms of collaboration between the researcher(s) and the researched such as those involved in participants cross-checking and/or analysing data do not only support the validity and credibility of each study. Philosophically and morally, they address concerns about respecting individuals, acknowledging their expertise in their own lives and also recognizing participants' willingness to open up their personal domains to the researcher in the interests of knowledge. From a purely methodological standpoint, collaboration also means that the researcher is able to more accurately exemplify lived lives and stories, thus representing them in ways which enhance understanding rather than 'affirming stereotypes' (Franzin,

2013: 417), something which would be contrary to all notions of social justice.

Conclusion

This chapter has illustrated a wide range of creative approaches that provide means of giving voice to often marginalized communities. As we stated in the introduction however, those discussed here are not inclusive. Data can take many forms although, unfortunately, many researchers all too often restrict themselves to those most commonly used (e.g. interviews and questionnaires) even where these are not actually fit for purpose (e.g. see Wellington, 2015: 108). This may be because they lack confidence. For example, researchers who are not 'digital natives' may not be as comfortable with the language of the digital medium and drawing on new and emerging technology mediums in their research.

The creativity in socially just research lies in finding methods and frameworks which are fit for purpose and underpinning those throughout with an ethic of respect which guides data collection, collation, analysis and presentation. For example, in this chapter Clare Woolhouse emphasized the importance of 'safe spaces' in which explicit value was placed on each contribution during the data gathering; Garth Stahl noted the importance of good relationships between himself and the young men he was researching in making their voices central to the study. Trust is a key feature of positive relationships, implied in both 'safe spaces' and positive, value-based relationships. Curtis Chin responded to the need for trust by recruiting a diverse film crew, noting that access to 'private moments' might not have been possible without this. Similarly, Vicky Duckworth and Rob Smith re-edited videos in collaboration with participants who were telling their story which included sharing personal details and experiences. Each of these case studies, therefore, emphasizes that ethic of respect for the individual and their communities. It is, perhaps, this that is the key difference between research which can claim to be socially just and research undertaken within other frameworks and paradigms where although there may be concerns about issues related to social justice, the research itself falls into the trap of using approaches and processes which are contrary to social justice. For example, concerns around the low reading attainment of some primary school children in certain geographical areas and from particular social groups have led to a wide range of studies. However, it is possible that where research emphasizes groups, it runs the risk of homogenizing individuals and their needs – something which is a significant issue in the concept of 'evidence-based education'. In contrast, where research is conducted from a social justice perspective, these issues are considered reflexively, and studies attempt to acknowledge the individual as well as the group, placing value on each person's uniqueness and contribution, as well as generating understandings and practices which can make a difference to educational lives.

Further reading

Dunne, L., Hallett, F., Kay, V., and Woolhouse, C. (2017), Visualising Inclusion: Employing a photo-elicitation methodology to explore views of inclusive education, *SAGE Research Methods Cases*. Part 2.

Duckworth, V., and Smith, R. (2019), 'Creative forms of doing and disseminating collaborative research', in F. Finnegan and B. Grummell (eds), *Doing Critical and Creative Research in Adult Education*. Rotterdam: Sense.

Franzen, S. (2013), 'Engaging a specific, not general, public: The use of ethnographic film in public scholarship', *Qualitative Research*, 13(4): 414–27.

Wang, C., and Burris, M. (1997), 'Photovoice: concept, methodology, and use for participatory needs assessment', *Health Education and Behavior*, 24: 369–87.

Woolhouse, C. (2017), 'Conducting photo methodologies: framing ethical concerns relating to representation, voice and data analysis when exploring educational inclusion with children', *International Journal of Research and Method in Education*.

Conclusion

As we have seen in the chapters in this book, social justice and its relationship with educational research and methodology are complex. Social justice is a multifaceted notion associated with diverse philosophical and sociological underpinnings, political ideologies and theoretical debates. The research presented clearly illustrates that carrying out research concerned with social justice involves a commitment to challenging local, national and international inequality. This focus includes participating in research as a means of exposing and addressing power and privilege on a structural level, as well as at the level of representation.

As such, there is an explicit understanding that social justice research has the potential to expose and address gaps in the distribution of resources which lead to social and educational inequality in the lives of people and their families and communities. It recognizes this unjust scale and places emphases on identity, respect and equal rights to participation. People who have been silenced and undervalued and whose identities are not acknowledged with respect are given voice; social justice research validates individuals and communities and offers diverse and valuable mechanisms for challenging the status quo.

It is ironic that, in contemporary times, when we might have imagined Dickensian streets to be behind us, socially just approaches have never been needed more. This is reflected in the fact that the gap between the richest and poorest has grown to its widest for several generations (Dorling, 2015). Cuts to welfare, wages and public services under austerity programmes have affected populations internationally in terms of widening inequalities, both in and beyond education.

Research for social justice calls for us to direct our energy and resources to creating genuine social and educational change.

For many of us, it is simply too easy to ignore the plight of children, young people and adults in our communities who have differentiated, 'divided and divisive' access to education. Indeed, the very structures of academia may be incongruent with social justice approaches, preferring instead research that generates income but without an authentic, socially just reach which addresses the complex social and political issues associated with educational in/equalities. This reflects the importance of finding critical spaces in which we can challenge the status quo and connect with like-minded practitioners and researchers. Our own journey is an example of this connectivity and, indeed, led to the conception and development of the book. For us the writing of this book was a moral and political imperative, which has allowed us to take our conversations from the personal to the public domain.

It has introduced us to a wide range of methodological approaches and has reflected on how different methods can be utilized in ways which promote social justice and equity. Key messages throughout the book are the importance of a moral, ethical and strongly theoretical basis to research and of taking a deeply reflexive approach throughout, something that is evident across all the research examples presented in this book. The notion of making quiet and/or silenced voices heard as a means of emancipation also emerges strongly, notwithstanding the risk of reifying historical oppressions. Participation and collaboration at many different levels are demonstrated as important strategies for respecting the other and addressing, at least in part, issues of representation. We have also seen the importance of using creativity in both method and methodology, whether as a means of gathering authentic data which more accurately reflects the lives of those we are researching – for example, some visual methods – or whether that creativity is applied to methods which are accessible to participant groups who may, for example, be young children, have learning disabilities or have limited literacy and/or verbal skills. Throughout, the book has highlighted that, in order to be socially just, research must not merely have a particular philosophical or theoretical underpinning, but that the researcher(s) must 'walk the walk' as well as 'talk the talk'. Research concerned with social justice, as our contributors reflect, is not merely about methodology or method but also about political engagement, activism and respect for others.

Dissemination is a key aspect of this: bodies of knowledge drawn from research for social justice not only have the potential but also have a moral imperative to provide empirical evidence that speaks back to and develops policy. This might include presenting empirical work to governmental evidence building panels at different levels nationally: for example, in the UK both the House of Commons and the House of Lords have committees concerned with education and in/equality, while in Australia policy might be developed at either state or national level as well as internationally. International examples might include European policy fora such as the European Agenda for Adult Learning (EAAL) or the European Centre for the Development of Vocational Training (CEDEFOP) or wider international bodies such as the United Nations Educational, Scientific and Cultural Organization (UNESCO) and/or the non-government organizations working in partnership with the United Nations (e.g. see BAICE, 2016). Disseminating research through organizations such as this can facilitate researchers to link local research with global issues.

It is equally important to disseminate at practitioner level, particularly in terms of contesting taken-for-granteds (such as that low-attaining youth have low aspirations) and interrogating everyday practices (e.g. setting or streaming by ability) and assumptions (that low attainment can be conflated with low ability). This can be achieved through practitioner fora, blogs, practitioner journals and conferences, and personal and professional networks and collaborations. These examples, all drawn from the research presented in this book, clearly demonstrate the power of socially just research to reach and influence domains beyond academia – stemming into local, national and international decision-making forums, thus providing a critical flow of research that moves across policy, practice and disciplines.

Finally, there is much still to do. Every child who is falling behind, who arrives at school hungry, every young person who becomes 'disengaged' and 'disaffected', every adult who needs help to complete a visa form or a benefits claim is an indictment of our failure to create a socially just education system. Worse, in policy terms, these people are seen in a deficit model of 'problem', something which effectively moves the responsibility for the impact of educational inequality from the state to the individual. It is our responsibility, as teachers and researchers, to address this. We can do this by 'walking the walk' and by continuing to engage in personal practice which is socially just. We can also continue to develop understandings and new knowledge through research.

Some possible broad topics, which can be sub-divided, for future socially just research could include the following:

- Education, representation and the media
- An exploration of ethics, values and moral education
- The impact of critical pedagogy across European and non-European nations
- Politics and education as a driver for change
- Power relations and education
- Mother-tongue-based and multilingual education
- The impact of technology on socially just research methodology
- Culture and schooling
- Ethical interventions and social justice

If we believe we can drive forward challenges to inequality and offer more equitable and socially just models of education, we also need to imagine how we can continue to develop and improve education, and access to education, at all levels and in all contexts. To do this we must continue to actively create spaces in academia and beyond that explore the many intersections of inequality and become advocates for social justice and active agents for meaningful change. The ability to expose and challenge inequality is perhaps the best legacy we can leave to younger generations so that they have a greater chance of living in a more socially just society based on humanity, care and equity.

GLOSSARY

Action research   Action research has its origins in the 1946 work of Kurt Lewin. It describes a related group of research methodologies which emphasize collective and self-reflective research involving ordinary people and which then lead to action that can result in greater social justice for disempowered and silenced groups.

Artefacts   Artefacts are objects which can have a symbolic meaning for a culture, group or individual. This can provide insights into the understandings, beliefs and values of groups and individuals. In historical research, artefacts can provide material, documentary evidence of the past – for example, in terms of religious or cultural practices. In education, artefacts from schools in different periods over time can tell us much about, for example, changing gender roles in education.

Capital   Capital refers to the assets individuals have access to which determine their social positioning in the context of a stratified society. According to the original theory of capital propounded by Pierre Bourdieu (1986), all forms of capital derive from labour and can take material or embodied forms. Bourdieu (1985) described three forms of capital. These were economic capital, referring to access to or ownership of tangible assets such as money or property; social capital which refers to established and enduring social networks which can be drawn upon for mutual advantage; and cultural capital which refers to education and qualifications and the societal advantages that they can be exchanged for.

Case study   Case study methodology is well established in the Social Sciences. If you want to learn more about a specific issue or you want to explore a particular problem or occurrence, then the case study is a meaningful approach. A *case* can refer to a group of people, a specific person or issue, a collective of ideas, and it is characterized by its boundaries (e.g. this school or those three universities). Case study research allows the deep exploration and illumination of complex issues. It is a robust method which is particularly useful when a holistic, in-depth investigation and analysis is required.

Co-inquiry   Co-inquiry refers to research conducted with a particular group to address shared concerns. In co-inquiry, the co-researchers are unlikely to be professional researchers, but members of a particular (often marginalized) community or employees of the organization which forms the site for research. Co-inquiry recognizes that these groups and individuals will have insights and knowledges that are different to those of professional researchers but of significant importance in relation to the research process. Co-inquiry is considered to be both empowering and a useful means of disrupting power relations by researching 'with' and not 'on'.

Critical discourse analysis   Critical discourse analysis is essentially an approach to language analysis, which addresses issues of language, power and ideology and which views language as a form of social practice.

Critical pedagogy   Critical pedagogy has its origins in the works of Paulo Freire. Critical pedagogy regards education as a political act concerned with emancipation for oppression, and thus Critical Pedagogues are specifically concerned with the influences of educational knowledge, and of cultural formations generally, that perpetuate or legitimate an unjust status quo. One of the aims of critical pedagogy is to develop a critical capacity in citizens as a means of enabling them to question the status quo, challenge social injustice and resist oppression.

Critical race theory   Critical race theory (CRT) refers to a critical social scientific approach to the study of race, racism and society. It is particularly concerned with the ways in which race, law and power are mediated in different social and cultural contexts and seeks to use critical and activist approaches to identify, challenge and de-construct racism in society.

Critical realism   Critical realism is a meta-theory for social sciences which is associated with the philosopher Roy Bhaskar.

It offers a series of philosophical positions on a range of matters including causation, structure, persons and forms of explanation in order to describe the interface between the natural and social worlds. Ontology and arguments for a new ontology are central to the theory.

Documentary evidence Research that draws on personal and official documents as a source material may be viewed as documentary evidence. Documents used by social scientists may include, for example, letters, newspapers, diaries, government statistical publications, websites, photographs, paintings and computer data. One of the key advantages in conducting documentary research is that you can get access to information that would be difficult to get in any other ways. Additionally, today, much of this information is online and in the public domain, making it readily accessible to the researcher.

Emancipatory research A perspective of generating knowledge that can empower marginalized and/or disadvantaged people. It is an umbrella term that can include many streams of critical theory–based research such as feminist, disability, race and gender theory.

Ethics/morality Morality refers to a value system and its understanding of right and wrong. Ethics forms the practical application of that value system in terms of individual actions. While all educational research is expected to be conducted 'within an ethic of respect for the person' (BERA, 2018), ethical issues are of particular concern in research concerned with social justice. This is because while the aim of socially just research is likely to be emancipatory, it is also likely to involve marginalized participants and researchers who are operating from a position of power and privilege (see power relations).

Ethnography Ethnography is the stem of anthropology that involves trying to understand how people live their lives. Ethnography is both a process and a product: the term can apply both to a methodology and to the written account of a particular ethnographic research study. Ethnographic research traditionally relies heavily on observation and interviewing, but can include a range of methods and can also combine qualitative and quantitative data.

Feminism   Feminism is the quest for the equality of the sexes. As a framework for research it actively seeks to remove the power imbalance between research and subject. It is politically motivated in that it seeks to change social inequality and it begins with the standpoints and experiences of women. A wide range of methods, both qualitative and quantitative, are available to feminist researchers.

Floorbooks   Floorbooks were initially used in early years' settings as a means of encouraging oracy and higher order thinking skills. A floorbook is something co-produced by the children with childcare professionals. Sustained shared thinking is central to the process, during which groups of children and their key adults work together in collaborative learning. These individuals will usually sit in a circle around the floorbook; children may draw, adults may scribe for the children and photographs may be included. In the nursery, floorbooks are an integral part of planning, but are also used for reflection upon activities and documenting achievement. They are available at all times, so children have ownership of them, and they may be revisited and added to over time. This learning approach has been adapted for use in research with young children, as it enables them to generate rich and meaningful data in a way which is familiar to them over time.

Group discussion   A group discussion is a means of collecting data in one go from several people who usually share common experiences and which focuses on their shared meanings. It is a term which is sometimes used interchangeably with group interview but which is generally understood to be less formal and more unstructured than a group interview.

Group interviews   Group interviews, including focus groups, are drawn on by researchers in the social and behavioural sciences to explore phenomena and are a useful and legitimate qualitative method. The group of people are selected and asked about their opinions or perceptions of the subject under investigation. Group size varies but is normally restricted to fewer than 12.

Insider research   Insider research is conducted by a researcher who is already a member of the organization they are investigating. In some respects, this is a privileged position which allows the researcher ready access to study a particular issue in depth and with special knowledge about that issue. However, it can also be problematic in terms of establishing clear lines between the different identities of researcher and professional (and meeting their different responsibilities). Insider research also raises significant ethical issues in terms of relationships within a particular context or organization and the power relations associated with them.

Institutional ethnography   Institutional ethnography describes an ethnographic approached developed by the sociologist Dorothy Smith which is focused on work processes and social relations (connections between work processes) within an organization. Typically data will be text based (e.g. in a college, enrolment forms, timetables) and the researcher uses these to explain the social relations within the organization.

Learning circles   A Learning Circle may include a group of individuals with a common interest who meet regularly to learn from each other, and others, about a self-identified topic and in a format the group has decided upon. Learning Circles are flexible, peer-directed learning experiences. Learning Circles are underpinned by democracy and are built on the premise that every member has something to contribute and that every member has something to learn.

Life history   Life history is an approach to qualitative research which has its origins in anthropology, specifically in studies of indigenous peoples. The approach uses interviewing (often on multiple occasions and for extended periods of time) to explore individual histories and the ways in which individuals understand those histories and their own place in the world, within a wider sociocultural and macro-historical framework. It enables the researcher to gather particularly rich data which offers greater insights into individual lives than some other methods and is written in narrative form.

Life worlds   The immediate experiences, activities and contacts that make up the world of an individual or corporate life.

Masculinities scholarship   Masculinities scholarship is a still-emerging interdisciplinary field which is an aspect of gender studies. It draws on a range of critical theoretical frameworks including feminism and queer theory to explore the social role and meanings of masculinities including issues such as men's own perceptions of their gender identities, sexualities and the family.

Multi-site ethnography   Multi-site ethnography is a method of data collection that follows a phenomenon or social problem through different field sites geographically and/or socially. It is utilized where it is not possible to account for the problem or phenomena by focusing on a single site.

Netnography   Netnography is a form of ethnography which draws data from virtual social worlds, as a means of understanding and interpreting online relationships and communications.

New literacy studies   Research from the New Literacy Studies understands literacy practices and events as being socially and culturally situated and extends conceptions of literacy beyond merely reading and writing (e.g. to texting, media, and digital literacies). It draws on anthropological and ethnographic methods as a means of data collection.

Observation   Observation is an ethnographic research method with its roots in anthropology. It allows the researcher to observe the population or culture they are investigating at close quarters and in a real-life context. This can provide insights that are unavailable using other methods. Observation occurs on a spectrum (Hammersley and Atkinson, 1983; Wellington, 2015, see also Gold, 1958) from complete participant (where the researcher is, or becomes, socialized into the group they are studying) to complete observer (where the observer is a completely detached 'outsider'). In addition, it can be structured or unstructured, undertaken over time or just to provide a 'snapshot' of a particular time and place.

Participatory action research   Participatory Action Research (PAR) is a qualitative research methodology that can promote empowerment, equality and social justice. It has the potential to bring people together to define for themselves what problems they face in their community, find solutions through, for example, talking with and gathering data from their peers and then implementing those solutions through informed actions.

Participatory analysis workshops   Participatory (analysis) workshops are aimed at sharing, analysing and discussing research data in order to interpret and make meaning from it. Participatory workshops will involve all participants, including non-academic users who may otherwise be marginalized from the cycle of the research process and its subsequent actions.

Photo-elicitation   When conducting photo-elicitation interviews (PEI), researchers introduce photographs into the interview context. Photo-elicitation refers to the use of a single photograph or sets of photographs to use as a stimulus during a research interview. In some cases, other images or artefacts, rather than photographs, are used to act as a stimulus.

Positionality (shifting positionality)   Positionality refers to intersecting subjectivities (e.g. class, race, gender, sexuality) and to personal and professional experiences, beliefs, values and/or characteristics which relate to the issue that you are investigating. Your positionality in research includes a recognition of how significant individual and cultural contexts allow access, rapport and trust to the participants in the study. It is important for researchers to maintain an informed reflexive consciousness as a means of contextualizing personal subjectivity in, for example, data interpretation and representation of experiences in the research process. The process of reflexivity and the personal insights gained from undertaking research can lead to shifts or changes in our view of the issue(s) under investigation, known as shifting positionality.

Power relations   Power relations refers to often subtle differences in power or privilege between people and the ways in which these influence behaviour, attitudes and (expected) roles in society. They can thus be associated with the domination of individuals or groups within society, particularly where power is unevenly distributed. However, the embodied nature of many of the differences between people which influence power relations (e.g. class fractions, gender, race) means that the relationships are often unquestioned and regarded as natural and normal by both the powerful and the powerless. Therefore, research concerned with social justice is always concerned with power relations and ways in which they might be influencing the researchers' and participants' interactions and understandings during the research process, as well as how they might be disrupted and changed to facilitate more just social relationships.

Queer theory   A theoretical perspective that rejects traditional categories of gender and sexuality.

Reflexivity   Reflexivity is a circular concept in research. It relates to the researchers' ability to consider her feelings, values, beliefs and behaviours in relation to the research, the participants' and her own actions in the research process as a means of understanding how she may influence the participants and/or different aspects of the research process. Critical reflexivity is considered imperative in the production of rigorous and ethical qualitative research.

Research circles   In the 1970s a participant-oriented method was developed at Lund University in Sweden and was given the name research circle. It is each circle's responsibility to come to an agreement about the democratic interplay between all participants. The overall purpose of a research circle is to produce new knowledge.

Research conversations   The term 'research interviews' is swapped for *research conversations* to illuminate the context and as a means of establishing a more democratic relationship whereby there is a greater sense of equality between the participants and the researchers, particularly in terms of their communication with and between each other.

Research diaries/journals   Research diaries (sometimes also known as research journals) are well-established methods for collecting data in the fields of educational and social research and are considered as part of a broad category together with other methods of recording such as research logs and field notes. The notes made can be useful for understanding and interpreting an event, or in terms of a self-reflexive process, as an event can be reflected on contemporaneously and at a distance, and the researcher's differing perspectives considered (see shifting positionality).

Semi-structured interviews   The semi-structured interview is a qualitative data collection strategy in which the researcher asks participants a series of predetermined but open-ended questions. They have in-built flexibility so the researcher can, if necessary, follow up something the participant has said.

Serendipitous data   This refers to anything unexpected, which might be used as data to answer a research question. Its use will necessarily need to be justified and appropriate in the context of that particular study.

Social justice   Social justice is a debated term which can have different meanings in different contexts and which is often associated with both social activism and (different forms of) political ideology. Broadly speaking, it refers to the equal worth of all people(s) and aims to achieve a more equitable state of society. In education terms, it refers to the drive for more equitable educational systems and approaches – and the life opportunities that can derive from that – globally and locally. In research terms, Social Justice has developed as a theoretical and philosophical framework, particularly in relation to qualitative social research, over the past two decades. As a theoretical framework, it is concerned with both identifying and addressing in/equalities.

Video ethnography   Video Ethnography is the video recording of the stream of action of subjects in their natural setting, with the aim of experiencing, interpreting and representing their lives and behaviour. It may be viewed as an important method in the twenty-first century as it has the capacity to explore multidimensional phenomena.

Video reflexivity   The camera and video lens is socially significant given both its ability to preserve interaction for re-presentation and participants' awareness of that ability. Therefore, reflexivity is vital as the researcher is an active participant in the situated activity that is being recorded. Video reflexivity may be a collaborative methodology involving researchers and/or participants.

Vignettes   Vignettes are short stories about a hypothetical person, presented to participants during qualitative research, for example, within an interview or focus group discussion, to ascertain information about their own set of beliefs and assumptions.

Voice   In this context, voice is a theoretical and ethical concept. Research concerned with social justice attempts to give voice to individuals and communities who are marginalized and thus might be described as having unheard or silenced voices. Therefore, much of this research uses the participants' own words and voice as generative of meaning and knowledge. However, concepts of voice are problematic in the ways in which researchers variously understand, interpret and mediate them. Therefore, the use of voice is a significant ethical issue, which is related to the power relations within the research project.

Walking tour interviews   The purpose of a walking tour interview is to situate the interview in a particular geographic space which has relevance to both the participant and the research. Undertaking the interview in a social and/or community space (rather than, e.g. in an office) can also be an effective means of addressing some of the concerns around power relations.

BIBLIOGRAPHY

Ade-Ojo, G., and Duckworth, V. (2015), *Adult Literacy Policy and Practice: From Intrinsic Values to Instrumentalism*, London: Palgrave Macmillan Pivotal.

Ade-Ojo, G., and Duckworth, V. (2016), 'Of cultural dissonance: The UK's adult literacy policies and the creation of democratic learning spaces', *International Journal of Lifelong Education*, 36(4): 1–18. http://www.tandfonline.com/doi/abs/10.1080/02601370.2016.12502 32.

Adler, P. A., and Adler, P. (2002), 'The reluctant respondent', in J. F. Gubrium and J. Holstein (eds), *Handbook of Interview Research: Context and Method*, pp. 515–35, Thousand Oaks, CA: SAGE.

Ahmed, S. (2000), *Strange Encounters: Embodied Others in Post-Coloniality*, London: Routledge.

Ahmed, S. (2004), *The Cultural Politics of Emotion*, Edinburgh: Edinburgh University Press.

Ainley, P., and Corney, M. (1990), *Training for the Future: The Rise and Fall of the Manpower Services Commission*, London: Cassell.

Ainscow, M., and Sandill, A. (2010), 'Developing inclusive education systems: The role of organisational cultures and leadership', *International Journal of Inclusive Education*, 14(4): 401–16.

Alaszewski, A. (2006), *Using Diaries for Social Research*, London: SAGE.

Alcoff, L. (1992), 'The problem of speaking for others', *Cultural Critique*, 20: 5–32.

Allan, D., and Duckworth, V. (2017), 'Voices of disaffection: Disengaged and disruptive youths or agents of change and self-empowerment?', *British Journal of Special Education*, 45(1): 43–60.

Allan, J. (2010), 'Questions of inclusion in Scotland and Europe', *European Journal of Special Needs Education*, 25(2): 199–208.

Anderson, E. (2012), *Inclusive Masculinity*, Abingdon: Routledge.

Angrosino, M., and Mays de Perez, K. (2000), 'Rethinking observation from method to context', in N. Denzin and Y. Lincoln (eds), *Handbook of Qualitative Research*, 2nd edn, London: Sage Publications.

Anthamatten, P., Shao-Chang Wee, B., and Korris, E. (2012), 'Exploring children's perceptions of play using visual methodologies', *Health Education Journal*, 72(3): 309–18.

Apple, M. (2004), *Ideology and Curriculum*, 3rd edn, London: Routledge.

Archer, M. S. (2003), *Structure, Agency and the Internal Conversation*, Cambridge: Cambridge University Press.

Archer, M. S. (2012), *The Reflexive Imperative in Late Modernity*, Cambridge: Cambridge University Press.

Aristotle (1911/1988), *The Politics* (ed. Stephen Everson), Cambridge: Cambridge University Press.

Aristotle (1998), *Nichomachean Ethics*, Mineola, NY: Dover Thrift Editions.

Association of Colleges (AoC) (2017), College Key Facts 2017/2018 online at https://www.aoc.co.uk/sites/default/files/Key%20Facts%20 2017–18%20.pdf. Accessed 3 November 2017.

Atkins, L. (2009), *Invisible Students, Impossible Dreams: Experiencing Vocational Education 14–19*, Stoke-on-Trent: Trentham Books.

Atkins, L. (2010a), 'Opportunity and aspiration, or the great deception? The case of 14–19 vocational', *Education Power and Education*, 2(3): 253–65.

Atkins, L. (2010b), 'Teaching for inclusion: Pedagogies for the "sector of the second chance"', in Susan Wallace (ed.), *Key Issues in the Lifelong Learning Sector: Writing about Teaching*, pp. 29–41, London: Learning Matters.

Atkins, L. (2013), 'Researching "with" not "on": Engaging marginalised learners in the research process', *Research in Post-compulsory Education Special Issue: Reclaiming the Disengaged: Critical Perspectives on Young People Not in Education, Employment or Training*, 18(1–2): 143–58.

Atkins, L. (2016a), 'The odyssey: School to work transitions, serendipity and position in the Field', *British Journal of Sociology of Education*, 38(5): 641–55.

Atkins, L. (2016b), 'Dis(en)abled: Legitimating discriminatory practice in the name of inclusion?', *British Journal of Special Education*, 43(1): 6–21.

Atkins, L., and Misselke, L. (2018), Skills with Meaning, Knowledge as Capital: Embracing the Transition Year, Presented at *Research in Post-compulsory Education*, Biennial Conference, University of Oxford, July 2018.

Atkins, L., and Duckworth, V. (2016), *How is social justice understood by intending teachers?* Paper presented at the British Educational Research Association Annual Conference, University of Leeds, September 2016.

Atkins, L., and Wallace, S. (2012), *Qualitative Research in Education*, London: BERA/SAGE.

Atkins, L., Flint, K., and Oldfield, B. (2011), *Practical Matters: What Young People Think about Vocational Education in England*, London: City and Guilds Centre for Skills Development.

Avis, J. (1996), 'The myth of the post-Fordist society', in J. Avis, M. Bloomer, G. Esland, D. Gleeson, and P. Hodkinson (eds), *Knowledge and Nationhood Education, Politics and Work*, pp. 71–82, London: Cassell.

Avis, J. (2016), *Social Justice, Transformation and Knowledge*, Abingdon: Routledge.

Avis, J., and Atkins, L. (2017), 'Youth transitions, VET and the "making" of class: Changing theorisations for changing times?', *Research in Post-Compulsory Education*, 22(2): 165–85.

Back, L. (1993), 'Gendered participation: Masculinity and fieldwork in a south London adolescent community', in D. Bell, P. Caplan and W. J. Karim (eds), *Gendered Fields: Women, Men and Ethnography*, pp. 215–33, London: Routledge and Kegan Paul.

Ball, S. J. (1981), *Beachside Comprehensive*, Cambridge: Cambridge University Press.

Ball, S. (1997), *Education Reform a Critical and Post-structural Approach*, Buckingham: Open University Press.

Ball, S. (2007), *Education PLC: Understanding Private Sector Participation in Public Sector Education*, Abingdon, Oxon: Routledge.

Ball, S. (2012), *Global Education Inc: New Policy Networks and the Neo-liberal Imaginary*, London: Routledge.

Ball, S. J., Maguire, M., and Macrae, S. (2000), *Choice, Pathways and Transitions Post-16 New Youth, New Economies in the Global City*, London: RoutledgeFalmer.

Ballard, K. (ed.) (1999), *Inclusive Education: International Voices on Disability and Justice*, London: Falmer Press.

Banks, J. A. (1998), 'The lives and values of researchers: Implications for educating citizens in a multicultural society', *Educational Researcher*, 27: 4–17.

Baradon, T., and Joyce, A. (2005), 'The theory of psychoanalytic parent–infant psychotherapy', in T. Baradon with C. Broughton, I. Gibbs, J. James, A. Joyce and J. Woodhead (eds), *The Practice of Psychoanalytic Parent–Infant Psychotherapy. Claiming the Baby*, New York, NY: Routledge.

Barr, K., and Truelove, L. (2015), 'Play and the achievement of potential', in J. Moyles (ed.), *The Excellence of Play*, 4th edn, Maidenhead: Open University Press.

Barrow, C. (2003), 'Children and social policy in Barbados: The unfinished agenda of child abuse', *The Caribbean Journal of Social Work*, 2: 36–53.

Barrow, C. (2008), 'Early childhood in the Caribbean', *Working Paper 47*. The Hague, The Netherlands: Bernard van Leer Foundation. ISBN 978-90-6195-102-5.

Bartlett, L., and Holland, D. (2002), 'Theorizing the space of literacy practices', *Ways of Knowing Journal*, 2(1): 10–22.

Barton, D., and Hamilton, M. (1998), *Local Literacies: Reading and Writing in One Community*, London: Routledge.

Barton, D., Hamilton, M., and Ivanic, R. (2000), *Situated Literacies: Reading and Writing in Context*, Abingdon: Routledge.

Barton, D., Ivanic, R., Appleby, Y., Hodge, R., and Tusting, K. (2006), *Relating Adults' Lives and Learning: Participation and Engagement in Different Settings*, London: NRDC.

Barton, D., Ivanic, R., Appleby, Y., Hodge, R., and Tusting, K. (2007), *Literacy, Lives and Learning*, London: Routledge.

Bassey, M. (1999), *Case Study Research in Educational Settings*, Buckingham: Open University Press.

Bates, E., McCann, J. J., Kaye L. K., and Taylor, J. C. (2017), '"Beyond words": A researcher's guide to using photo elicitation in psychology', *Qualitative Research in Psychology*, 14(4): 459–81.

Bathmaker, A. M. (2001), '"It's a Perfect Education": Lifelong learning and the experience of foundation-level GNVQ students', *Journal of Vocational Education and Training*, 53(1): 81–100.

Bauman, Z. (2007), *Liquid Times: Living in an Age of Uncertainty*, Cambridge: Polity.

Bearne, E., and Marsh, J. (ed.) (2007), *Literacy and Social Inclusion: Closing the Gap*, Stoke on Trent: Trentham Books.

Beddall-Hill, N., Jabbar, A., and Al Shehri, S. (2011), 'Social mobile devices as tools for qualitative research in education: iPhones and iPads in ethnography, interviewing, and design-based research', *Journal of the Research Center for Educational Technology*, 7(1): 67–90.

Beebe, B. (2003), 'Brief mother–infant treatment: Psychoanalytically informed video feedback', *Infant Mental Health Journal: Official Publication of the World Association for Infant Mental Health*, 24(1): 24–52.

Beebe, B., Friedman, D. D., Jaffe, J., Ross, D., and Triggs, S. (2010), 'Microanalysis of 4-month Infant vocal affect qualities and maternal postpartum depression', *Clinical Social Work*, (38): 8–16.

Bélisle, R. (2006), 'Socialisation à l'écrit et pluralité du rapport à l'écrit d'acteurs du communautaire', in R. Bélisle and S. Bourdon (eds), *Pratiques et apprentissage de l'écrit dans les sociétés éducatives*, pp. 145–72, Québec: Presses de l'Université Laval.

Berger, J. (1972/1980), 'Photographs of agony', in J. Berger (ed.), *About Looking*, London: Bloomsbury.

Bergold, J., and Thomas, S. (2012), Participatory research methods: A methodological approach in motion [110 paragraphs]. *Forum Qualitative Sozialforschung/Forum: Qualitative Social Research*, 13(1), Art. 30, http://nbn-resolving.de/urn:nbn:de:0114-fqs1201302. Accessed 6 January 2017.

Biesta, G. (2007), 'Towards the knowledge democracy? Knowledge production and the civic role of the university', *Studies in Philosophy and Education*, 26(5): 467–79.

Bigby, C., Frawley, P., and Ramcharan, P. (2014), 'Conceptualising inclusive research with people with learning disabilities', *Journal of Applied Research in Intellectual Disabilities*, 27: 3–12.

Billett, S., Thomas, S., Sim, C., Johnson, G., Hay, S., and Ryan, J. (2010), 'Constructing productive post-school transitions: An analysis of Australian schooling policies', *Journal of Education and Work*, 23(5): 471–89.

Björnsdóttir, K., and Svensdóttir, A. S. (2008), 'Gambling for capital: Learning disability, inclusive research and collaborative life histories', *British Journal of Learning Disabilities*, 36: 263–70.

Bloomer, M. (1996), 'Education for studentship', in J. Avis et al. (eds), *Knowledge and Nationhood Education, Politics and Work*, London: Cassell.

Blunkett, D. (2000), 'Influence or irrelevance: Can social science improve government?', *Research Intelligence*, 71: 12–21.

Boal, A. (1979), *Theatre of the Oppressed*, London: Pluto Press.

Boas, F., edited by Helen Codere (1966), *Kwakiutl Ethnography*, Chicago: Chicago University Press.

Bornstein, M. H., Britto, P. R., Nonoyama-Tarumi, Y., Ota, Y., Petrovic, O., and Putnick, D. L. (2012), 'Child development in developing countries: Introduction and methods', *Child Development*, 83(1): 16–31.

Bourdieu, P. (1985), 'The social space and the genesis of groups', *Theory and Society*, 14(6): 723–44.

Bourdieu, P. (1986), 'The forms of capital', in J. Richardson (ed.), *Handbook of Theory and Research for the Sociology of Education*, pp. 241–58, New York, NY: Greenwood.

Bourdieu, P. (1977), *Outline of a Theory of Practice*, Cambridge: Cambridge University Press.

Bourdieu, P. (1991), *Language and Symbolic Power*, Cambridge, MA: Harvard University Press.

Bourdieu, P. (1996/92), *The Rules of Art*, Cambridge: Polity Press.

Bourdieu, P. (2010), *Outline of a Theory of Practice*, Cambridge: Cambridge University Press.

Bourdieu, P., and Passeron, J.-C. (1990), *Reproduction in Education, Society and Culture*, 2nd edn, London: SAGE.

Bourdieu, P., and Wacquant, L. J. D. (1992), *An Invitation to Reflexive Sociology*, Chicago: University of Chicago Press.

Bourke, B. (2014), 'Positionality: Reflecting on the research process', *The Qualitative Report*, 19(33): 1–9. Retrieved from https://nsuworks.nova.edu/cgi/viewcontent.cgi?article=1026&context=tqr, 26 May 2018.

Bowles, S., and Gintis, H. (1979), *Schooling in Capitalist America: Educational Reform and the Contradictions of Economic Life*, New York, NY: Basic Books Inc.

Boxall, K., and Ralph, S. (2009), 'Research ethics and the use of visual images in research with people with intellectual disability', *Journal of Intellectual and Developmental Disability*, 34(1): 45–54.

Brenkman, J. (2007), *The Cultural Contradictions of Democracy: Political Thought since September 11*, Princetown: Princetown University Press.

British Educational Research Association (2011), *Ethical Guidelines for Educational Research*, online available at: www.bera.ac.uk/publications/guidelines/

British Educational Research Association (2018), *Ethical Guidelines for Educational Research* online available at BERA.ac.uk. Accessed 20 June 2018.

Brown, P. (1987), *Schooling Ordinary Kids: Inequality, Unemployment and the New Vocationalism*, London: Tavistock.

Brown, J., and Johnson, S. (2008), 'Childrearing and child participation in Jamaican families', *International Journal of Early Years Education*, 16(1): 31–40.

Buckland, T. J. (ed.) (1999), *Dance in the Field: Theory, Methods and Issues in Dance Ethnography*, New York, NY: St Martin's Press.

Burnard, P. (2004), 'Using critical incident charting for reflecting on musical learning'. *The Mountain Lake Reader: Conversations on the Study and Practice of Music Teaching*, Spring: 8–21.

Burnard, P. (2012), 'Rethinking creative teaching and teaching as research: Mapping the critical phases that mark times of change and choosing as learners and teachers of music', *Theory Into Practice*, 51(3): 167–78.

Burns, D., and Worsley, S. (2015), *Navigating Complexity in International Development*, Rugby, England: Practical Action.

Burrell, J. (2009), 'The field site as a network: A strategy for locating ethnographic research', *Field Methods*, 21: 181–99.

Butler, J. (2007), *Gender Trouble*, 2nd edn, Oxon: Routledge.

Calderón López, M., and Thériault, V. (2017), Accessing a 'very, very secret garden': Exploring children's and young people's literacy practices using participatory research methods. *Language and Literacy*. https://journals.library.ualberta.ca/langandlit/index.php/langandlit/article/view/28366.

Campbell, E. (2008), 'The ethics of teaching as a moral profession', *Curriculum Inquiry*, 38: 357–85.

Canal, G. O. (2004), 'Photography in the field', in S. Pink, L. Kúˊrti and A. I. Afonso (eds), *Working Images: Visual Research and Representation in Ethnography*, pp. 31–46, London; New York, NY: Routledge.

Cannella, G., and Lincoln, Y. (2013), 'Ethics, research regulations and critical social science', in N. Denzin and Y. Lincoln (eds), *Landscape of Qualitative Research*, 4th edn, pp. 169–87, Los Angeles: SAGE.

Carr, W. (1995), *For Education*, Buckingham: Open University Press.

Carr, W., and Kemmis, S. (1986), *Becoming Critical: Education, Knowledge and Action Research*, Lewes: Falmer Press.

Carrol, K. (2009), 'Outsider, insider, alongsider: Examining reflexivity in hospital-based video research', *International Journal of Multiple Research Approaches*, 3(3): 246–63.

Castells, M. (2000), *The Information Age: Economy, Society and Culture Volume 3: End of the Millennium*, 2nd edn, Oxford: Blackwell Publishers.

Castells, M. (2009), *Communication Power*, Oxford: Oxford University Press.

Checkoway, B. (2013), 'Social justice approach to community development', *Journal of Community Practice*, 21: 472–86.

Cheek, J. (2000), 'An untold story? Doing funded qualitative research', in N. K. Denzin and Y. S. Lincoln (eds), *Handbook of Qualitative Research*, pp. 401–20, Thousand Oaks, CA: SAGE.

Children and Families Act (2014) (Chapter 3) HMSO, London. Available at: http://www.legislation.gov.uk/ukpga/2014/6/part/3/enacted. Accessed 10 November 2016.

Chilisa, B. (2012), *Indigenous Research Methodologies*, Los Angeles: SAGE.

Chilisa, B., and Ntseane, G. (2011), 'Resisting dominant discourses: Implications of indigenous, African feminist theory and methods for gender and education research', *Gender and Education*, 22(6): 617–32. https://doi.org/10.1080/09540253.2010.519578.

Chilton, P., Tian, H., and Wodak, R. (2010), 'Reflections on discourse and critique in China and the West', *Journal of Language and Politics*, 9(4): 489–507.

Christians, C. (2013), 'Ethics and politics in qualitative research', in N. Denzin and Y. Lincoln (eds), *The Landscape of Qualitative Research*, 4th edn, Thousand Oaks, CA: SAGE.

Church, J. (n.d.), Ethnographic approaches to education research [Online]. Available at http://www.tecks.co.nz/home/Typesofresearchevidence/Approachestoresearchintolearningandteaching/Naturalsciencesocialscienceandethnographicapproachestoresearch/Ethnographicapproachestoeducationresearch. Accessed 22 November 2017.

Cin, M., and Walker, M. (2013), 'A capabilities-based social justice perspective: Three generations of west Turkish women teachers' lives', *International Journal of Educational Development*, 33(4): 394–404.

Clark, C., and Dugdale, G. (2008), *Literacy Changes Lives – The Role of Literacy in Offending Behaviour*, London: National Literacy Trust.

Clay, M. (1991), *Becoming Literate – The Construction of Inner Control*, London: Heinemann.

Clifford, J. (1986), 'Introduction', in J. Clifford and G. E. Marcus (eds), *Writing Culture: The Poetics and Politics of Ethnography*, pp. 1–26, California: University of California.

Cohen, L., Manion, L., and Morrison, K. (2007), *Research Method in Education*, 6th edn, London: Routledge.

Coleman, M. (2012), 'Leadership and Diversity', *Educational Management Administration & Leadership*, 40(5): 592–609.

Colley, H. (2003), *Mentoring for Social Inclusion: A Critical Approach to Nurturing Mentor Relationships*, London: RoutledgeFalmer.

Colley, H. (2006), 'Learning to labour with feeling: Class, gender and emotion in childcare education and training', *Contemporary Issues in Early Childhood*, 7(1): 15–29.

Colley, H., James, D., Tedder, M., and Diment, K. (2003), 'Learning as becoming in vocational education and training: Class, gender and the role of vocational habitus', *Journal of Vocational Education and Training*, 55(4): 471–97.

Comte, A. (1974 reprint), *The Positive Philosophy of Auguste Comte Freely Translated and Condensed by Harriet Martineau*, New York, NY: AMS Press.

Connell, R. (2000), *The Men and the Boys*, Cambridge: Polity.

Connolly, P., Kelly, B., and Smith, A. (2009), 'Ethnic habitus and young children: A case study of Northern Ireland', *European Early Childhood Education Research Journal*, 17(2): 217–32.

Côté, James E. (2005), 'Identity capital, social capital and the wider benefits of learning: Generating resources facilitative of social cohesion', *London Review of Education*, 3(3): 221–37.

Country Assessment of Living Conditions (2012), Sir Arthur Lewis Institute of Social and Economic Studies 2012, 'Barbados county assessment of living conditions 2010 volume 1: Human development challenges in a global crisis: Addressing growth and social inclusion', *Caribbean Development Bank country poverty assessment report*. Available at: http://www.caribank.org/uploads/2012/12/Barbados-CALC-Volume-1-MainReport-FINAL-Dec-2012.pdf.

Creswell, J. W., and Plano-Clark, V. L. (eds) (2011), *Designing and Conducting Mixed Methods Research*, 2nd edn, Thousand Oaks, CA: SAGE.

Crewe, B. (2012), *The Prisoner Society*, Croydon: Macmillan.

Croghan, R., Griffin, C., Hunter, J., and Phoenix, A. (2008), 'Young people's construction of self: Notes of the use and analysis of the photo-elicitation methods', *International Journal of Social Research Methodology*, 11(4): 345–56.

Cronin, C. (2014), 'Using case study research as a rigorous form of inquiry', *Nurse Researcher*, 21(9): 19–27.

Cunliffe, A. L., and Karunanayake, G. (2013), 'Working within hyphen-spaces in ethnographic research: Implications for research identities and practice', *Organizational Research Methods*, 16(3): 364–92.

Dagley, V. (2004), 'Making the invisible visible: A methodological and substantive issue', *Educational Action Research*, 12(4): 613–30.

Daniels, D. (2008), 'Exploring Ethical Issues when using visual tools in educational research', in P. Liamputtong (ed.), *Doing Cross-Cultural Research: Ethical and Methodological Considerations*, pp. 119–33, The Netherlands: Springer.

Danny the Champion of the World (1989), 'Directed by Gavin Millar USA', TV Movie (DVD).

Davies, C. A. (2008), *Reflexive Ethnography: A Guide to Researching Selves and Others*, 2nd edn, London: Routledge.

Davies, W. (2014), *The Limits of Neoliberalism: Authority, Sovereignty and the Logic of Competition*, London: SAGE.

Davis, N. (2017), 'Rural deprivation and ill-health in England "in danger of being overlooked"', *Guardian*, 18 March 2017 available at https://www.theguardian.com/society/2017/mar/18/rural-deprivation-and-ill-health-in-england-in-danger-of-being-overlooked.

Defeyter, G., Graham, P., Atkins, L., Harvey-Golding, L., and Crilley, E. (2017), *Evaluation of Premiership Rugby's HITZ Learning Academy Programme Premiership*, Rugby: Northumbria University.

Delgado, R., and Stefancic, J. (2017), *Critical Race Theory: An Introduction*, New York, NY: New York University Press.

Denis, A. (2008), 'Intersectional analysis: A contribution of feminism to sociology', *International Sociology*, 23: 677–94.

Denscombe, M. (1998), *The Good Research Guide*, Buckingham: Open University Press.

Denscombe, M. (2010), *The Good Research Guide for Small-scale Social Research Projects*, 4th edn, Maidenhead: Open University Press.

Denzin, N. (1970), *The Research Act in Sociology*, Chicago: Aldine.

Denzin, N. (2009), 'The elephant in the living room: Or extending the conversation about the politics of evidence', *Qualitative Research*, 9(2): 139–60.

Denzin, N., and Lincoln, Y. (2000), 'Introduction: The discipline and practice of qualitative research', in N. Denzin and Y. Lincoln (eds), *Handbook of Qualitative Research*, 2nd edn, pp. 1–30, London: SAGE.

Denzin, N., and Lincoln, Y. (2005), 'Introduction: The discipline and practice of qualitative research', in N. Denzin and Y. Lincoln (eds), *Handbook of Qualitative Research*, 3rd edn, pp. 1–32, London: SAGE.

Denzin, N., and Lincoln, Y. (eds) (2011), *Handbook of Qualitative Research*, 4th edn, London: SAGE.

Denzin, N., and Lincoln, Y. (2013), 'Epilogue: Towards a "Re-functioned Ethnography"', in N. Denzin and Y. Lincoln (eds), *The Landscape of Qualitative Research*, pp. 579–88, Thousand Oaks, CA: SAGE.

Denzin, N., and Lincoln, Y. (2013), 'Paradigms and Perspectives in Contention', in N. Denzin and Y. Lincoln (eds), *The Landscape of Qualitative Research*, pp. 189–98, Thousand Oaks, CA: SAGE.

Denzin, N., and Lincoln, Y. (2013), 'Part II: Paradigms and perspectives in contention', in N. Denzin and Y. Lincoln (eds), *The Landscape of Qualitative Research*, Thousand Oaks, CA: SAGE.

Department for Business Innovation and Skills (DBIS) (2012), The 2011 Skills for Life Survey: A survey of literacy, numeracy and ICT levels in England BIS Research Paper Number 81 online at: file:///D:/the_2011_skills_for_life_survey_-_december_2012%20(1).pdf. Accessed 27 December 2017.

Department for Education and Employment (2000), *Blunkett Rejects Anti-Intellectualism and Welcomes Sound Ideas (DfEE News 43/00)*, London: DfEE.

Department for Education and Skills (2003a), *14-19 Opportunity and Excellence*, London: The Stationery Office.

Department for Education and Skills (July 2003b), *21ˢᵗ Century Skills: Realising Our Potential Individuals, Employers, Nation*, London: The Stationary Office.

Department for Education and Skills (2005), *14–19 Education and Skills*, Annesley: DfES Publications.

Department for Education and Skills (2006), *Further Education: Raising Skills, Improving Life Chances*, Norwich: The Stationary Office.

Department for Education (DfE) (2011), Wolf Review of Vocational Education: Government Response online at: https://www.gov.uk/government/uploads/system/uploads/attachment_ data/file/180504/DFE-00031-2011.pdf.

Department for Education (DfE) (2013), Teachers standards guidance for school leaders, school staff and governing bodies (introduction updated 2013), DfE: Crown copyright.

Department for Education (DfE) (2014a), Promoting fundamental British values as part of SMSC in schools departmental advice for maintained schools DfE: Crown copyright.

Department for Education (DfE) (2014b), Special Educational Needs (SEN) Code of Practice: for 0 to 25 years: Statutory guidance for organisations who work with and support children and young people with SEN, London: DfE.

Department for Education (DfE) (2017), Permanent and Fixed Period
  Exclusions in England: 2015–2016 SFR 35/2017, 20 July 2017 at:
  https://www.gov.uk/government/uploads/system/uploads/attachment_
  data/file/645075/SFR35_2017_text.pdf.
de Sousa Santos, B. (ed.) (2007), *Another Knowledge Is Possible: Beyond
  Northern Epistemologies*, New York, NY: Verso.
Dewey, J. (1916), *Democracy and Education*, New York, NY: Free Press.
Dickens, C. (1854), *Hard Times*, London: Bradbury and Evans.
Dillard, C., and Okpalaoka, C. (2013), 'The sacred and spiritual nature of
  endarkened transnational feminist praxis in qualitative research', in N.
  Denzin and Y. Lincoln (eds), *The Landscape of Qualitative Research*,
  pp. 305–38, Thousand Oaks, CA: SAGE.
Dixon, M., and Hadjialexiou, M. (2005), 'Photovoice: Promising practice
  in engaging young people who are homeless', *Youth Studies Australia*,
  24(2): 52–6.
Donaldson, M. (1993), 'What is hegemonic masculinity?' *Theory and
  Society*, 22(5): 643–57.
Dorling, D. (2015), *Inequality and the 1%*, 2nd edn, London: Verso.
Dover, A. G. (2013), 'Teaching for social justice: from conceptual
  frameworks to classroom practices', *Multicultural Perspectives*,
  15(1): 3–11.
Duckworth, V. (2013), *Learning Trajectories, Violence and Empowerment
  amongst Adult Basic Skills Learners*, London: Routledge.
Duckworth, V., and Ade-Ojo, G. (2016), 'Journeys through transformation:
  A case study of two adult literacy learners', *Journal of Transformative
  Education*, 14(4): 285–304.
Duckworth, V., and Hamilton, M. (2016), 'Linking research and practice
  in adult literacy in the UK', in K. Yasukawa and S. Black (eds),
  *Beyond Economic Interests: Critical Perspectives in Adult Literacy
  & Numeracy in a Globalised World (International Issues in Adult
  Education, Volume 18)*, pp. 167–84, Netherlands: Sense Publishers.
Duckworth, V., and Maxwell, B. (2015), 'Extending the mentor role
  in initial teacher education: Embracing social justice', *International
  Journal of Mentoring and Coaching in Education*, 4(1): 4–20.
Duckworth, V., and Smith, R. (2017a), Further education in England –
  Transforming lives and communities: Interim Report. UCU.
Duckworth, V., and Smith, R. (2017b), Transformational Further
  Education: Empowering People & Communities. FE NEWS 19 April
  2017. https://www.fenews.co.uk/fe-voices/transformational-further-
  education-empowering-people-communities-13755.
Duckworth, V., and Smith, R. (2018a), 'Transformative learning in
  English further education', in C. Borg, P. Mayo and R. Sultana (eds),
  Skills for Sustainable Human Development of the International

Handbook on Vocational Education and Training for Changing the World of Work. Switzerland: Springer International Publishing, Springer Nature.

Duckworth, V., and Smith, R. (2018b), 'Adult literacy: Further education as a space for resistance', *RaPAL Journal*, 93(Winter): 2017.

Duckworth, V., Smith, Rob (2018c), 'Breaking the Triple Lock: Further Education and Transformative Teaching and Learning', *Education + Training*, 60(6): 529–543, https://doi.org/10.1108/ET-05-2018-0111 .

Duckworth, V., and Smith, R. (2018d), 'Women, adult literacy education and transformative bonds of care', *Australian Journal of Adults Learning*, 58(2): 161–87.

Duckworth, V., and Smith, R. (2019a), 'Further educations: Transformative teaching and learning for adults in times of austerity', in N. James and E. Boeren (eds), *Being an Adult Learner in Austere Times*, London: Palgrave-Macmillan.

Duckworth, V., and Smith, R. (2019b), 'Research, criticality & adult and further education: Catalysing hope and dialogic caring', in M. Hamilton and L. Tett (eds), *Resisting the Neo-liberal Discourse in Education: Local, National and Transnational Perspectives*, Bristol: Policy Press.

Duckworth, V., and Smith, R. (2019c), 'Creative, Critical and Democratic Research Dissemination', in F. Finnegan and B. Grummell (eds), *Doing Critical and Creative Research in Adult Education*, Rotterdam: Sense.

Dunne, L., Hallett, F., Kay, V., and Woolhouse, C. (2017), *Visualising Inclusion: Employing a Photo-elicitation Methodology to Explore Views of Inclusive Education*, SAGE Research Methods Cases. Available at http://methods.sagepub.com/case/visualizing-inclusion-photo-elicitation-methodology-inclusive-education.

Durkheim, E. (1895/1982), *The Rules of the Sociological Method and Selected Texts on Sociology and Its Method*, New York, NY: The Free Press.

Ecclestone, K. (2004), 'Learning or therapy? The demoralisation of education', *British Journal of Educational Studies*, 52(2): 112–37.

Eglinton, K. A. (2013), 'Between the personal and the professional: Ethical challenges when using visual ethnography to understand young people's use of popular visual material culture, *Young*, 21(3): 253–71.

Elton-Chalcraft, S., Lander, V., Revell, L., Warner, D., and Whitworth, L. (2016), 'To promote, or not to promote fundamental British values? Teachers' standards, diversity and teacher education', *British Educational Research Journal*, 43(1): 29–48.

England, K. (1994/2008), 'Getting personal: Reflexivity, positionality, and feminist research', in H. Bauder and S. Engel-Di Mauro (eds), *Critical Geographies: A Collection of Readings*, Praxis (e) Press Critical Topographies Series.

Engle, P. L., Fernald, L. C., Alderman, H., Behrman, J., O'Gara, C., Yousafzai, A., and Global Child Development Steering Group (2011), 'Strategies for reducing inequalities and improving developmental outcomes for young children in low-income and middle-income countries', *The Lancet*, 378: 1339–53. http://dx.doi.org/10.1016/S0140-6736(11)60889-1.

Equality Challenge Unit (ECU) (2017), *ASSET 2016: Experiences of gender equality in STEMM academia and their intersections with ethnicity, sexual orientation, disability and age Summary report*. Equality Challenge Unit.

Erel, U., Reynolds, T., and Kaptani, E. (2017), 'Participatory theatre for transformative social research', *Qualitative Research*, 17(3): 302–12.

Erickson, F. (2013), 'A history of qualitative inquiry in social and educational research', in N. Denzin and Y. Lincoln (eds), *The Landscape of Qualitative Research*, pp. 89–124, Thousand Oaks, CA: SAGE.

Etherington, K. (2004), *Becoming a Reflexive Researcher: Using Our Selves in Research*, London: Jessica Kingsley.

European-American Collaborative Challenging Whiteness, collaborative@eccw.org. Presented at the Sixth International Transformative Learning Conference, Michigan State University, 6–9 October 2005.

Falk, J., and Commonwealth Environment Protection Agency (Australia) and University of Wollongong Technological Change and Environmental Strategies Group (1993), *Social Equity and the Urban Environment: Report to the Commonwealth Environment Protection Agency*, Canberra: Australian Govt. Pub. Service.

Fals Borda, O. (1979), 'Investigating reality in order to transform it: The Colombian experience', *Dialectical Anthropology*, 4(1): 33–55.

Fals Borda, O., and Rahman, M. A. (1991), *Action and Knowledge: Breaking the Monopoly with Participatory Action-Research*, New York, NY: Apex Press.

Farrell, F. (2014), '"We're the mature people": A study of masculine subjectivity and its relationship to key stage four Religious Studies', *Gender and Education*, 27(1): 19–36.

Farrell, F. (2016a), '"Learning to listen": boys' gender narratives – implications for theory and practice', *Education + Training*, 58(3): 283–97.

Farrell, F. (2016b), 'Why all of a sudden do we need to teach fundamental British values? A critical investigation of religious education student teacher positioning within a policy discourse of discipline and control', *Journal of Education for Teaching*, 42(3): 280–97.

Field, J. (2000), *Lifelong Learning and the New Educational Order*, Stoke-on-Trent: Trentham Books.

Field, J. (2008), *Social Capital*, London: Routledge.

Field, J., Gallacher, A. and Ingram, R. (2009), *EDS Researching Transitions in Lifelong Learning*, London: Routledge.

Fielding, M. (2004), 'Transformative approaches to student voice: Theoretical underpinnings, recalcitrant realities', *British Educational Research Journal*, 30(2): 295–311.

Fine, M. (1992), *Disruptive Voices*, Ann Arbour: University of Michigan Press.

Fine, M. (1994), 'Dis – stance and other stances: Negotiations of Power inside Feminist Research', in A. Gitlin (ed.), *Power and Method: Political Activism and Educational Research*, London: Routledge.

Fine M., Weis, L., Weseen, S., and Wong, L. (2000), 'For whom? Qualitative research, representations, and social responsibilities', in N. Denzin and Y. Lincoln (eds), *Handbook of Qualitative Research*, 2nd edn, London: SAGE.

Finlay, L. (2002), '"Outing" the researcher: The provenance, process and practice of reflexivity', *Qualitative Health Research*, 12(3): 531–45.

Finnegan, F., and Merrill, B. (2017), '"We're as good as anybody else": A comparative study of working-class university students' experiences in England and Ireland', *British Journal of Sociology of Education*, 38(3): 307–24.

Fitch, B. D., and Normore, A. H. (2012), *Education-Based Incarceration and Recidivism*, Charlotte: Information Age Publishing.

Fleming, T., Loxley, A., and Finnegan, F. (2017), *Access and Participation in Irish Higher Education*, London: Palgrave.

Flewitt, R. (2005), 'Conducting research with young children: Some ethical considerations', *Early Child Development and Care*, 175(6): 553–65.

Fogel, A., and Garvey, A. (2007), 'Alive communication', *Infant Behavior and Development*, 30(2): 251–7.

Foley, D., and Valenzuela, A. (2005), 'Critical ethnography: The politics of collaboration', in N. K. Denzin and Y. S. Lincoln (eds), *The Sage Handbook of Qualitative Research*, 3rd edn, pp. 217–34, Thousand Oaks, CA: SAGE.

Fonagy, P., Gergely, G., and Target, M. (2007), 'The parent–infant dyad and the construction of the subjective self', *Journal of Child Psychology and Psychiatry*, 48(3/4): 288–328.

Fontana A., and Frey, J. (2000), 'The interview: From structured questions to negotiated text', in N. Foote Whyte, William (1955), *Street*

Corner Society. The Structure of an Italian Slum, Chicago: Chicago University Press.

Foster, V., Kimmel, M., and Skelton, C. (2001), 'What about the boys? An overview of the debates', in W. Martino and B. Meyenn (eds), *What About the Boys?*, pp. 1–24, Buckingham: Open University Press.

Foucault, M. (1977), *Discipline and Punish: The Birth of the Prison*, New York, NY: Pantheon Books.

Foucault, M. (1997), in P. Rabinow (ed.), *Ethics: Subjectivity and truth. Essential Works of Michel Foucault 1954–1984 (Vol. 1)*, Allen Lane: The Penguin Press.

Foucault, M. (2002), *The Archaeology of Knowledge*, London: Routledge.

Foucault, M. in Forney-Betancourt, R., Becker, H., Gomez-Müller, A., and Gauthier, J. D. (1987), 'The ethic of care for the self as a practice of freedom', *Philosophy and Social Criticism*, 12(2–3): 112–31.

Francis, B. (2000), *Boys, Girls and Achievement: Addressing the Classroom Issues*, London: RoutledgeFalmer.

Frankham, J. (2009), *Partnership Research: A Review of Approaches and Challenges in Conducting Research in Partnership with Service Users*, ESRC National Centre for Research Methods Review Paper 013, http://eprints.ncrm.ac.uk/778/1/Frankham_May_09.pdf.

Franklin, B. (1995), 'The case for children's rights: a progress report', in B. Franklin (ed.), *The Handbook of Children's Rights: Comparative Policy and Practice*, London: Routledge.

Franzen, S. (2013), 'Engaging a specific, not general, public: The use of ethnographic film in public scholarship', *Qualitative Research*, 13(4): 414–27.

Fraser, N. (2013), *Fortunes of Feminism: From State-Managed Capitalism to Neoliberal Crisis*, London; New York, NY: Verso.

Fraser, N., and Honneth, A. (2003), *Redistribution or Recognition? A Political-Philosophical Exchange*, London: Verso.

Freire, P. (1970), *Pedagogy of the Oppressed*, London: Bloomsbury.

Freire, P. (1985), *The Politics of Education: Culture, Power, and Liberation*, South Hadley, MA: Bergin & Garvey.

Freire, P. (1990), 'Conscientizing as a way of liberating', *Liberation Theology: A Documentary History*, 5–13, Maryknoll: NY: Orbis Books.

Freire, P. (1996), *Pedagogy of the Oppressed*, London: Penguin.

Freire, P. (2004), *Pedagogy of Indignation*, London: Paradigm Publishers.

Freire, P. (2005), *Pedagogy of the Oppressed*, 30th Anniversary Edition, New York, NY: Continuum.

Freire Institute (2017), *Paulo Freire* online at: www.freire.org/paulo-freire

Frith, S. (2004), 'Towards an aesthetic of popular music', in S. Frith (ed.), *Popular Music: Critical Concepts in Media and Cultural Studies*, pp. 32–47. London: Routledge.

Garrido, E., Pimenta, G. S., Moura, O. M., and Fusari, M. F. R. (1999), 'Collaborative research as an approach to foster teacher development, teachers' production of knowledge and changes in school practices', *Educational Action Research*, 7(3): 385–98.

Gaventa, J. (1991), 'Towards a knowledge democracy: Viewpoints on participatory research in North America', in O. Fals-Borda and M. A. Rahman (eds), *Action and Knowledge: Breaking the Monopoly with Participatory Action-Research*, pp. 121–31, New York, NY: Apex Press.

Gibb, K. (2017), Theresa May's speech and the challenge to expand English social housing The Conversation (5 October 17) at: https://theconversation.com/theresa-mays-speech-and-the-challenge-to-expand-english-social-housing-85218.

Giroux, H. (1997), *Pedagogy and the Politics of Hope: Theory, Culture, and Schooling*, Boulder, CO: Westview.

Gitlin, A. (1994), 'The shifting terrain of methodological debates', in A. Gitlin (ed.), *Power and Method Political Activism and Educational Research*, pp. 1–12, New York, NY: Routledge/Falmer.

Gitlin, A., and Russell, R. (1994), 'Alternative methodologies and the research context', in A. Gitlin (ed.), *Power and Method Political Activism and Educational Research*, pp. 181–202, New York, NY: Routledge/Falmer.

Goffman, E. (1959/1971), *The Presentation of Self in Everyday Life*, 2nd edn, New York, NY: Doubleday and Anchor Books (1971), London: Penguin.

Goffman, E. (1963), *Stigma: Notes on Management of Spoiled Identity*, London: Cox and Wyman.

Goffman, E. (1969), *Asylums*, Harmondsworth: Penguin.

Goffman, E. (1989), 'On fieldwork', *Journal of Contemporary Ethnography*, 18(2): 123–32.

Goodley, D. (2007), 'Towards socially just pedagogies: Deleuzoguattarian critical disability studies', *International Journal of Inclusive Education*, 11(3): 317–34.

Goodson, I. (1992), 'Studying teachers' lives: An emergent field of inquiry', in I. Goodson (ed.), *Studying Teachers' Lives*, pp. 1–17, London: Routledge.

Goodson, I. F., and Sikes, P. (2001), *Life History Research in Educational Settings: Learning from Lives*, Buckingham: Open University Press.

Gorard, S., and Huat See, B. (2017), *The Trials of Evidence-based Education: The Promises, Opportunities and Problems of Trials in Education*, London: Routledge.

Graham, L. J., and Slee, R. (2008), 'An illusory interiority: Interrogating the discourse/s of education', *Educational Philosophy and Theory*, 40(2): 277–93.

Greene J. C. (2008), 'Is mixed methods social inquiry a distinctive methodology?' *Journal of Mixed Methods Research*, (2): 1.

Grek, S. (2010), 'International organisations and the shared construction of policy "problems": Problematisation and change in education governance in Europe', *European Educational Research Journal*, 9(3): 396–406.

Grenfell, M., and James, D. (2004), 'Change *in* the field – Chang*ing* the field: Bourdieu and the methodological practice of educational research', *British Journal of Sociology of Education*, 25(4): 507–23.

Griffiths, M. (1998), *Educational Research for Social Justice: Getting off the Fence*, Buckingham: Open University Press.

Griffiths, M. (2003), *Action Research for Social Justice in Education: Fairly Different*, Buckingham: Open University Press.

Grove, J. (2017), Target UK's black female professor deficit 'with bespoke strategy': Broad-brush efforts to support female and ethnic minority academics will not address 'multidimensional inequality', says Warwick professor *Times Higher Education* 10 November 2017. https://www.timeshighereducation.com/news/target-uks-black-female-professor-deficit-bespoke-strategy

Grube, V. (2009), 'Admitting their worlds: Reflections of a researcher/teacher on the self-initiated art making of children', *International Journal of Education and the Arts*, 10(7). http://www.ijea.org/v10n7/.

Guberman, N., and Maheu, P. (2003), 'Beyond cultural sensitivity: Universal issues in caregiving', *Generations*, 27(4): 39–43.

Gunter, H. M. (2005), 'Conceptualizing research in educational leadership', *Educational Management Administration and Leadership*, 33(2): 165–80.

Guzmán, N. (1997), 'Leadership for successful inclusive schools: A study of principal behaviours', *Journal of Educational Administration*, 35(5): 439–50.

Habermas, J. (1974), *Theory and Practice*, London: Heinemann.

Habermas, J. (1987), *The Theory of Communicative Action. Vol 2, Lifeworld and System: A Critique of Functionalist Reason*, Cambridge: Polity.

Hadfield, M., and Haw, K. (2012), 'Video: Modalities and methodologies', *International Journal of Research & Method in Education*, 35(3): 311–24.

Hall, B. L. (1992), ' From margins to center? The development and purpose of participatory research', *The American Sociologist*, 23: 15–28.

Hall, B. L. (2001), 'I wish this were a poem of practices of participatory research', in P. Reason and H. Bradbury (eds), *Handbook of Action Research,* pp. 171–8, London: SAGE.

Hallett, F., and Allan, D. (2017), 'Architectures of oppression: Perceptions of individuals with Asperger's syndrome in the Republic of Armenia', *Journal of Research in Special Educational Needs,* 17(2): 123–31.

Hamilton, M. (2014), 'Survey literacies', in V. Duckworth and G. Ade-Ojo (eds), *Landscapes of Specific Literacies in Contemporary Society: Exploring a Social Model of Literacy,* pp. 47–60, London: Routledge Research in Education.

Hamilton, M. (2017), 'How international large-scale skills assessments engage with national actors: Mobilising networks through policy, media and public knowledge', *Critical Studies in Education,* 58(3): 280–94.

Hammersley, M. (2007), 'Educational research and teaching: A response to David Hargreaves TTA Lecture', in M. Hammersley (ed.), *Educational Research and Evidence-based Practice,* pp. 18–42, Milton Keynes: Open University Press/SAGE Publications Ltd.

Hammersley, M. (2009), 'Against the ethicists: On the evils of ethical regulation', *International Journal of Social Research Methodology,* 12(3): 211–25.

Hammersley, M., and Atkinson, P. (1983), *Ethnography: Principles in Practice,* London: Tavistock Publications.

Hammersley, M., and Atkinson, P. (2007), *Ethnography: Principles in Practice,* Oxon: Routledge.

Hanley, L. (2007), *Estates: An Intimate History,* London: Granta Publications.

Hanley, L. (2017), 'Look at Grenfell Tower and see the terrible price of Britain's inequality' *The Guardian,* 16 June 2017 at: https://www.theguardian.com/commentisfree/2017/jun/16/grenfell-tower-price-britain-inequality-high-rise.

Haraway, D. J. (1991), *Simians, Cyborgs and Women. The Reinvention of Nature,* London: Routledge.

Harding, S. (1987), 'Introduction: Is there a feminist method?', in S. Harding (ed.), *Feminism and Methodology,* pp. 1–14, Bloomington, IN: Indiana University Press.

Harding, S. (1991), *Whose Science? Whose Knowledge? Thinking from Women's Lives,* Ithaca: Cornell University Press.

Harding, S. (2008), *Sciences from Below: Feminisms, Postcolonialities, and Modernities,* Durham, NC: Duke University Press.

Hargreaves, D. (1967), *Social Relations in the Secondary School,* London: Routledge and Kegan-Paul.

Hargreaves, A. (1986), *Two Cultures of Schooling: The Case of Middle Schools*, London: Falmer Press.

Hargreaves, D. H. (1996), *Teaching as a Research-based Profession: Possibilities and Prospects Teacher Training Agency Annual Lecture*, London: Teacher Training Agency.

Hargreaves, D. H. (2007), 'In defence of research for evidence-based teaching: A rejoinder to Martyn Hammersley', in M. Hammersley (ed.), *Educational Research and Evidence-based Practice*, pp. 43–60, Milton Keynes: Open University Press/SAGE Publications Ltd.

Harper, D. (2002), 'Talking about pictures: A case for photo-elicitation', *Visual Studies*, 17(1): 13–26.

Harper, G. W., Jamil, O. B., and Wilson, B. D. (2007), 'Collaborative community-based research as activism: Giving voice and hope to lesbian, gay, and bisexual youth', *Journal of Gay & Lesbian Psychotherapy*, 11(3/4): 99–119.

Hatch, J. A. (2002), *Doing Qualitative Research in Education Settings*, Albany, USA: State University of New York Press.

Heckman, J. J. (2013), *Giving Kids a Fair Chance*, Cambridge, MA: MIT Press. ISBN:9780262019132.

Hedd-Jones, C. (2017), Combining daycare for children and elderly people benefits all generation in The Conversation 4 January 2017 at: http://theconversation.com/combining-daycare-for-children-and-elderly-people-benefits-all-generations-70724. Accessed 18 November 2017.

Heller, M. (2011), *Paths to Post-nationalism*, Oxford: Oxford University Press.

Hertz, R. (ed.) (1997), *Reflexivity and Voice*, Thousand Oaks, CA: SAGE Publications Inc.

Hickling-Hudson, A. (2014), Caribbean schooling and the social divide – what will it take to change neo-colonial education systems? In CIES 2015 Annual Conference of the Comparative and International Education Society, 8–13 March 2015, Washington, USA.

Hine, C. (2007), 'Connective ethnography for the exploration of e-science', *Journal of Computer-Mediated Communication*, https://onlinelibrary.wiley.com/doi/abs/10.1111/j.1083-6101.2007.00341.x. Accessed 28 May 2018.

Hine, C. (2009), 'How can qualitative internet researchers define the boundaries of their projects?', in A. N. Markham and N. K. Baym (eds), *Internet Inquiry: Conversations about Method*, Los Angeles: SAGE.

Hines, J. M. (2012), 'Using an anti-oppressive framework in social work practice with lesbians', *Journal of Gay & Lesbian Social Services*, 24(1): 23–39.

Hitlin, S. (2003), 'Values as the core of personal identity: Drawing links between two theories of self', *Social Psychology Quarterly*, 66(2): 118–37.

Hodder, I. (2000), 'The interpretation of documents and material culture', in N. Denzin and Y. Lincoln (eds), *Handbook of Qualitative Research*, 2nd edn, London: SAGE.

Hodkinson, A. (2012), 'Illusionary inclusion – what went wrong with New Labour's landmark educational policy?', *British Journal of Special Education*, 39(1): 4–11.

Hodkinson, P. (2008), 'Understanding career decision-making and progression: Careership revisited', *John Killeen Memorial Lecture*, Woburn House, London, 16 October 2008.

Holland, S., Renold, E., Ross, N., and Hillman, A. (2008), *Rights, 'Right On' Or The Right Thing to Do?*. ESRC National Centre for Research Methods NCRM Working Paper Series 07/08.

Holmes, S. M., and Casteneda, H. (2016), 'Representing the "European refugee crisis" in Germany and beyond: Deservingness and difference, life and death', *American Ethnologist*, 43(1): 12–24.

hooks, b. (1989), *Talking Back: Thinking Feminist, Thinking Black*, Boston, MA: South End Press.

hooks, b. (1994), *Teaching to Transgress: Education as the Practice of Freedom*, New York: Routledge.

hooks, b. (2000), *Feminism Is for Everybody: Passionate Politics*, Cambridge, MA: South End Press.

hooks, b. (2009), *Belonging: A Culture of Place*, New York; London: Routledge.

House of Lords Select Committee on Social Mobility (2016), *Overlooked and left behind: Improving the transition from school towork for the majority of young people*, 8 April 2016.

Hume, D. (1740/2000), *A Treatise of Human Nature*, D. F. Norton and M. J. Norton (eds), Oxford: Oxford University Press.

Humphreys, L. (1970), *Tearoom Trade: Impersonal Sex in Public Places*, London: Gerald Duckworth.

Huws, J. C., and Jones, R. S. P. (2010), '"They just seem to live their lives in their own little world": lay perceptions of autism', *Disability and Society*, 25(3): 331–44.

Huws, J. C., and Jones, R. S. P. (2015), '"I'm really glad this is developmental": Autism and social comparisons – an interpretative phenomenological analysis', *Autism: the International Journal of Research and Practice*, 19(1): 84–90.

Ingram, N. (2011), 'Within school and beyond the gate: The complexities of being educationally successful and working class', *Sociology*, 45(2): 287–302.

Iredale, A. (2018), *Teacher Education in Lifelong Learning: Developing Professionalism as a Democratic Endeavour*, London: Palgrave Macmillan.

Janssens, W., Rosemberg Montes, C., and van Spijk, J. K. N. (2009), *The impact of home-visiting early childhood intervention in the Caribbean on cognitive and socio-emotional child development*. (AIID Research Series; No. 09-01/1) Amsterdam: Amsterdam Institute for International Development. Available from: https://research.vu.nl/en/publications/the-impact-of-home-visiting-early-childhood-intervention-in-the-c.

Janssens, W., and Rosemberg, C. (2014), 'The impact of a Caribbean home-visiting child development program on cognitive skills', *Economics of Education Review*, 39: 22–37.

Johnson, C., Duckworth, V., McNamara, M., and Apelbaum, C. (2010), 'A tale of two adult learners: From adult basic education to degree completion', *National Association for Developmental Education*, 5(5): 57–67.

Johnson, C., and Duckworth, V. (2018), 'A tale of two adult leaners', in A. Benoit, J. S. Olson, and C. Johnson (eds), *Leaps of Faith: Stories from Working-Class Scholars*, Charlotte, NC: Information Age Publishing.

Johnston, R. (2000), 'Whose side, whose research. Whose learning, whose outcomes? Ethics, emancipatory research and unemployment', in H. Simons and P. Usher (eds), *Situated Ethics in Educational Research*, London: RoutledgeFalmer.

Jones, S. (2018), *Portraits of Everyday Literacy for Social Justice: Reframing the Debate for Families and Communities*, London: Palgrave Macmillan.

Jones, C., and Lyons, C. (2004), 'Case study: Design? Method? Or comprehensive strategy?', *Nurse Researcher*, 11(3): 70–6.

Jones, P. (1995), *Drama as Therapy, Theatre as Living*, London: Routledge.

Kalmanson, B. (2009), 'Echoes in the nursery: Insights for treatment of early signs of autism in a baby sibling', *Journal of Infant, Child, and Adolescent Psychotherapy*, 8(1).

Kara, H. (2015), *Creative Research Methods in the Social Sciences: A Practical Guide*, Bristol: Policy Press.

Karapetyan, S., Manasyan, H., Mirzakhanyan, A., Norekian, M., and Harutyunyan, N. (2011), *Armenia: Social Protection and Social Inclusion (Country Report)*, Yerevan, Armenia: Armenia Eurasia Partnership Foundation.

Kazdin, A. E. (2003), *Research Design in Clinical Psychology*, 4th edn, Boston: Allyn and Bacon.

Keep, E. (2014), Vocational qualifications and their interaction with the labour market – The challenges of weak incentives to learn. Keynote

Address at Research in Post-compulsory Education, Inaugural
  Conference, University of Oxford, July 2014.
Kellett, M. (2010), *Re-thinking Children and Research: Attitudes in
  Contemporary Society*, London: Continuum.
Kemmis, S., and McTaggart, R. (eds) (1988), *The Action Research
  Planner*, Geelong, Vic: Deakin University Press.
Kemmis, S., and McTaggart, R. (2000), 'Participatory action research', in
  N. Denzin and Y. Lincoln (eds), *Handbook of Qualitative Research*,
  2nd edn, pp. 567–605, Thousand Oaks, CA: SAGE.
Kemmis, S., and McTaggart, R. (2005), 'Participatory action research',
  in N. K. Denzin and Y. S. Lincoln (eds), *The Sage Handbook of
  Qualitative Research*, 3rd edn, pp. 559–604, Thousand Oaks,
  CA: SAGE.
Kilgore (2001), 'Critical and postmodern perspectives on adult learning',
  New Directions for Adult and Continuing Education, 89(Spring
  2001): 53–61.
Kincheloe, J., and McLaren, P. (2000), 'Rethinking critical theory and
  qualitative research', in N. Denzin and Y. Lincoln (eds), *Handbook
  of Qualitative Research*, 2nd edn, pp. 279–313, Thousand Oaks,
  CA: SAGE.
Kincheloe, J., McLaren, P., and Steinberg, S. (2011), 'Critical pedagogy
  and qualitative research: Moving to the bricolage', in N. Denzin and Y.
  Lincoln (eds), *Landscape of Qualitative Research*, 4th edn, pp. 339–70,
  Los Angeles: SAGE.
Knight, S. (ed.) (2011), *Forest School for All*, London: SAGE.
Knowles, R. (2010), *Theatre and Interculturalism*, Basingstoke: Palgrave
  Macmillan.
Kohlberg, L., and Kramer, R. (1969), 'Continuities and discontinuities
  in childhood and adult moral development', *Human Development*,
  12: 93–120.
Kozinets, R. (2010), *Netnography: Doing Ethnographic Research Online*,
  London: SAGE.
Kozinets, R. V. (2015), *Netnography: Redefined*, 2nd edn,
  London: SAGE.
Krishnakumar, A., Buehler, C., and Barber, B. K. (2004), 'Cross-ethnic
  equivalence of socialization measures in European American
  and African American Youth', *Journal of Marriage and Family*,
  66(3): 809–20.
Kugelmass, J. W., and Ainscow, M. (2004), 'Leadership for inclusion: A
  comparison of international practices', *Journal of Research in Special
  Educational Needs*, 4(3): 133–41.
Kvale, S., and Brinkmann, S. (2009), *InterViews: Learning the Craft of
  Qualitative Research Interviewing*, London: Sage Publications.

Ladson-Billings, G., and Donner, J. (2005), 'The moral activist role of critical race theory scholarship', in N. Denzin and Y. Lincoln (eds), *The SAGE Handbook of Qualitative Research*, 3rd edn, pp. 279–302, Thousand Oaks, CA: SAGE.

Lamphere, L. (1994), 'Critical qualitative methodology', in A. Gitlin (ed.), *Power and Method*, pp. 217–26, London: Routledge.

Lander, V. (2016), 'Introduction to fundamental British values', *Journal of Education for Teaching*, 42(3): 274–9.

Landy, R. J., and Montgomery, D. T. (2012), *Theatre for Change*, New York, NY: Palgrave Macmillan.

Lather (1986), 'Research as praxis', *Harvard Educational Review*, 56(3): 257–78.

Lawrence-Lightfoot, S. (n.d.), Portraiture. Origins and Purpose. [Online]. Available: http://www.saralawrencelightfoot.com/origin--purpose.html. Accessed 3 April 2016.

Lawthom, R. with Stamford, C. (2004), '"I'd never met a vegetarian, never mind a lesbian": Coleen's life story', in D. Goodley, R. Lawthom, P. Clough and M. Moore (eds), *Researching Life Stories: Method, Theory and Analyses in a Biographical Age*, pp. 15–25. London: RoutledgeFalmer.

Lazuka, R. (2009), 'What is Art?', in Arts at the Core. The National Task Force on the Arts in Education, p. 6. https://advocacy.collegeboard.org/ sites/default/files/arts-at-the-core.pdf. Accessed 23 March 2016.

Ledwith, M. (2007), 'Listening as emancipatory research', *Journal of Critical Health*, 5(3): 15–18.

Lee, D. (1955/1987), *Plato The Republic*, London: Penguin Books.

Lefebvre, H. (1991), *The Production of Space*, Oxford: Blackwell.

Leo, E., and Barton, L. (2006), 'Inclusion, diversity and leadership: Perspectives, possibilities and contradictions', *Educational Management Administration & Leadership*, 34(2): 167–80.

Lieblich, A., Tuval-Mashiach, R., and Zilber, T. (1998), *Narrative Research: Reading, Analysis and Interpretation (Vol. 47)*, London: Sage Publications.

Lincoln, Y., and Denzin, N. (2002), 'The seventh moment: Out of the past', in N. Denzin and Y. Lincoln (eds), *Handbook of Qualitative Research*, 2nd edn, Thousand Oaks, CA: SAGE.

Lincoln, Y., and Denzin, N. (2013), 'Epilogue', in N. Denzin and Y. Lincoln (eds), *Landscape of Qualitative Research*, pp. 579–87, Thousand Oaks, CA: SAGE.

Lincoln, Y., and Guba, E. G. (1985), *Naturalistic Inquiry*, Beverly Hills, CA: SAGE.

Lincoln, Y., and Guba, E. (2000), 'Paradigmatic controversies, contradictions, and emerging confluences', in N. Denzin and Y. Lincoln (eds), *Handbook of Qualitative Research*, 2nd edn, pp. 163–88, Thousand Oaks, CA: SAGE.

Lincoln, Y., Lynham, S., and Guba, E. (2013), 'Paradigmatic controversies, contradictions, and emerging confluences, revisited', in N. Denzin and Y. Lincoln (eds), *The Landscape of Qualitative Research*, pp. 199–266, London; Los Angeles: SAGE.

Locke, K. D. (2014), 'Agency and communion in social comparisons', in Z. Krizan and F. X. Gibbons (eds), *Communal Functions of Social Comparison*, pp. 11–38, Cambridge: Cambridge University Press.

Lumby, J., and Morrison, M. (2010), 'Leadership and diversity: Theory and research', *School Leadership & Management*, 30(1): 3–17.

Luttrell, W. (1997), *School-smart and Mother-wise: Working-class Women's Identity and Schooling*, New York, NY: Routledge.

Lynch, K., and O'Riordan, C. (1998), 'Inequality in higher education: A study of class barriers', *British Journal of Sociology of Education*, 19(4): 445–78.

Lyons, H. Z., Bike, D. H. Ojeda, L., Johnson, A. Rosales, R., and Flores, L. Y. 'Qualitative research as social justice practice with culturally diverse populations', *Journal for Social Action in Counseling and Psychology* [Special Issue on Research and Social Justice] 5(2): 10–25. Accessed 28 May 2018. http://psysr.org/jsacp/Lyons-Etal-V5N2-13_10-25.pdf.

Mac an Ghaill, M. (1994), *The Making of Men: Masculinities, Sexualities and Schooling*, Buckingham: Open University.

MacDonald and Marsh (2005), *Disconnected Youth? Growing Up in Britain's Poor Neighbourhoods*, Basingstoke: Palgrave Macmillan.

Macedo, D. (1994), *Literacies of Power: What Americans Are Not Allowed to Know*, Boulder, CO: Westview.

Machin, S. (2006), *Social Disadvantage and Education Experiences, OECD Social, Employment and Migration Working Papers No. 32*, Paris: OECD.

MacIntyre, A. (1981), *After Virtue: A Moral Theory*, London: Duckworth.

Madison, D. S. (2005), *Critical Ethnography: Methods, Ethics, and Performance*, Thousand Oaks, CA: SAGE.

Madison, D. S. (2012), *Critical Ethnography: Method, Ethics, and Performance: Volume 2*, 2nd edn, Thousand Oaks, CA: SAGE.

Madriz, E. (2000), 'Focus groups in feminist research', in N. Denzin, and Y. Lincoln (eds), *Handbook of Qualitative Research*, 2nd edn, London: SAGE.

Magnat, V. (2012), 'Can research become ceremony? Performance ethnography and indigenous epistemologies', *Canadian Theatre Review*, 151: 30–6.

Mahlomaholo, S. M. (2013), 'Indigenous research and sustainable learning', *International Journal of Science Education*, 5: 317–22.

Malloy, J. K. (2007), 'Photovoice as a tool for social justice workers', *Journal of Progressive Human Services*, 18(2): 39–55.

Margaret, W., and Kas, M. (2015), 'Exploring the social milieu of disability: Themes of poverty, education, and labour participation', *Labor et Education*, (3): 155–72.

Martino, W. (1999), '"Cool boys," "party animals," "squids" and "poofters": Interrogating the dynamics and politics of adolescent masculinities in school', *British Journal of Sociology of Education*, 20(2): 239–63.

Marx, K. (1998), *Das Kapital*, Oxford: Oxford University Press.

McCorkel, J., and Myers, K. (2003), 'What difference does difference make? Positon and privilege in the field', *Qualitative Sociology*, 26(2): 199–231.

McCormack, M. (2012), *The Declining Significance of Homophobia*, New York, NY: Oxford University Press.

McCulloch, G. (1991), *Philosophers and Kings Education for Leadership in Modern England*, Cambridge: Cambridge University Press.

McCulloch, G. (1998), *Failing the Ordinary Child? The Theory and Practice of Working Class Secondary Education*, Buckingham: Open University Press.

MacDonald, R., and Marsh, J. (2005), *Disconnected Youth? Growing up in Britain's Poor Neighbourhoods*, London: Palgrave.

Maynard, M., and Purvis, J. (1995), *Researching Women's Lives from a Feminist Perspective*, pp. 1–9. London: Taylor and Francis.

McDonough, S. (2005), 'Interaction guidance: Promoting and nurturing the caregiving relationship', in A. J. Sameroff, S. C. McDonough, K. L. Rosenblum (eds), *Treating Parent–Infant Relationship Problems*, New York, NY: Guildford Press.

McDowell, L. (2000), 'The trouble with men? Young people, gender transformations and the crisis of masculinity', *International Journal of Urban and Regional Research*, 24(1): 201–9.

McKenna, T., Vicars, M., and Cacciattolo, M. (eds) (2013), *Engaging the Disengaged*, Cambridge: Cambridge University Press.

McRobbie, A. (2006), 'Yummy mummies leave a bad taste for young women', *The Guardian*, 2 March 2006, available at: http://www.guardian.co.uk/world/2006/mar/02/gender.comment.

Mead, M. (1930/2001), *Coming of Age in Samoa*, New York, NY: HarperCollins.

Mead, M. (1995), 'Visual anthropology in a discipline of words', in P. Hockings (ed.), *Principles of Visual Anthropology*, 2nd edn, pp. 3–10, Berlin/New York, NY: Mouton de Gruyter.

Mercer, J. (2007), 'The challenges of insider research in educational institutions: Wielding a double-edged sword and resolving delicate dilemmas', *Oxford Review of Education*, 33(1): 1–17.

Merrill, B., and West, L. (2009), *Using Biographical Methods in Social Research*, Los Angeles/London: SAGE.

McAteer, M., and Wood, L. Enacting the civic role of the university in a community-based participatory action research project. Under review: Higher Education.

Miles, M. B., and Huberman, A. M. (1984), *Qualitative Data Analysis: A Source Book of New Methods*, Beverly Hills, CA: SAGE.

McNiff, J., and Whitehead, J. (2009), *Doing and Writing Action Research*, London: SAGE.

Merton, R. (1972), 'Insiders and outsiders: A chapter in the sociology of knowledge', *American Journal of Sociology* 78: 9–47.

Milligan, L. (2016), 'Insider-outsider-inbetweener? Researcher positioning, participative methods and cross-cultural educational research', *Compare: A Journal of Comparative and International Education*, 46(2): 235–50.

Mills, C. (2008), 'Reproduction and transformation of inequalities in schooling: The transformative potential of the theoretical constructs of Bourdieu', *British Journal of Sociology of Education*, 29(1): 79–89.

Milner, A. (2005), *Literature, Culture and Society*, Abingdon: Routledge.

Ministry of Justice (2015), *Proven Reoffending Statistics Quarterly Bulletin*, London: Ministry of Justice.

Minogue, K. (1998), 'Social justice in theory and practice', in D. Boucher and P. Kelly (eds), *Social Justice from Hume to Walzer*, London: Routledge.

Mishra, R. K., and Raveendran, J. (eds) (2014), *Millennium Development Goals: The Indian Journey*, New Delhi: Allied Publishers.

Mitzen, J. (2006), 'Ontological security in world politics: State identity and the security dilemma', *European Journal of International Relations*, (12): 341–70.

Moss, J., Deppeler, J., Astley, L., and Pattison, K. (2007), 'Student researchers in the middle: Using visual images to make sense of inclusive education', *Journal of Research in Special Educational Needs*, 7(1): 46–54.

Mottron, L., Bouvet, L., Bonnel, A., Samson, F., Burack, J., Dawson, M., and Heaton, P. (2013), 'Veridical mapping in the development of exceptional autistic abilities', *Neuroscience and Biobehavioral Reviews*, 37: 209–28. http://www.sciencedirect.com/science/article/pii/S0149763412002060.

Narayan, U. (1989), 'The project of feminist epistemology', in S. Bordo and A. Jaggar (eds), *Gender/Body/Knowledge: Feminist*

Reconstructions of Being and Knowing, pp. 256–72. Rutgers, NJ: Rutgers University Press.

National Education Union, NUT Section (2017), Edu Facts: Child Poverty at https://www.teachers.org.uk/edufacts/child-poverty.

Nicholson, H. (2015), *Applied Drama: The Gift of Theatre*, New York, NY: Palgrave.

Nilholm, C. (2006), 'Special education, inclusion and democracy', *European Journal of Special Needs Education*, 21(4): 431–45.

Nind, M. (2011), 'Participatory data analysis: A step too far', *Qualitative Research*, 11: 349–63.

Nind, M. (2014a), 'Inclusive research and inclusive education: Why connecting them makes sense for teachers' and learners' democratic development of education', *Cambridge Journal of Education*, 44(4): 525–40.

Nind, M. (2014b), *What Is Inclusive Research?* London: Bloomsbury Academic.

Nind, M., and Vinha, H. (2012), 'Doing research inclusively: Bridges to multiple possibilities in inclusive research', *British Journal of Learning Disabilities*, 42: 102–9.

Nind, M., and Vinha, H. (2013), National Centre for Research Methods Methodological Review paper *Practical considerations in doing research inclusively and doing it well: Lessons for inclusive researchers* NCRM/ESRC.

Nind, M., Hall, K., and Curtin, A. (2016), *Research Methods for Pedagogy*, London: Bloomsbury.

Nixon, J., Walker, M., and Clough, P. (2003), 'Research as thoughtful practice', in P. Sikes, J. Nixon and W. Carr (eds), *The Moral Foundations of Educational research: Knowledge, Inquiry and Values*, Maidenhead: Open University Press.

Nutbrown (2011), 'Naked by the pool? Blurring the image? Ethical issues in the portrayal of young children in Arts-based educational research', *Qualitative Inquiry*, 17(1): 3–14.

OECD (2018), *Equity in Education: Breaking Down Barriers to Social Mobility*, Paris: PISA, OECD Publishing.

Olesen, V. (2000), 'Feminisms and qualitative research at and into the millennium', in N. Denzin and Y. Lincoln (eds), *Handbook of Qualitative Research*, 2nd edn, Thousand Oaks, CA: SAGE.

Olesen, V. (2013), 'Feminist qualitative research in the millennium's first decade: developments, challenges, prospects', in N. Denzin and Y. Lincoln (eds), *The Landscape of Qualitative Research*, pp. 267–304, Thousand Oaks, CA: SAGE.

Oliffe, J. L., and Bottorff, J. L. (2007), 'Further than the eye can see? Photo elicitation and research with men', *Qualitative Health Research*, 17: 850–8.

Ollis, T., Starr, K., Ryan, C., Angwin, J., and Harrison, U. (2017), 'Second chance learning in neighbourhood houses in Victoria', *Australian Journal of Adult Learning*, 57: 1–28.

Ollis, T., Williams, J., Townsend, R., Harris, A., and Jorquera, J. (2014), 'The Popular Education Network of Australia (PENA) and twenty-first century critical education', in M. Peters and T. Besley (eds), *Paulo Friere: The Global Legacy*, New York, NY: Peter Lang.

O'Neill, C. (1992), *Telling It Like It Is*, Dublin: Combat Poverty Agency.

Otto, H.-U., Walker, M., and Holger, Z. (eds) (2017), *Capability-promoting Policies: Enhancing Individual and Social Development*, Bristol: Policy Press.

Oxfam Blogs (20/06/2017), Grenfell Tower is a Hurricane Katrina moment, revealing the shameful state of Britain at https://oxfamblogs.org/fp2p/grenfell-tower-is-a-hurricane-katrina-moment-revealing-the-shameful-state-of-britain/.

Pahl, K., and Rowsell, J. (2010), *Artifactual Literacies: Every Object Tells a Story*, New York, NY: Teachers College Press.

Papen, U. (2010), 'Literacy mediators, scribes or brokers? The central role of others in accomplishing reading and writing', *Langage et société*, septembre (133): 63–82.

Papen, U., and Thériault, V. (2016), 'Youth Workers as literacy mediators: Supporting young people's learning about institutional literacy practices', *Journal of Adolescent & Adult Literacy*, 60(2): 185–93.

Patai (1994), 'When method becomes power', in A. Gitlin (ed.), *Power and Method: Political Activism and Educational Research*, London: Routledge.

Perepa, P. (2014), 'Cultural basis of social "deficits" in autism spectrum disorders', *European Journal of Special Needs Education*, 29(3): 313–26.

Persson, S. (2009), *Research Circles – A Guide*, Malmo: Centre for Diversity in Education.

Pink, S. (2007a), *Doing Visual Ethnography: Images, Media and Representation in Research*, London: SAGE.

Pink, S. (2007b), 'Walking with video', *Visual Studies*, 22(3): 240–52.

Pink, S. (2013), *Doing Visual Ethnography: Images, Media, and Representation in Research*, 3rd edn, London: SAGE.

Plummer, K. (1995), *Telling Sexual Stories: Power, Change and Social Worlds*, London: Routledge.

Plummer, K. (2013), 'Critical humanism and queer theory: Living with the tensions postscript 2011 to living with the contradictions', in N. Denzin and Y. Lincoln (eds), *The Landscape of Qualitative Research*, pp. 407–42, Thousand Oaks, CA: SAGE.

Pole, C., and Morrison, M. (2003), *Ethnography for Education*, Maidenhead: Open University Press.

Pollack, W. (1999), *Real Boys: Rescuing Our Sons from the Myths of Boyhood*, New York, NY: Henry Holt and Company.

Pope, C., De Luca, R., and Tolich, M. (2010), 'How an exchange of perspectives led to tentative ethical guidelines for visual ethnography', *International Journal of Research & Method in Education*, 33(3): 301–15.

Prentki, T., and Preston, S. (2013), 'Applied theatre: An introduction', in T. Prentki, and S. Preston (eds), *The Applied Theatre Reader*, pp. 9–16, Oxon: Routledge.

Proudfoot, J. (2015), 'Anxiety and phantasy in the field: The position of the unconscious in ethnographic research', *Environment and Planning D: Society and Space*, 33(6): 1135–52.

Prosser, J., and Loxley, A. (2007), 'Enhancing the contribution of visual methods to inclusive education', *Journal of Research in Special Educational Needs*, 7(1): 55–68.

Prosser, J., and Schwartz, D. (1998), 'Photographs within the sociological research process', in J. Prosser (ed.), *Image-based Research*, pp. 115–30, London: Falmer Press.

Punch, K., and Oancea, A. (2014), *Introduction to Research Methods in Education*, London: SAGE.

Putnam, D. (2009), We are the people we've been waiting for', available at: www.youtube.com/watch?v¼x-B0fJfXADU

Ramazanoglu, C. (2002), *Feminist Methodology: Challenges and Choices*, London: SAGE.

Ramsaran, D. (2004), 'State reaction to globalization, a class centered analysis: The case of Barbados and Trinidad and Tobago', *International Journal of Comparative Sociology*, 45(1–2): 111–30.

Rawls, J. (1999), *A Theory of Justice Revised Edition*, Oxford: Oxford University Press.

Rawls, J. (1971), *A Theory of Justice*, Cambridge, Massachusetts/London, England: The Belknap Press of Harvard University Press.

Rayner, S. (2009), 'Educational diversity and learning leadership: A proposition, some principles and a model of inclusive leadership?' *Educational Review*, 61(4): 433–47.

Reason, P. (1994), 'Three approaches to participative inquiry', in N. Denzin and Y. Lincoln (eds), *Handbook of Qualitative Research*, London: SAGE.

Reason, P., and Bradbury, H. (2001), 'Introduction: Inquiry and participation in search of a world worthy of human aspiration', in P. Reason and H. Bradbury (eds), *Handbook of Action Research: Participative Inquiry and Practice*, London: SAGE.

Reason, P., and Bradbury, H. (2007), *Handbook of Action Research*, London: SAGE.

Reason, P., and Heron, J (1995), 'Co-operative Inquiry', in J. Smith, R. Harre and L. Langenhove (eds), *Rethinking Methods in Psychology*, London: SAGE.

Reay, D. (1998), 'Cultural reproduction: Mothers involvement in their children's primary schooling', in M. Grenfell and D. James (eds), *Bourdieu and Education Acts of Practical Theory*, pp. 55–70, London: Falmer Press.

Reay, D. (2004), 'Exclusivity, exclusion, and social class in urban education markets in the United Kingdom', *Urban Education*, 39(5): 537–60.

Reay, D. (2006), 'The zombie stalking English schools: Social class and educational inequality', *British Journal of Educational Studies*, 54(3): 288–307.

Reay, D. (2012), 'What would a socially just education system look like?: Saving the minnows from the pike', *Journal of Education Policy*, 27(5): 587–99.

Reay, D. (2017), *Miseducation*, Bristol: Policy Press, University of Bristol.

Reay, D., David, M. E., and Ball, S. J. (2005), *Degrees of Choice: Class, Race, Gender and Higher Education*. Stoke-on-Trent: Trentham Books.

Richardson, L. (2000), 'Writing: A method of inquiry', in N. Denzin and Y. Lincoln (eds), *Handbook of Qualitative Research*, 2nd edn, London: SAGE.

Richardson, L., and St. Pierre, E. A. (2008), 'Writing: A method of inquiry', in N. Denzin and Y. Lincoln (eds), *Collecting and Interpreting Qualitative Materials*, 3rd edn, London: SAGE.

Riehl, C. J. (2000), 'The principal's role in creating inclusive schools for diverse students: A review of normative, empirical, and critical literature on the practice of educational administration', *Review of Educational Research*, 70(1): 55–81.

Roberts, S. (2012), '"I just got on with it": The educational experiences of ordinary, yet overlooked, boys', *British Journal of Sociology of Education*, 33(2): 203–21.

Robbins, D. (1998), 'The Need for an Epistemological "Break"', in M. Grenfell and D. James (eds), *Bourdieu and Education Acts of Practical Theory*, London: Falmer Press.

Robinson-Pant, A. (2016), *Promoting Health and Literacy for Women's Empowerment*. UNESCO Institute for Lifelong Learning (UIL). http://uil.unesco.org/literacy-and-basic-skills/focus-women/investigating-relationship-between-literacy-health-and-womens. Accessed 30 July 2017.

Roggman, L. A., Innocenti, M. S., Cook, G. A., Jump, V. K., and Akers, J. F. (2007), *Parenting Interactions with Children: Checklist of Observations Linked to Outcomes (PICCOLO)*. Paper presented at the Society for Research in Child Development, Boston, MA.

Roopnarine, J. L. (2006), 'Cultural bases of childrearing and socialization in African Caribbean and indo Caribbean families', in S. G. Williams, J. Brown, and J. L. Roopnarine (eds), *Child Rearing in the Caribbean: A Literature Review*, Caribbean Child Support Initiative.

Roopnarine, J. L., Shin, M., Jung, K., and Hossain, Z. (2003), 'Play and early development and education. The instantiation of parental belief systems', in O. Saracho and B. Spodek (eds), *Contemporary Perspectives on Play, Early Childhood Education*, pp. 115–32, New York, NY: Information Age Publishing.

Rose, G. (1997), 'Situating knowledges: Positionality, reflexivities and other tactics', *Progress in Human Geography*, 21(3): 305–20.

Rose, G. (2016), *Visual Methodologies: An Introduction to Researching with Visual Materials*, 4th edn, London: SAGE.

Said, E. W. (1978), *Orientalism*, New York, NY: Vintage Books, A Division of Random House, Inc.

Sales, N. J. (2017), Single mothers aren't all disasters. But you wouldn't know that from TV. *The Guardian*, 14 November 2017. https://www.theguardian.com/commentisfree/2017/nov/14/single-mothers-hot-messes-smilf-frankie-shaw.

Sameroff, A. (ed.) (2009), 'The transactional model of development: How children and contexts shape each other', *American Psychological Association*, pp. 3–21. Washington, DC, US: A doi.org/10.1037/11877-001

Sameroff, A. J., McDonough, S. C., and Rosenblum, K. L. (eds) (2005), *Treating Parent–Infant Relationship Problems. Strategies for Intervention*, New York, NY: The Guildford Press.

Save the Children International (2012), *Assessment of Success and Challenges of Projects Implemented for People with Disabilities in Armenia (report)*. Armenia: Save the Children International LIFE Programme.

Sandberg, E. H., and Spritz, B. L. (2013), *A Brief Guide to Autism Treatments*, London: Jessica Kingsley Publishers.

Sayer, A. (1992), *Method in Social Science: A Realist Approach*, 2nd edn, London/New York, NY: Taylor & Francis.

Sayre, J. M., Pianta, R. C., Marvin, R. S., and Saft, E. W. (2001), 'Mothers' representations of relationships with their children: Relations with mother characteristics and feeding sensitivity', *Journal of Pediatric Psychology*, 26(6): 375–84.

Schechter, D. S., Myers, M. M., Brunelli, S. A., Coates, S. W., Zeanah, C. H., Davies, M., and Liebowitz, M. R. (2006), 'Traumatized mothers can change their minds about their toddlers: Understanding how a novel use of video feedback supports positive change of maternal attributions', *Infant Mental Health Journal*, 27(5): 429–47. doi:10.1002/imhj.20101

Schostak, J. F. (2002), *Understanding, Designing and Conducting Qualitative Research in Education*, Buckingham: Open University Press.

Schostak, J. F. (2006), *Interviewing and Representation in Qualitative Research Projects*, Maidenhead: Open University Press.

Schwandt, T. A. (1998), 'Constructivist, interpretivist approaches to human inquiry', in N. Denzin, and Y. Lincoln (eds), *The Landscape of Qualitative Research*, Thousand Oaks, CA: SAGE.

Sebba, J., and Ainscow, M. (1996), 'International developments in inclusive schooling: Mapping the issues', *Cambridge Journal of Education*, 26(1): 5–18.

Seguin, C. A., and Ambrosio, A. L. (2002), 'Multicultural vignettes for teacher preparation', *Multicultural Perspectives*, 4(4): 10–16.

Shakespeare Behind Bars (2017), Shakespeare Behind Bars. Retrieved from ww.shakespearebehindbars.org: http://www.shakespearebehindbars.org/programs/kentucky/llcc/.

Shaw, I. (2008), 'Ethics and the practice of qualitative research', *Qualitative Social Work*, 7(4): 400–14.

Sheller, M. (2013), *Sociology After the Mobilities Turn from: The Routledge Handbook of Mobilities*, Routledge. Accessed 26 May 2018.

Shor, I. (1992), *Empowering Education: Critical Teaching for Social Change*, Chicago, IL: University of Chicago Press.

Sikes, P., and Goodson, I. (2003), 'Living research: Thoughts on educational research as moral practice', in P. Sikes, J. Nixon and W. Carr (eds), *The Moral Foundations of Educational Research: Knowledge, Inquiry and Values*, Maidenhead: Open University Press.

Sikes, P., and Piper, H. (eds) (2010), 'Ethical research, academic freedom and the role of ethics review committees and review procedures in educational research', *International Journal of Research and Method in Education*, 33(3): 205–13.

Sikes, P., and Potts, A. (2008), *Researching Education from the Inside: Investigations from Within*, Abingdon: Routledge.

Sikes, P., Nixon, J., and Carr, W. (eds) (2003), *The Moral Foundations of Educational Research: Knowledge, Inquiry and Values*, Maidenhead: Open University Press.

Silverman, D. (2009), *Doing Qualitative Research*, 3rd edn, London: SAGE.

Simons, H. (2000), 'Damned if you do, damned if you don't: ethical and political dilemmas in evaluation', in H. Simons and P. Usher (eds), *Situated Ethics in Educational Research*, London: RoutledgeFalmer.

Sir Arthur Lewis Institute of Social and Economic Studies (SALISES) (2012), *Barbados Country Assessment of Living Conditions Human Development Challenges in a Global Crisis: Addressing Growth and Social Inclusion*, University of the West Indies, Cave Hill, Barbados.

Skeggs, B. (1997), *Formations of Class and Gender*, London: SAGE.

Skeggs, B. (2002), *Formations of Class and Gender*, Online: SAGE Knowledge.

Skelton, C., and Francis, B. (2009), *Feminism and 'The Schooling Scandal'*, Abingdon: Routledge.

Skropeta, C. M., Colvin, A., and Sladen, S. (2014), An evaluative study of the benefits of participating in intergenerational playgroups in aged care for older people, *BMC Geriatrics* 14, 109 online at https://bmcgeriatr.biomedcentral.com/track/pdf/10.1186/1471-2318-14-109?site=bmcgeriatr.biomedcentral.com. Accessed 1 January 2018.

Slade, A. (2005), 'Parental reflective functioning: An introduction', *Attachment and Human Development*, 7: 269–81.

Slade, A. (2009), 'Mentalizing the unmentalizable: Parenting children on the spectrum', *Journal of Infant, Child, and Adolescent Psychotherapy*, 8(1): 7–21.

Slee, R. (2006), 'Limits to and possibilities for educational reform', *International Journal of Inclusive Education*, 10(2–3): 109–19.

Smith, B., Bundon, A., and Best, C. (2016), 'Disability Sport and activist identities: A qualitative study of narratives of activism among elite athletes with impairment', *Psychology of Sport and Exercise*, 26: 139–48.

Smith, D. (1987), *The Everyday World as Problematic: A Feminist Sociology*, Boston, MA: Northeastern University Press.

Smith, D. (1997), 'From the margins: Women's standpoint as a method of inquiry in socialsciences', *Gender, Technology and Development*, 1: 113–35.

Smith, D., and Katz, S. (2000), HEFCE Fundamental Review of Research Policy and Funding Collaborative Approaches to Research HEPU/University of Leeds/SPRU, University of Sussex online at http://users.sussex.ac.uk/~sylvank/pubs/collc.pdf. Accessed 13 December 2017.

Smith, L. (1999), *Decolonizing Methodologies: Research and Indigenous Peoples*. New York, NY: Zed Books.

Spence, M. (2011), Globalization and Unemployment: The Downside
of Integrating Markets in Foreign Affairs, online at http://www.
foreignaffairs.com/articles/67874/ michael-spence/globalization-and-
unemployment. Accessed 20 July 2016.

Spindler, G. and Spindler, L. (eds) (2014), *Interpretive Ethnography of
Education at Home and Abroad*, New York, NY: Psychology Press.

Stahl, G. (2015), *Aspiration, Identity and Neoliberalism: Educating White
Working-Class Boys*, London: Routledge.

Stahl, G. (2016), 'Relationship-building in research: Gendered identity
construction in researcher-participant interaction', in M. R. M. Ward
(ed.), *Gendered Identity Construction in Researcher-Participant
Interaction*, pp. 145–64, London: Emerald.

Stake, R. (2000), 'Case studies', in N. Denzin and Y. Lincoln (eds),
Handbook of Qualitative Research, 2nd edn, London: SAGE.

Stalker, K. (1998), 'Some ethical and methodological issues in research
with people with learning disabilities', *Disability & Society* 13: 5–20.

Stanley, L., and Wise, S. (1993), *Breaking Out Again: Feminist Ontology
and Epistemology*, London: Routledge.

Stenhouse, L. (1975), *An Introduction to Curriculum Research and
Development*, London: Heinemann.

Strack, R. W., Magill, C., and McDonagh, K. (2004), 'Engaging youth
through photovoice', *Health Promotion Practice*, 5: 49–58.

Strand, S. (2014), 'Ethnicity, gender, social class and achievement gaps at
Age 16: Intersectionality and "Getting it" for the white working class',
Research Papers in Education 29(2): 131–71.

Swift, C. (2016), N*egotiating Contexts for Reading: Becoming 'Someone
who Reads' (Unpublished doctoral dissertation)*, The University of
York: York, UK.

Teater, B. (2016), 'Intergenerational programs to promote active
ageing: The experiences and perspectives of older adults' activities',
Adaptation and Ageing, 40(1): 1–19.

Tedlock, B. (2000), 'Ethnography and ethnographic representation', in N.
Denzin and Y. Lincoln (eds), *Handbook of Qualitative Research*, 2nd
edn, pp. 455–86, Thousand Oaks, CA: SAGE.

Thériault, V. (2016), 'Literacy mediation as a form of powerful literacies
in community-based organisations working with young people in a
situation of precarity', *Ethnography and Education*, 11(2): 158–73.

Thieme, S. (2012), '"Action": Publishing research results in film, *Forum:
Qualitative Social Research Sozialforschumg* 13, 1 article 31,
online at http://www.qualitative-research.net/index.php/fqs/article/
download/1671/3327.

Thurlby-Campbell, I., and Bell, L. (2017), *Agency, Structure and the
NEET Policy Problem*, London: Bloomsbury.

Tierney, W. G. (2000), 'Undaunted courage: Life history and the post-modern challenge', in N. Denzin, and Y. Lincoln (eds), *Handbook of Qualitative Research*, 2nd edn, London: SAGE.

Tin, O., and Stenning, E. (2016), *Situation Analysis of the Monastic Education System in Myanmar Final Report*, Myanmar: Myanmar Education Consortium.

Tomlinson, S. (1997), 'Education 14–19: Divided and divisive', in S. Tomlinson (ed.), *Education 14–19: Critical Perspectives*, London: Athlone Press.

Tomlinson, S. (2001), 'Education policy 1997–2000: The effects on top, bottom and middle England', *International Studies in the Sociology of Education*, 11(3): 261–78.

Tomlinson, S. (2013), *Ignorant Yobs? Low Attainers in a Global Knowledge Economy*, London: Routledge.

Troyna, B. (1995), 'Beyond reasonable doubt? Researching "race" in educational settings', *Oxford Review of Education*, 21: 395–408.

Tuhiwai Smith, L. (2012), *Decolonizing Methodologies: Research and Indigenous Peoples*, 2nd edn, London: Zed Books Limited.

Tummons, J., and Duckworth, V. (2012), *Doing Your Research Project in the Lifelong Learning Sector*, Maidenhead: Open University Press.

UNESCO (1994), *The Salamanca Statement and Framework for Action on Special Needs Education*. World Conference on Special Needs Education, Access and Quality. Salamanca, Spain.

UNESCO (2015), *The Right to Education for Persons with Disabilities*, Paris: United Nations Educational, Scientific and Cultural Organization.

UNICEF (2012), *The Right of Children with Disabilities to Education: A Rights-Based Approach to Inclusive Education*, Geneva: UNICEF Regional Office for Central and Eastern Europe.

United Nations (1948/2018), *Universal Declaration on Human Rights* at http://www.un.org/en/universal-declaration-human-rights/.

Urry, J. (2007), *Mobilities*, Cambridge: Polity.

Usher, P. (2000), 'Feminist approaches to situated ethics', in H. Simons and P. Usher (eds), *Situated Ethics in Educational Research*, pp. 22–38, London: RoutledgeFalmer.

Vasiljevic, M., and Viki, G. T. (2013), 'Dehumanisation, moral disengagement, and public attitudes to crime and punishment', in P. G. Bain, J. Vaes, and P. Leyens (eds), *Advances in Understanding Humanness and Dehumanization*, pp. 129–46, New York, NY: Psychology Press.

Vicars, M. (2016), 'A Code of our own: Making meaning queerly', in L. Ling and P. Ling (eds), *Methods and Paradigms in Education Research*, Pennsylvania: IGI Global Publishers.

Vidich, A., and Lyman, S. (2000), 'Qualitative methods: Their history in sociology and anthropology', in N. Denzin and Y. Lincoln (eds), *Handbook of Qualitative Research*, 2nd edn, London: SAGE.

Wainwright, H. (2009), *Reclaim the State: Experiments in Popular Democracy*, Calcutta: Seagull Books.

Walford, G. (1994), 'The new christian schools: A survey', *Educational Studies*, 20(1): 127–43.

Walford, G. (2009), 'For ethnography', *Ethnography and Education*, 4(3): 271–82.

Walker, M. (2003), 'Framing social justice in education: What does the capabilities approach have to offer?' *British Journal of Educational Studies*, 51(2): 168–87.

Walker, M. (2016), *The Development of the Mechanics' Institute Movement in Britain and Beyond: Supporting Further Education for the Adult Working Classes*, London: Routledge.

Walker, M. (2017), 'Aspirations and equality: Gender in a South African university', *Cambridge Journal of Education*, http://dx.doi.org/10.1080/0305764X.2016.1254159.

Walker, M., and Loots, S. (2014), 'Social citizenship formation at university: A South African case study', *Compare: A Journal of Comparative and International Education*, 46(1): 48–68.

Walker, M., and Loots, S. (2017), Transformative change in higher education through participatory action research: A capabilities analysis Educational Action Research. DOI: http://dx.doi.org/10.1080/0965079 2.2017.1286605.

Wang, C. (1999), 'Photovoice: A participatory action research strategy applied to women's health', *Journal of Women's Health*, 8(2): 185–92.

Wang, C., and Burris, M. (1997), 'Photovoice: Concept, methodology, and use for participatory needs assessment', *Health Education and Behavior*, (24): 369–87.

Wang, C. C., and Pies, C. A. (2008), 'Using photovoice for participatory assessment and issue selection: Lessons from a family, maternal, and child health department', In M. Minkler and N. Wallerstein (eds), *Community-based Participatory Research for Health: From Process to Outcomes*, pp.183–97, San Francisco, CA: Jossey-Bass.

Warden, C. (2015), *Talking and Thinking Floorbooks. Consultation, Observation, Planning and Assessment in Children's Learning*, 3rd edn, Crieff: Mindstretchers.

Warren, C., and Hackney, J. (2000), *Qualitative Research Methods: Gender Issues in Ethnography*, Thousand Oaks, CA: SAGE.

Warren, H. (2015), Reading England's Future – Mapping how well the poorest children read. Save the Children Fund.

Warin, J. (2010), *Stories of Self: Tracking Children's Identity and Well-being Through the School Years*, London: Trentham Books.

Wason, K. D., Polonsky, M. J., and Hyman, M. R. (2002), 'Designing vignette studies in marketing', *Australasian Marketing Journal*, 10(3): 41–58.

Weiler, K. (1991), 'A feminist pedagogy of difference', *Harvard Educational Review*, 61(4): 449–74.

Wellington, J. (2000), *Educational Research Contemporary Issues and Practical Approaches*, London: Continuum.

Wellington, J. (2015), *Educational Research Contemporary Issues and Practical Approaches*, 2nd edn, London: Continuum.

Wellington, J., and Cole, P. (2004), 'Conducting evaluation and research with and for "disaffected" students: Practical and methodological issues', *British Journal of Special Education*, 31(2): 100–4.

West, L. (2016), *Distress in the City: Racism, Fundamentalism, and a Democratic Education*, London: UCL Institute of Education Press.

Whitburn, B. (2016), 'Voice, post-structural representation and the subjectivity of "included" students', *International Journal of Research & Method in Education*, 39(2): 117–30.

Whitehead, S. (2002),' *Men and Masculinities: Key Themes and New Directions*, Cambridge: Polity.

Wight-Felske, A. (2003), 'History of advocacy tool kit. Making equality: History of advocacy and persons with disabilities in Canada', pp. 321–38.

Wilkinson, C. (2016), '"Babe, I like your lipstick": Rethinking researcher personality and appearance', *Children's Geographies*, 14(1): 115–23.

Wilkinson, S., and Kitzinger, C. (2013), 'Representing our own experience: Issues in "Insider" research', *Psychology of Women Quarterly*, 37(2): 251–55.

Williams, J., Brown, S., and Roopnarine, J. (2006), *Childrearing in the Caribbean: A Literature Review* (ed. L. Walker) Director (p. 160), Caribbean Child Support Initiative and Bernard van Leer Foundation.

Willis, P. (1977), *Learning to Labour: How Working Class Kids Get Working Class Jobs*, Farnborough: Saxon House.

Wolf, A. (2011), Review of Vocational Education – The Wolf Report. www.gov.uk/government/ publications/review-of-vocational- education-the-wolf-report

Wood, L., and McAteer, M. (2017), 'Levelling the playing fields in PAR: The intricacies of power, privilege and participation in a university-community-school partnership', *Adult Education Quarterly*, 67(4): 251–65.

Woolhouse, C. (in press), 'Conducting photo methodologies: Framing ethical concerns relating to representation, voice and data analysis when exploring educational inclusion with children', *International Journal of Research and Method in Education*.

Workers Educational Association (2017), *Who we are* online at: www.wea.org.uk/about-us/who-we-are

World Bank List of Economies (2016), Available from http://www.iaprd-world-congress.com/tl_files/IAPRD/layout/World%20Bank%20country%20classification%20by%20income_web.pdf.

Yin, R. K. (2003), *Case Study Research Design and Methods*, 3rd edn, London: SAGE.

Yin, R. K. (2009), *Case Study Research: Design and Methods*, 4th edn, Thousand Oaks CA: SAGE.

Zuber-Skerritt, O. (1982), *Action Research in Higher Education*, London: Kegan.

Zuber-Skerritt, O. (ed.) (1996), *New Directions in Action Research*, London: Falmer.

INDEX